A Torch Kept Lit

A Torch Kept Lit

Great Lives of the Twentieth Century

William F. Buckley, Jr.
EDITED BY JAMES ROSEN

CROWN
FORUM
NEW YORK

Library of Congress Cataloging-in-Publication Data
Names: Buckley, William F., Jr., 1925–2008, author. |
Rosen, James, 1968– editor.
Title: A torch kept lit : great lives of the twentieth century /
William F. Buckley, Jr. ; edited by James Rosen.
Description: New York : Crown Forum, 2016.
Identifiers: LCCN 2016017488| ISBN 9781101906217 (hardback) |
ISBN 9781101906224 (electronic)
Subjects: LCSH: United States—History—20th century—Biography.
| Biography—20th century. | Eulogies—United States. | BISAC:
BIOGRAPHY & AUTOBIOGRAPHY / Editors, Journalists, Publishers. |
HISTORY / United States / 20th Century. | HISTORY / Social History.
Classification: LCC E747 .B95 2016 | DDC 973.91—dc23
LC record available at https://lccn.loc.gov/2016017488

ISBN 978-1-101-90621-7
eBook ISBN 978-1-101-90622-4

Printed in the United States of America

Book design by Maria Elias
Frontispiece photograph: Ron Galella/Getty Images
Jacket design by Alison Forner
Jacket photograph: Jerry Engel/*New York Post* Archives/
© NYP Holdings, Inc. (via Getty Images)

10 9 8 7 6 5 4 3 2 1

First Edition

To Aaron and Gray,
joys of my life

Contents

Introduction   1

Presidents

Dwight Eisenhower   13

John F. Kennedy   18

Lyndon B. Johnson   24

Richard Nixon   31

Ronald Reagan   43

Family

Patricia Taylor Buckley   55

William F. Buckley, Sr.   61

Aloise Steiner Buckley   78

L. Brent Bozell, Jr.   85

Arts and Letters

Truman Capote   95

Johnny Carson   101

Alistair Cooke   105

Milton Friedman   113

Jerry Garcia   117

Vladimir Horowitz   121

Russell Kirk   125

John Lennon   129

Norman Mailer   134

Vladimir Nabokov   140

Elvis Presley   144

A. M. Rosenthal   148

William Shawn   153

Rosalyn Tureck   163

Generals, Spies, and Statesmen

Winston Churchill   171

William Colby   176

Princess Diana   179

Allen Dulles   183

Barry Goldwater   187

Richard Helms   194

E. Howard Hunt   198

Martin Luther King, Jr.   203

Golda Meir   208

John Mitchell   211

Jacqueline Onassis   215

Vernon Walters   218

Friends

Whittaker Chambers   225

Richard Clurman   238

Evan Galbraith   241

John Kenneth Galbraith   244

Tom Hume   250

Nan Kempner   254

Hugh Kenner   258

Allard Lowenstein   267

David Niven   270

Warren Steibel   274

Charles Wallen   278

Nemeses

Alger Hiss   289

John V. Lindsay   295

Ayn Rand   298

Nelson Rockefeller   302

Eleanor Roosevelt   306

Arthur Schlesinger, Jr.   311

Acknowledgments   319

A Torch Kept Lit

Introduction

—◆ ◆—

"I'm tired of *life*," William F. Buckley, Jr., declared to Charlie Rose in March 2006. "I really am. I'm utterly prepared to stop *living on*. You know, there are no enticements to me that justify the weariness, the repetition—"

Suddenly it dawned on Buckley how *morose* he sounded. Still possessed of the showman's instincts, he hastened to add "my hours of exercise" to his list of laments. Rose, a close friend, got the joke: Though he had been an avid sailor and splendidly fit most of his life, Bill Buckley *hated* exercising. He used to refer to it, borrowing from Scripture, as "the unhappiest hour of my week, the Mortification of the Flesh." But the quip hardly masked the underlying sentiment.

Not long after the Rose interview, addled by diabetes, emphysema, and hearing loss, Buckley suffered a fatal heart attack at his home in Stamford, Connecticut, at the age of eighty-two.*

Buckley's weariness with life, so in contrast with the zest with which he had always lived it, became acute after the death eight months earlier of Pat Buckley, his wife of fifty-seven years. To close students of Buckley and his works, however, the stealthy onset of a certain fatalism that was hard to fathom in a life so charmed had been in evidence for some time. As Fox News cameras rolled, I interviewed Buckley at his East 73rd Street maisonette in October 2000. The occasion was his seventy-fifth birthday, which was then a month away. I was startled by how disaffected the great man seemed. "You're celebrating a milestone birthday soon," I began the interview. "How do you feel?"

"Who said I was celebrating it?" he shot back with a chuckle. "*You're* celebrating it."

In more than a half century on the national stage, William F. Buckley, Jr., achieved unique stature as the architect of modern American conservatism. He founded *National Review* and, from 1966 to 1999, welcomed viewers to *Firing Line,* the longest-running television talk show with a single host. For nearly fifty years, he produced a syndicated column that was read in hundreds of newspapers across the country and republished in best-selling anthologies year after year; wrote a dozen best-selling spy novels; sailed the Atlantic and Pacific Oceans and wrote best-selling books about *that;* and played the harpsichord with professional

---

* *Charlie Rose,* [aired] March 24, 2006. The relevant interview can be viewed at https://www.charlierose.com/videos/18124. See also William F. Buckley, Jr., *Cruising Speed: A Documentary* (1971), pp. 24–25.

orchestras. Handsome and witty, he was a forerunner, in his seeming omnipresence, to today's multimedia celebrities. Bill Buckley met everybody, knew everybody, hosted everybody you ever wanted to meet, skewered everybody who needed skewering, carried on lengthy and amusing correspondence with everybody worth writing to, and in general lived life on a grand scale in a way that inspired countless young conservatives and delighted even many who rejected his politics.

One of Buckley's greatest strengths, however, remains neglected in his vast catalogue of published works: his mastery of that elusive art form *the eulogy*. Outside of WFB's explicit writings on Catholicism—a frequent subject over the course of his career, capped by the publication of *Nearer, My God: An Autobiography of Faith* (1997)—none of WFB's enterprises so closely fused his religious faith and literary gift.

A keen observer of people and mannerisms, Buckley used his eulogies both to mourn and as a kind of conjuring act: a final chance to *savor* the deceased as he had. Often drawing on his own experiences or private correspondence, WFB recalled memorable moments spent with The Departed, revealed their hidden sides, heralded their greatness—or, as occasion warranted, reminded the living why certain individuals, notwithstanding the grace that death can bestow, should be remembered as abject failures or, worse still, evil.

Part of what readies a man for death, of course, is his steady exposure to it. First comes the passing of elders: one's parents, aunts and uncles, teachers; later one suffers the loss of one's contemporaries, friends and cousins, classmates and colleagues, acquaintances and antagonists, spouses. Buckley never imagined himself immune to or estranged from the immutable laws of mortality. Death is a part of life, and WFB understood the fortifying effect that death, even when tragic, can visit upon those who survive and bear witness. More deeply, WFB thought that we are all inheritors of what he liked to call The Patrimony, the corpus of objective truths, earthly and celestial, established by humankind over the millennia and handed down by our elders, the first among which is: *People die, God endures.*

At all points, these remembrances bring us Buckley's distinct *voice:* the greatest pleasure of this volume. As a literary stylist, WFB was renowned for elegant prose and a light comic touch, ironic formalism married to an addiction to obscure words. Buckley also imbibed the New Journalism as practiced by his friend Tom Wolfe and other contemporaries, taking full advantage, as the conventions of "literary journalism" evolved, of all the techniques suddenly available to the writer of nonfiction: dialogue, shifting point of view, sentence fragments, sound effects, made-up words, Ironic Capitalization, and subtle rhetorical devices such as *antonomasia* (the practice, usually derisive, of describing an individual by a certain characteristic and then using that as the individual's name). WFB's embrace of the New Journalism sprang from the revolutionary precincts of his personality, marking the rare terrain on which he did not venerate the patrimony—and we are the richer for it.

Each of these essays bequeaths to the legacies of the deceased a fitting tribute, or unsparing verdict, consistent with the lives, careers, accomplishments, mercies, and misdeeds that Buckley, with his oceanic view of the world, deemed worthy of final summation. In 1993, C-SPAN host Brian Lamb asked how often WFB wrote such pieces.

WFB: I do a fair amount. I've been doing it for *National Review* for years and years and years. I mean, I don't know how many I've done. Maybe five hundred [*sic*]. I don't know.

LAMB: [. . .] But is there some way to describe what it takes to get you to write somebody's obituary? I mean, do you have to like them?

WFB: Or dislike them, one or the other, or they have to have been a friend of the *National Review* or of mine or have had some historical importance.

Known for dashing off his columns in twenty minutes, a chore cheerfully disposed of on a portable typewriter as his limousine navigated Midtown traffic and a King Charles Cavalier panted beside him, Buckley appears to have devoted especial care to his eulogies. The solemnity of these occasions, their emotional impact, summoned him to greatness, demanded he use his gifts fully, and he answered the charge.

We have many anthologies of Buckley's syndicated columns; a thick volume of annotated *Firing Line* transcripts; a reader of excerpts from the Blackford Oakes spy novels; even a volume, published in tandem with the documentary film *Best of Enemies* (2015), collecting the transcripts of Buckley's epic TV debates against his nemesis of nemeses, Gore Vidal (who outlived Buckley and thus is not included here). Yet until now no one has collected Buckley's eulogies—consistently brilliant, sometimes shattering works—in one place.

Using the restricted online archives of *National Review*

and the resources of Hillsdale College, whose website contains original PDF images for almost the entire canon of Buckley's works—an invaluable resource for students of WFB and his times—I identified some 250 eulogies he penned across his career: an average, roughly, of two per year, although weighted, naturally, toward the end of his life, and steady enough an exposure to death to make even the most joyful and energetic soul ready, at ripe age, to receive it himself.

A Torch Kept Lit collects the best of WFB's eulogies, more than fifty in all, a far-ranging survey of the famous and obscure, the heroic and villainous, the charmed and doomed.

Inevitably, and happily, these writings shed as much light on Buckley—his personality and extraordinary life—as on the tumultuous times in which he flourished and on the subjects themselves. We see Buckley shuttling between his multiple selves, a son, husband, and father, editor, writer, and TV celebrity, sailor, skier, harpsichordist, and controversialist. We travel back in time to an era when men of affluence smoked cigars after dinner and proposed to women within a week of meeting them. We find Buckley swimming in the ocean outside Claudette Colbert's house with Ronald Reagan, tricking Vladimir Horowitz into performing a private recital, buying a King Charles puppy for a friend who has lapsed into melancholy.

We observe up close the rituals WFB observed: lunch or dinner, once a year in Switzerland, with Nabokov and his dour, watchful Vera; midday meals, once a quarter, with his erudite English-born friend ("What a piece of luck, lunching with Alistair Cooke for 30 years"); participation in "a little club" of New Yorkers, "some of them decisive voices

in American journalism," including *New York Times* editor
A. M. Rosenthal, who lunched with Buckley "five or six
times every year."

We learn that Buckley's father, usually described as
being upright to the point of sternness, was "inept in manual pursuits" and enjoyed his first taste of alcohol at the
age of forty. We frolic on the grounds of Great Elm, the
idyllic Buckley family compound in Sharon, Connecticut,
as the young WFB and his nine brothers and sisters grow
up, privileged and driven, engaged with great issues yet iso-
lated from the corrupting influences of the impious world
around them.

Last but not least, we witness up close the postwar ascendancy of *National Review* and the broader conservative
movement that lives on to this day.

Thematic organization readily suggested itself over strict
chronological order, and so I have grouped the eulogies
into the categories, distinct and self-explanatory, listed in
the Contents. However, a warning is necessary up front:
namely, that between the categories I devised, a certain
blurring of the lines was inescapable. Case in point: Whittaker Chambers was surely a man of arts and letters, but
WFB's anthology of their correspondence was, after all, titled *Odyssey of a Friend* (1969), so in which category does
Chambers belong? Guessing at what Bill would have preferred, I chose Friend.

In that category the reader is introduced to some obscure names: stricken Yale classmates, longtime pen pals,
and other nonfamous people, their time often come too
soon and for whom, no less than with presidents or Pulitzer
winners, Buckley was determined to bear witness. To pay

tribute to these "ordinary" men and women, record their unsung workaday heroics and private suffering, and chronicle their impact on the world and WFB himself, Buckley deployed all his gifts, ensuring that the reader experiences emotion as profoundly as when the subject is a household name. Indeed, in these pieces—the eulogy for Charles Wallen is an example—Buckley summons extraordinary tenderness. The gentility is all the more impressive when we remember that in many cases, the writer was wracked by grief and working on deadline.

For each eulogy I have crafted a prefatory note designed to acquaint Buckley fans and more casual readers with the nature and background of his relationship to The Departed and to present facets of those relationships that the eulogies sometimes omit. Often I've used these notes to show how Buckley's relationship with an individual, or an epoch, evolved, producing the eulogy that follows. In this endeavor I've drawn on the online resources referenced above as well as the archive of *Firing Line* synopses and transcripts maintained on the website of the Hoover Institution.

Some of the eulogies were actually delivered at memorial services or are remarks that sometimes were republished in *National Review*. Elsewhere Buckley might have used his column to remember the freshly deceased, and he sometimes republished the work in *NR;* in these cases, they often appeared in varied form, reflecting space needs. I have sought here always to provide the fullest version of a particular eulogy. In a few instances (e.g., John F. Kennedy, Truman Capote), Buckley produced *two* eulogies, featuring different observations, perhaps tailored for different audiences—and I have presented both, in chronological order, to give Buckley's fullest measure of a man.

Only sparingly have I ranged beyond the corpus of eulogies to include a piece of writing not explicitly prepared to commemorate a death. In these cases (e.g., Lyndon Johnson, Elvis Presley) the essay was written with such attentiveness to the overall legacy of the individual—either very close to the end of the subject's life or career or maybe decades afterward—that it constituted Buckley's Final Word on a renowned figure.

Inevitably, space constraints mandated the exclusion of many fine pieces, including tributes to individuals who figured prominently in Buckley's intellectual development, helped launch *National Review,* and so on.

Yet the roll call in these pages presents a panoramic view of the twentieth century, from the stylish sublimity of Jacqueline Onassis to the moral blackness of Alger Hiss. One of the hallmarks of the sixties and seventies was a newfound taste for eclecticism, a Warholian conflation of high and low, that brought celebrities from different walks of life—athletes, politicians, novelists—to the same TV couch. Buckley himself had guested on Woody Allen's TV shows in the sixties, and his appearances on *The Tonight Show Starring Johnny Carson* in the seventies found the conservative commentator paired with the likes of the impersonator Rich Little and the psychic Jeane Dixon.

The elite salons of the Upper East Side were no exception. How much *fun* it must have been to arrive at the Buckleys' at night and find Truman Capote talking to George Plimpton or Henry Kissinger . . . or to take in a *Firing Line* taping, the air thick with electricity as WFB matched wits with Allen Ginsberg or Muhammad Ali. . . . *Anything was possible!* So it is here, in *A Torch Kept Lit:* Where else but the shimmering orbit of Bill Buckley will we find Milton Friedman rubbing elbows with Jerry Garcia?

In his review of *Execution Eve and Other Contemporary Ballads* (1975), WFB's collection of Watergate-era columns, the learned scholar Ernest van den Haag noted the "cheerfulness" that intruded even upon the most "mournful" of WFB's writings. Many colleagues remarked, during Buckley's time, on his gift for eulogy—but van den Haag paid the ultimate compliment: "Buckley has re-elevated the art of eulogy to the high standard from which it had long ago fallen. So much so, that I am firmly resolved to leave this world before he does, for his eulogy is bound to be much better than mine."*

---

* Ernest van den Haag, "Cheerfulness Is Always Breaking In," *National Review,* October 24, 1975. Upon his death in 2002, at the age of eighty-seven, van den Haag got his wish. WFB's eulogy, not included here for space reasons, appeared in the April 22 edition of *National Review* and included Buckley's own supreme compliment: "In my lifetime I have not known so satisfying a companion, intellectually and psychologically."

PRESIDENTS

Dwight Eisenhower

(1890–1969)

From the start, William F. Buckley, Jr., and *National Review* exhibited an oppositional temperament, as captured in the magazine's opening declaration that it "stands athwart history, yelling Stop." But it was also clear from the outset that those whom WFB intended to Stop were not just liberals but their handmaidens in the Republican Party, the RINOs of the day whose capitulations to liberals, in and out of Congress, contributed to the left's cultural hegemony. Chief among WFB's Republican targets at that time was the much-revered Dwight D. Eisenhower. Even before *National Review* launched—in November 1955, roughly midway through Ike's presidency—Buckley had begun registering his disappointment with the former Supreme Allied Commander of World War II. In some of his earliest published writing, WFB lamented that there existed between the two major parties an "ephemeral battle line dividing two almost identical streams of superficial thought," that only "trivia" separated "the 1952 Republican from the 1952 Democrat." By June 1955, in an article titled "The Liberal Mind," published in *Facts Forum News,* Buckley was likening Ike to the sitting Soviet premier:

[W]e know more about the workings of the mind of Nikolai Bulganin than we know about the workings of the mind of Dwight Eisenhower.... [T]he life of Bulganin makes sense in a way that the life of Eisenhower does not.

NR's debut issue also lamented the growth of "a gigantic, parasitic bureaucracy." A decade later, when WFB ran for mayor of New York City, the Republican target of the oppositional temperament would be John V. Lindsay—but even then, the betrayal of Eisenhower weighed heavily on Buckley, as recorded in *The Unmaking of a Mayor* (1966):

Even under the moderate Eisenhower—the Republican exemplar, according to the rules of prevailing opinion—the registration figures continued to polarize, as they had during the preceding two decades. Two years before the good general came into office, the national registration figures were 45 percent to 33 percent in favor of the Democrats, according to Dr. Gallup. When he left the pulpit, eight years later, the infidels had in fact increased, the figures having separated to 46 percent Democrats and 30 percent Republicans.

What did emerge in the post-Eisenhower years among Republicans was a hunger for orthodoxy, for an intellectual discipline in the formulation of policy. It was fueled in part by the long diet of blandness that had produced a body lacking in tone and coordination....

WFB's eulogy was prepared in advance as Eisenhower lay dying.

The accomplishments of Dwight Eisenhower will be copiously recorded now that he is gone, that being the tradition, and tradition being what one has come to associate with General Eisenhower, who comes to us even now as a memory out of the remote past. During his lifetime he had his detractors. There are those who oppose Dwight Eisenhower because he was the man who defeated Adlai Stevenson. In their judgment it was profanation for anyone to stand in the way of Adlai Stevenson. And so, when Eisenhower was inaugurated, they took up, and forever after maintained, a jeremiad on America the theme of which was: America is a horrible country because a banal and boring general with not an idea in his head gets to beat a scintillating intellectual who is in tune with the future. These gentry did President Eisenhower a certain amount of harm, and in later years they took to referring routinely to his tenure as "boring," "lacking in ideals," and "styleless."[*]

Their criticisms never actually took hold. America wanted Eisenhower in preference to Stevenson; and however keenly we felt the death of Stevenson, it wasn't—speaking for the majority—because we had failed to confer the presidency upon him. Stevenson was born to be defeated for the presidency.

Among the critics of Mr. Eisenhower also from the liberal end of the world are a few who reckoned him as quite different from what it is generally supposed that he was. There are those—one thinks of the singularly acute Mr. Murray Kempton, who all along has led that particular pack—who saw Mr. Eisenhower as perhaps the most highly

---

[*] Buckley's grammatical piety fluctuated; his use of the serial comma, for example, was inconsistent. In part this reflected contemporaneous standards and style guides. In this volume we have sometimes corrected for WFB's inconsistencies (e.g., the serial comma), and elsewhere, when context benefited (e.g., capitalization), preserved them.

efficient political animal ever born in the United States. They believe that his aspect of indifference to practical political matters was one of the most successful dissimulations in political history. He had, they maintain, the most accomplished sense of political danger that any man ever developed, and he always knew—they maintain—how to defend himself against the ravages of political decisiveness by a) setting up another guy, who would easily fall victim; and b) appearing to be innocently disinterested in the grinding of political gears.

The record is certainly there, that over a period of a dozen years, it was, somehow, always somebody else who stood between him and the tough decisions: a Sherman Adams, a Richard Nixon, a CIA. General Eisenhower never really developed any mass opposition. His critics were either formalistic (the Democratic Party); or personal—men who held him responsible not for what he did, but for what he failed to do.

It is I think this category of critics of the General which is the most interesting. Not the liberals, but the conservatives. It is hardly a surprise that liberals would have faulted Eisenhower's performance as president, they having so hotly desired the election of another man. But the conservatives, or at least many of them, were genuinely disappointed that he let the federal government grow at a rate no domesticated Democrat could reasonably have exceeded. Disappointed by his failure to take decisive action against the Soviet Union notwithstanding unique historical opportunities, as for instance in Hungary, Egypt, and Cuba. Disappointed by his dismal unconcern with the philosophy of conservatism (of which he was a purely intuitive disciple) at a point in the evolution of America when a few conservative philosophers at his side might have accomplished more for the ends he sought to serve than the battery of sycophantic (and opportunistic) big businessmen with whom he loved to while away the hours.

The critique of General Eisenhower from the right will perhaps be the most interesting historical critique (to use the Army term): and one somehow feels that the General, retired from office, had an inkling of this. Never was he so adamantly and philosophically conservative as when he last addressed the nation, via the Republican Convention at Miami Beach, a fortnight ago.

Meanwhile we are left to mourn the (imminent— Editors: Please supply if necessary) passing of an extraordinary man, a genius of personal charm, a public servant manifestly infected with a lifetime case of patriotism. His country requited his services. No honor was unpaid to him. If he was, somehow at the margin deficient, it was because the country did not rise to ask of him the performance of a thunderbolt. He gave what he was asked to give. And he leaves us (or "will leave") if not exactly bereft, lonely; lonely for the quintessential American.

END.

John F. Kennedy

(1917–1963)

As early as 1957, WFB described John F. Kennedy as an "ideological wraith," marveling at how the junior senator from Massachusetts had mastered "the art of voting Liberal and appearing conservative." When, a year later, Senator Kennedy proposed that the United States adopt an "underdog" strategy with the Soviet Union, pursuing diplomacy through disarmament, *NR* recoiled in "utter amazement":

> [W]e suppose Senator Kennedy was merely making a campaign speech. We hope his dreams of reducing "the [missile] gap" by reliance on calls for disarmament are not unduly disturbed by memories of a book he once wrote. The title was *Why England Slept* [1940].

During the 1960 election, WFB again scored JFK for weakness on foreign policy, anticipating the themes later to inform David Halberstam's *The Best and the Brightest* (1972): "The most educated men in our midst and the most highly-trained—and those who trained the Kennedys—have not been understanding the march of history, in which [Fidel] Castro is a minor player, though at the moment great shafts of light converge upon him and give him a spectacular brilliance." After the Bay of Pigs, *NR* condemned Kennedy's "contemptible" inaction, arguing that it "left . . . 700 brave Cubans to die, and 6 million others to live in slavery." Nor did Buckley believe the USSR had "blinked" in the Cuban Missile Crisis: "President John F. Kennedy, 35th president of the United States, has formally given our bitterest enemy a pledge that we will enforce the nonenforcement of the Monroe Doctrine! . . . How can it be maintained that we have won a great victory when Khrushchev is, in October, ahead of where he was in May?"

Kennedy took note of his erudite critic. Upon receiving his honorary degree from Yale in June 1962, the president told the graduates he was "particularly glad to become a Yale man because as I think about my troubles, I find that a lot of them have come from other Yale men . . . not to mention William F. Buckley, Jr., of the class of 1950."

With JFK's death, WFB found himself, rhetorically, in a tight spot: He had to acknowledge the intense mourning, yet he also felt compelled to remind his readers that JFK was a real, and controversial, person and that the conservative challenge to the Kennedy program needed, perforce, to be carried to his successor. WFB penned two JFK eulogies, the first somewhat rushed, presumably produced on tight deadline, and the second longer, more thoughtful—and more barbed.

"*J.F.K., 1917–1963*"

National Review, December 10, 1963.

The grief was spontaneous and, in most cases, wholly sincere. Not because Mr. Kennedy's policies were so universally beloved, but because he was a man so intensely charming, whose personal vigor and robust enjoyment of life so invigorated almost all who beheld him. The metabolism of the whole nation rose on account of the fairyland quality of the First Family. After all, no divine typecaster could have done better than to get JFK to play JFK, Jackie to play the First Lady, and the children to play themselves.

The assassination of President Kennedy was the act presumably of a madman, heir to the madmen who killed Lincoln and McKinley and, for that matter, Christ, reminding us that the beasts are always with us, and that they continue to play decisive roles in history, and in human affairs.

Even his most adamant political opponents acknowledged the personal courage Mr. Kennedy showed during his young and dazzling lifetime. Now, no doubt, he would desire that his countrymen also act heroically, by enduring their grief; and by demonstrating to his bereaved family not only their compassion, but also their fortitude.

"The Morning After"

National Review, December 17, 1963.

Norman Mailer, reviewing Victor Lasky's book on John Kennedy several weeks ago for the *New York Herald Tribune,* remarked that Kennedy's political genius rested in his apprehension of the main point in American politics towards the close of the '50s, namely, that the American people were ready, in Mailer's words, to turn away from the father image (Eisenhower), and accept as ruler someone cast in the role of the young hero; someone in the Hollywood image, as Mailer put it.

Mailer seems to have been right, as he very often is. What happened, two and one-half weeks ago, was the Morte d'Arthur. The grief was that of a nation that had lost a young king, a young king whose own fairyland rise to power recapitulated the national experience; whose personal radiance warmed the whole nation—and whose great failures were charitably disregarded, for were we not, really, forgiving ourselves? And are we not, really, grieving for ourselves? "A part of me has gone with him," one orator said, and a great chorus responded to the theme: and they are all exactly correct, they *have* lost a part of themselves. Much of America, the intelligentsia especially, succeeded in anthropomorphizing itself in the image of John Kennedy, whereon it had to follow that when he lay bleeding, they lay bleeding; and that the great ache, the anxiety expressed so effusively, lay in the numbing realization that though their king was dead, they were still alive, and would have to learn again to act for themselves. And, God help us, to *think* for themselves.

For it gives one the grues. The assassination itself, yes, obviously. We know what death is, and what evil is in the twentieth century. We live with violence, and apocalypse is camped just over the horizon. We have lived with violent endings, for individuals, and for nations, and for whole races. We know the unyielding finality of death, and one's helplessness before recurrent acts of individual and collective depravity. But what is this other thing that seems to be going on? Pay the man all the many compliments to which he is entitled, and sing the praises he is due. But not all this, no indeed; and for the reason, first among the others, that it tends to undermine those qualities in national life that John Kennedy at his best exemplified: courage, dignity, fortitude, toughmindedness, independence.

The rhetoric has gone quite out of control. The symbol of our emotional, if not neurotic excess, is the Eternal Flame at Arlington, a few hundred yards from the shrines we built to the memories of George Washington (86 years after he died), Thomas Jefferson (117 years), and Abraham Lincoln (57 years); who have no eternal flames. The lovely and tormented Mrs. Kennedy needs a gentle hand lest in her understandable grief, she give the air of the Pharaoh, specifying his own magnitude.

John F. Kennedy lived a life of tough controversy, and while it is correct that an individual's weaknesses should be buried with him, it is not ever possible to bury the public issues on which a public figure committed himself. Mr. Kennedy told us the fight would last beyond his lifetime; and his successor has pledged himself on the same side of those policies. It is sobering to recall that there was great dissension, left and right, in respect of John Kennedy's policies, right up until the moment he died. The issue of *Time* magazine dated the awful day of the assassination carried, for instance, the news of a growing campus "disenchantment" with President Kennedy's policies, "now spread far and wide." "At conservative Georgia Tech," said *Time*, "the complaint is that 'he's interfering with my personal life' through Big Government. At liberal Reed, where 'he doesn't inspire respect as Stevenson did,' the gripe is Kennedy's caution on the civil rights bill. At exuberant Wisconsin, 'he's liked in a negative way,' faulted for lack of political conviction." The restlessness, as we see, was not partisan, not only from the Right.

Are we now being emotionally stampeded into believing that Kennedy was the incarnation, and that respect for him requires that we treat his program like the laws of the Medes and the Persians? What we need is a period of dignified mourning for a graceful human being who passed through our midst with style and energy, a mourning more intense in virtue of the treachery of his end; but less intense than that which degenerates into abject pity for ourselves, or that asks that we place our personal grief above the best interests of our country as we understand them; which interests many people thought of as calling for the retirement of Mr. Kennedy from public life one year from now. Jack Kennedy wouldn't want a caterwauling public besotted by its own tears for its own self, or accepting his program for sentimentality's sake. He asked us to keep the torch lit. And that means work, each one of us according to his own lights, to keep this country at least as strong and as free, stronger, we can hope, and freer, than it was when John F. Kennedy last knew it.

Lyndon B. Johnson

(1908–1973)

Long before he became president, Lyndon B. Johnson excited Buckley's instinct, and talent, for ridicule. "It is widely known that whenever Senator Johnson feels the urge to act the statesman at the cost of a little political capital," WFB wrote in June 1958, "he lies down until he gets over it." By the end of Johnson's presidency, Buckley would describe LBJ as "a man of his most recent word." The twin failings of the Great Society—as ambitious a redistributionist program as the post-Enlightenment world has seen—and the Vietnam War became apparent just as Buckley was reaching the apex of his multimedia influence: The introduction of *Firing Line* in 1966 meant the nation's foremost conservative polemicist now had a TV show to go along with his magazine, syndicated column, and lectures. Buckley's first mention of the Great Society asked what, exactly, it would encompass.

> We know that we are at war with poverty and with ill health and that we will never surrender; and we suspect that it is going

to be a very long war indeed. But what else, other than step up the antipoverty program, and move in the direction of socializing medicine, does President Johnson plan to do? It is of course misleading to suggest that great bureaucracies cannot find enough to do: On that subject Parkinson's Law is absolutely binding, that work suggests itself equal to the amount of money available to perform it. But apart from the housekeeping chores of monster government, what might Lyndon Johnson do to leave his mark on destiny, now that the weapons are all at his disposal?

Monster government came, coupled with protracted war. WFB supported the war as vital to the Cold War struggle against Soviet expansionism, but he faulted Johnson, as in 1968, for pressing an escalatory exercise, writing: "Our participation in the Vietnam war is justified only if Vietnam is the contemporary salient of the world enterprise, however loosely organized, that aims ultimately at the security of United States.... If that is not what Vietnam is all about, then we should get the hell out."

The first piece below appeared in December 1968, a kind of political obituary ruminating on why such a gifted tactician should have left the White House so widely condemned; the second was a proper eulogy but one that did not mince words.

"LBJ Packs Up"

Syndicated column, December 12, 1968.

We read these days about Lyndon Johnson's staggered good-byes to his many staffs. The other day it was the gardeners at the White House, then the secret service men, then the telephone operators, and so on. Truly he is sorry to go and desires to extract as much ceremony as he can out of the painful act of separation, like John McCormack, who made something like six world tours in order adequately to bid his fans adieu.

It is more than punctilio that moves the president. Nor is he by nature given to preoccupation with those little attentions to which an altogether different kind of man is given. Lyndon Johnson's favors are conceived on a far grander scale, and it is no doubt supremely galling to him that he leaves office lonely, unloved, and discredited, after giving us the Great Society, which he defined in a speech in 1964 as society concerned more for the quality of its goals than for the quality of its goods.

There never was a man, in all of history, who conferred such prodigious favors on his subjects. I beg you to be patient as I catalog the programs passed during Mr. Johnson's reign, because although like any list it is tedious, still, it is hard to grasp the appetite of the government under Mr. Johnson to look after us unless one plows through it. The whole of it is costing $25 billion per year, which is two and one-half times as much as Ike was spending at the end there, and more than twice as much as JFK was spending.

Under LBJ we got antipoverty programs, mass transportation bills, model cities help, rent supplements, crime control, antisegregation acts, voting acts, housing acts, a communication relations act, acts on water and air pollution, on waste, roads, recreation and parks, on meat and poultry and fabrics and farm prices, on truth in lending, on fair packaging, on electronic radiation, on traffic; aid for elementary schools, for higher education, for teacher corps, aid to the poor, adult education, job opportunity training, the job corps, business aid, aid for Appalachia, an increase in the minimum wage, Medicare for the elderly, Medicaid for the nonelderly, doctors' training, nurses' training, mental health, immunization, health centers, and child health.

A few questions suggest themselves:

(1) How is it that the people are so dissatisfied? I mean those among the people who are critical of the government for not spending more? Is it as easy as this, that if one can find a single poor family, or a derelict building, or a contaminated creek, or an illiterate child, the government has not spent as much money as it ought to have spent?

(2) Why is it that so many observers of government have chosen this moment to disavow government spending as an efficacious means of bringing about a socially desirable end, such as the diminution of poverty? Was it Johnson's handling of the money; or is the problem inherent in government spending?

And (3) Do the people feel as much better off—as much more secure—as one would expect that they should, as beneficiaries of goods and services valued at approximately $1,250 per family? Granted, the wiser among them realize that the money Johnson gave them was the same money Johnson took away from them; still, were there enough people who calculated that after all is said and done, they managed not only to get their own back, but also a little of their neighbor's?

If not, (4) Could it be that under Johnson we came finally to the end of the period exultantly memorialized by Harry Hopkins, who thought he had the perpetual key to political success when he announced: Tax and tax, spend and spend, elect and elect?

All of which, in Mr. Johnson's case, reduced him, at the

prime of his life, to ceremonial leavetakings at the White House, whose staff probably value more highly the little bauble the president left them, than all these splendors of the Great Society which left America cold.

—————•••—————

"Lyndon Johnson, R.I.P."

Syndicated column, January 27, 1973.
[ellipses in original]

SAN ANTONIO—The lady is middle-aged, shrewd, politically active, impeccably kind, civic-minded, born in Texas and raised here, and she spoke as if she were facing such a problem for the very first time in her life. Well, obviously not the first time: when acknowledged monsters like Hitler and Stalin died, people did not, for the most part, scratch about to find something redeeming to say about them. LBJ was clearly of another category, but the lady now remarked, "What am I supposed to say? I didn't like what I knew about him personally. I didn't admire his domestic programs. And I thought his foreign policy was a mess. So what am I supposed to say?"

I counseled her to say nothing, absolutely nothing at all. Having done so, I regretfully acknowledge that my advice is only one part discretion, nine parts funk. Accordingly, into the breach. . . .

Even if history justifies Lyndon Johnson's determination to stand by South Vietnam, it is very difficult to believe that history will applaud his conduct of the war. We set out, in Vietnam, to make a resonant point. We did not make it resonantly. In international affairs as in domestic affairs, crime is deterred by the predictability of decisive and conclusive retaliation. The Soviet Union knows that it can count on a dozen years between separatist uprisings in its empire because when it moves, it moves conclusively. If the Soviet Union had sent a few battalions into Hungary, and a dozen years later into Czechoslovakia, the Soviet Union would not have made its point.

Johnson, reminiscing in the White House a year before he was evicted, told two reporters that there was no way he might have avoided a showdown in Indochina, that not only John Kennedy (who told him shortly before leaving for Dallas that he intended to make a stand there) but Dwight Eisenhower (who told him in the early sixties that Southeast Asia would be the principal challenge of the presidency) agreed on the strategic point. But what, one wonders, has been achieved under the circumstances?

To begin with, nobody can predict that, a year or two from now, South Vietnam will still be free. But of greater importance than that, no one in his right mind will predict that the United States, facing a comparable challenge a year or two from now, would respond with military decisiveness. If, in that part of the world, the decision is to gobble up Thailand, what are we going to do about it? Exactly. And if, in another part of the world, they decide to go after Yugoslavia, or even Greece—what would we do about it?

It was the strangest aspect of this strange man that, once having decided on a course of action, he did not pursue it characteristically—i.e., with exclusive concern for its success. By his failure to do so, he undermined the very purpose of the intervention. And if the great communist superpowers exercise restraint at this point, it will not be because they have learned the lesson of Vietnam, in the way that Stalin learned the lesson of Greece and Iran. It will be merely because of the coincidence of their mutual hostility and their desire for American economic aid.

So what of his great domestic accomplishments? What great domestic accomplishments? He sought a Great Society. He ushered in bitterness and resentment. He sought to educate all the population of America, and he bred a swaggering illiteracy, and a cultural bias in favor of a college education so adamant and so preposterous that if John Milton applied for a job with Chock Full o'Nuts, they would demand first to see his college diploma. The rhetoric of LBJ was in the disastrous tradition of JFK—encouraging the popular superstition that the state could change the quality, no less, of American life. This led necessarily to disappointment, and the more presumptuous the rhetoric, the more bitter the disappointment.

The Great Society did not lead us into eudaemonia. It led us into frustration—and to the lowest recorded confidence-vote in the basic institutions of this country since the birth of George Gallup. But: He was a patriot, who cared for his country, who was unsparing of himself, and who acquired at least a certain public dignity which lifted him from buffoonery, into tragedy. And he was the object of probably the greatest sustained vituperation in American political history. He paid a very high price for the office he discharged. And his detractors, as it happened, are America's worst friends, if that was any consolation.

Richard Nixon

❥

(1913–1994)

No president—no public figure—vexed WFB the way Richard
Nixon did. During Buckley's rise to fame and peak celebrity, Nixon
was the preeminent Man of the Right; indeed, the "Age of Nixon"
that Senator Bob Dole tearfully proclaimed at Nixon's funeral was
also the Age of Bill Buckley, as evidenced by the frequent arm's-
length references to WFB on the Nixon tapes. As a self-proclaimed
"pragmatic conservative," RN saw Buckley not as just another commentator but as the leader of a faction, an Interest Group unto
himself—and thus a force to be reckoned with. In October 1966,
as Nixon launched his comeback, he told Robert Novak that "the
Buckleyites" were more dangerous to the GOP than the John Birch
Society. "What Nixon meant," Novak explained on *Firing Line,*

> was that the Buckleyites are very persuasive, they're very able,
> they have an outlet in the *National Review* and other publica-
> tions, they are extremely intelligent...that the Buckleyites are

to the right of the mainstream of the Republican Party and because they do have this forensic and persuasive ability...that
they represent a greater threat.

Appearing on *Firing Line* the next year, RN courted a new generation of conservatives who were forgetful of the Hiss case and
enchanted with California governor Ronald Reagan. "Naturally I'm a
prejudiced witness," Nixon said in his lawyerly way,

but I believe that as this campaign in 1968 unfolds, that the nation will see that the new Republican Party is one which advocates change, but advocates change in a different way from the
"irresponsibles." And I mean by that that in changing those things
that are wrong in America, we must not destroy the things that
are right. That to me is the essence of true conservatism.

Nixon was the first POTUS to whom WFB enjoyed direct access. Nixon attempted co-option: appealing to Buckley's vanity
with symbolic appointments. WFB told *Playboy* in 1970:

I have discovered a new sensual treat, which, appropriately, the
readers of *Playboy* should be the first to know about. It is to
have the president of the United States take notes while you are
speaking to him....

In the Nixon White House conservatives were bound to be disappointed: He was a Californian who understood the tribulations
of small business owners but who could expand, as president, the
regulatory state; a hawkish anticommunist who could cozy up to
Red China; a law and order man who could become ensnared in
a criminal conspiracy in the Oval Office. By late 1971, WFB had
moved from defending RN, as in the famous column "Is Nixon One

of Us?" ("Did anyone really expect that Richard Nixon would dis-mantle the welfare state?"), to declaring a "suspension" of support for the president.

In his long friendship with E. Howard Hunt, WFB had a personal connection to Watergate, and he bristled in his column when Nixon and his men could be heard on the tapes cynically plotting to ex-ploit that friendship. Below are two postmortems.

"Richard Nixon, RIP"

National Review, May 16, 1994.
[ellipses in original]

Clare Booth Luce once remarked that all public figures come to be associated with a single achievement, never mind how complex their career. And, true, we can say about Lincoln that he won the Civil War, about Edison that he harnessed electricity, about FDR that he created the New Deal. But with what achievement will Richard Nixon be associated, a generation from now? A negative achieve-ment: he is the only American president in history to be kicked out of office. Even so, in America and in much of the world, he was the dominant political figure. It can hap-pen only to a man who takes very large strides in history, that he could win reelection with a runaway majority, and in less than two years leave the White House in greater ignominy than was ever before suffered by a departing American president.

His excommunication from public life was so decisive, his subsequent return has to be credited to him alone, the most spectacular reopening in contemporary political history. Remarkable not only because he came back, so to speak, into power, but that he did so notwithstanding the implacability of those who were hostile to him. In the darkest days of August 1974, it looked unlikely that a single member of the press corps could be persuaded to be civil to Richard Nixon. Ten years later, after he addressed their convention in Washington, he was given a standing ovation.

It is an important part of his singular story that, really, he disposed of no spectacular personal talent. He was not a great orator, nor a great writer. His one professional skill he was formally disbarred from using. He had only the force of his extraordinary personality, his unswerving determination to succeed, and his mastery of the political craft. He competed during his career in forty state political primaries. He lost one.

Alexander Haig was his chief of staff when Nixon left the White House. "As you'd have guessed," General Haig reminisced a few years ago, "when Nixon got to Casa Pacifica in California late that afternoon in August, his White House line was still connected. He was in a daze: President of the United States until noon; one minute later—nothing. He was master of a villa which, without a president to preside over it, was simply a big house on the Pacific Ocean. But when Nixon got there, he used the telephone to the White House exactly as he'd been doing for six years. He must have called ten, fifteen times a day, and of course the White House operators didn't want to be responsible for breaking the trance, so they'd put him straight through to me, as though I were still his chief of staff."

How did he get the message that it was all over?

"On the fifth day I recognized that reality had to get to him. So when he called the next morning, I told the operator to put him on hold. . . . It had the magical effect, the necessary effect. Suddenly he realized he wasn't president."

But Mr. Nixon didn't abandon his sense of priorities, the first being to tell his story and to make a living for his family. A day or so later he reached by telephone, in Geneva, Irving Lazar. The exchange was as follows.

"Mr. Lazar, you are known as the number-one agent in America."

"Well, thank you very much, Mr. President. Yes, I suppose I'd have to own up to that reputation."

"Well, I'd like to see you tomorrow morning here in California."

"Mr. President! I have five days' appointments backed up here in Europe, appointments made weeks and months ago!"

"I take it you do not want to handle my memoirs? I have been told by someone who knows his way around in the publishing world that my memoirs may be worth as much as a million dollars. . . ."

"Of course I'd be glad to handle your memoirs, but there simply is no way I can get to you by tomorrow."

"Well, then, make it the day after tomorrow."

Irving Lazar finally succeeded, so to speak, in putting President Nixon on hold, but by the time he got to Casa Pacifica a week later, he arrived with contracts for two and one-half million dollars.

Nixon had begun the return journey. Retirement suited him singularly well. Henry Kissinger, in his own memoirs, remarked on how little Nixon actually enjoyed the life he had struggled so hard to achieve in the White House. He hated meeting with the press, hated state functions. He engaged in much that chiefs of state engage in with a visible detestation of ceremony and light talk.

That now was all gone, and he had only his tiny staff, his yellow pads, and the publishers, waiting for book after book. He resumed those travels he did enjoy—briefing foreigners, being briefed by them; renewing the company of men and women he had met when he was sun-king.

Gradually the agents of power everywhere in the world acknowledged that Richard Nixon's prestige did not derive exclusively from the office of president. He had a feeling for the American political scene invaluable to those who needed a confident grasp of it. And although meetings with Mr. Nixon would (except for two, perhaps three of his closest friends) never be confused with going down to the club and having a drink with old Tricky Dick, his company was thought rewarding by the men and women who ran the affairs of Europe, the Soviet Union, and Asia. He did not deceive them about what to expect from America, or indeed from Richard Nixon. When most recently he visited Moscow and Yeltsin canceled an appointment, indignant because Nixon had given interviews to Russian rivals, the sympathy was immediately with Nixon, rather than with his host: Nixon was being Nixon, and that, after all, was why he continued to be so eminent a figure. It did not surprise the diplomatic community that Yeltsin backed down, and that one of the earliest tributes logged by the hospital in New York, bidding Nixon adieu, was from Boris Yeltsin.

In America, Nixon was always thought of as a towering figure of the conservative camp, yet this was so only when the perspectives were narrowly confined. At the earliest conspicuous moment in his career, he had been spotted

as the man who believed Whittaker Chambers, and disbe-
lieved Alger Hiss. During the Fifties, the anti-Communists
mobilized against the anti-anti-Communists, and when Eisenhower permitted himself to reveal that he had not yet
decided whether to put Nixon back on the ticket in 1956,
the American Right spoke threateningly to General Eisenhower, who had learned all about *force majeure* at West
Point; and Nixon stayed on. During the Goldwater upheaval, Nixon was the loyalist, but he had learned in 1962,
in California, the lesson he never forgot. He was driving
through Central Park in 1967 after a television program
and told his companion, "I learned in 1962 that you can't
do without the support of conservatives. But I learned also
that you can't win with just the conservatives."

One year later he won the presidency. During those ill-
fated years he lost the Vietnam War, pulled out of the Bret-
ton Woods alliance, declared wage and price controls, and
traveled to China, where he toasted the achievements of
Mao Tse-tung. Not exactly a majestic roll for a right-wing
American president. For all the talk about the triumphant
resumption of diplomatic relations with China, it has never
been clear just what was achieved by going to Peking in
1972, instead of waiting another few years until Mao, and
the Cultural Revolution, had run their course. Indeed, one
more remarkable achievement of Richard Nixon is how he
earned the special affection and admiration of U.S. conservatives without ever significantly advancing their cause.

In the final analysis, he was a heroic, intensely personal
figure, whose life was lived on the public stage. He was
at once the weakest of men, and the strongest; a master
of self-abuse, and of self-recovery. Stained by worldliness,
and driven by the hunger to serve. For Americans under

seventy, there never was a world without Richard Nixon. Not many people can pitch whole generations into loneliness, as he has now done, R.I.P. —WFB

———•———

"The Watergate Moment"

New York Times, August 8, 1994.

To look back on it: On Feb. 1, 1974, I urged President Richard Nixon to invoke the 25th Amendment and declare Gerald Ford to be acting President, on the explicit understanding that Mr. Nixon would resume the office if the impeachment proceedings came to rest without expelling him.

That became, in the nature of things, the position of *National Review,* and early in March my brother, Senator James Buckley, publicly called on the President to resign. This rank-breaking severely rattled the White House, but Mr. Nixon's strategists remained confident that the President would survive. It wasn't until April 29 that Mr. Nixon finally succumbed to pressures from all sides and released the transcripts of the tapes. That was the moment, as I reflect on it, when one knew that the king must die.

In April 1974, the mind of America hadn't closed on a script for the last act of Watergate. Moral and legal conclusions were everywhere being peddled. The smoking gun transcript sat ticking away, three months off.

Though the publication of other tape transcripts had

seeded a moral consensus, deliberative men and women hadn't all concluded, by April, that a legal offense had been committed on a scale that justified overturning the emphatic decision of the people, given in November 1972, to keep Richard Nixon in the White House.

And the moralists (those of them who stayed sober) were asking sophisticated questions—among them, can we opine convincingly on the matter at hand when dealing with the king? Are not a President's temptations and extravagances reasonably measured by standards different from those that apply to others?

On July 27, 1974, Mr. Nixon lost the special House committee, which voted to impeach him on three counts. It could now be predicted that the whole House would vote to impeach—but not yet that the Senate would vote to convict. That certainty was still a week off. But by the time the smoking gunshot was heard, confirming that Mr. Nixon had conspired to obstruct justice and that he had lied about doing so, the tapes had reached into the consciousness of America. Their effect was devastating.

P[resident]: You've got to have something where it doesn't appear that I am doing this in, you know, just in a—saying to hell with the Congress and to hell with the people, we are not going to tell you anything because of executive privilege. That, they don't understand. But if you say, "No, we are willing to cooperate," and you've made a complete statement, but make it very incomplete. See, that is what I mean. I don't want a, too much in chapter and verse as you did in your letter. I just want just a general——

Dean: An all-around statement.

P.: That's right. . . .

Toward the end, Mr. Nixon brought in a Jesuit priest who, from the White House steps, pronounced the President to be "the greatest moral leader of the last third of this century." For those who would not take the priest's word for it, he asked merely that they show charity. One reaction at the time (my own):

"Charity has nothing to do with keeping us from giving to the transcripts the kind of attention that Mr. Nixon asked us to give to them—from dwelling on the contradictions, remarking the selfishness of their concern, expressing a not uncosmopolitan dismay at the quality of the discourse. The only thing that charity absolutely requires is that no further analysis be made of the remarks of Father McLaughlin." (This is the John McLaughlin who now presides over *The McLaughlin Group* on television.) It would have been stirring if on first learning that their existence had been detected, Richard Nixon had piled the tapes onto the Rose Garden grill and set a match to them. He'd have reaffirmed by concrete act the Presidential stakes he had described so apocalyptically—that the office of the President would be destroyed if ever the tapes of Presidential conversations were released. He might then with some dignity have invited Congress and the courts to do with him as they willed; he was prepared to go to the stake to protect the office.

But he could do nothing effective. It crept into the mind of America that Richard Nixon had lost political savoir faire. He had begun by denouncing Watergate as insignificant. Soon after, he declared the need to probe Watergate fully and to expose all who were guilty. Dismayed observers were beginning to wonder whether his mind was misfiring: in one speech (April 30, 1973), he declared John Ehrlichman and Bob Haldeman the two greatest civil servants in American history and, in the same speech, fired them.

The ongoing assertions of innocence galvanized a painful dilemma. Either his words had directly to be doubted or it was necessary to construct a scaffolding that supported both those words and the developing data—pleas of guilt by Mr. Nixon's associates, revelations of incriminating tapes, missing portions of individual tapes. But such a structure would no longer stand up. The mind of America was closing on the question.

I recall a visit to the Oval Office in 1970. "Bring along any one person you wish," the President's aide had said, so I invited James Burnham, the renowned political philosopher and my colleague at *National Review*. The other two in the room with the President were Attorney General John Mitchell and the chief of staff, H. R. Haldeman. The President came quickly to the point, informing me that he intended, notwithstanding that James Buckley was running against a Republican incumbent, obliquely to support my brother for the Senate in the election six weeks down the road.

He then thought to give me some political advice to pass along to Candidate Buckley. "Tell him when he is being heckled at one of his speeches to go right up to spitting distance of the protester. The television cameras will catch that face-to-face encounter and that means votes for the law and order candidate."

Mr. Haldeman took it from there. "Bill, get a couple of guys from Young Americans for Freedom. Tell them to dress up like Woodstock protesters and have them throw an egg or some ketchup at your brother. That will make it into the evening television news."

The President leaned over to me, a Madame Tussaud smile on his face: "I didn't hear that, Bill."

During those final months, he lost his capacity not to hear bad counsel, lost any capacity to listen to whatever angels struggled in his nature. When on Aug. 9 the helicopter flew him off the White House lawn to exile, there were only two policemen patrolling the street outside against the possibility of mob protests. No more were needed. The mind of America had set on the Watergate drama.

Ronald Reagan

(1911–2004)

"I was way behind in apprehending his potential," WFB admitted of Ronald Reagan. Chatting with Nelson Rockefeller in 1967, Buckley declared, "There's no way a former actor could go for president." "Anybody who wins the California election with 1 million votes," replied Rockefeller, "is presidential material." In Reagan, WFB ultimately came to see heroic qualities: a man of intellectual and physical rigor in whose character Buckley located the central factor in the West's triumph over communism. WFB also experienced RR as a charming friend who credited WFB, and *National Review,* as singularly influential in the president's intellectual development. Still, for Bill, the best part of the whole deal, secretly, was Nancy Reagan, with whom the Buckleys would carry on a deep friendship beyond Ronnie's death. The saddest moment in *The Reagan I Knew* (2008), WFB's posthumously published memoir, recounted their final meeting, in 1990, in which an afternoon taping of *Firing Line* (his ninth, depending on how one counts them, designed to promote Reagan's memoir) preceded a private dinner with Nancy and Ron, Jr., at the Reagans' Bel Air home.

> After a few minutes it became plain that the conversation was not expected at a pitch high enough to guarantee [the former president's] hearing of it and participation in it. From time to time he would initiate a talking point, and the conversation would be general. But soon his voice quivered, and his attention was paid to the food, not to whatever was on the mind of his wife, son, and old friend.

Of the mystery surrounding Reagan—the emotional distance he kept even from close companions—Buckley got an early glimpse. In November 1967, Governor Reagan, freshly named the Chubb Fellow at Yale, shook hands on a receiving line with WFB at his side. "I would have the same experience with Reagan two or three times again," Buckley noted.

> What happened was that at a certain moment a faintly detectable glaze fell over his eyes. *Nothing else was noticeable.* His pleasantries were spontaneous, his head often bowed slightly to catch every word. But when the glaze set in, whatever faculty it is that informs you on the matter of who it is you're talking to, in Reagan, simply cut out.... About the twenty-third guest came by, and I knew that Reagan was no longer distinguishing them. Then an electric moment. A particular guest had grabbed Reagan's hand firmly and was leaning just slightly toward him, a summons to that extra little intimacy often seen on receiving lines. But while Reagan's smile was warm, his hand actively engaged in the guest's hand, suddenly the guest withdrew his hand. "Ronnie," he said, in a voice just a little strained. "This is me, George Bush." The glaze lifted, and there was some lively

patter between the Chubb Fellow who thirteen years later would become president and the man who would become his vice president and successor.

The remarks below originally were delivered at Reagan's eighty-eighth birthday at the Ronald Reagan Presidential Foundation and Library celebration in Simi Valley in February 1999.

"Ronald Reagan: 1911–2004, the Keynote Address"

National Review, June 28, 2004.
[originally delivered at the Ronald Reagan Presidential Library
on February 4, 1999]

I recall that Henry Mencken described an introduction to him on a celebratory occasion as having evoked "a full moon, the setting sun, and the aurora borealis." In this perspective, if all the things Mark Burson has said really belong to me, how am I expected even to intimate the achievements of Ronald Reagan? Well, I can do that, really, in one sentence.

He succeeded in getting Nancy Reagan to marry him.

The country is familiar with the legend of Nancy, familiar with her accomplishments as companion, aide, monitor, wife, and lover. There was never anyone who more devotedly served a husband. She has renewed for us all the meaning of the pledge to stand by in sickness and in health.

This being a convocation of friends and admirers, in celebration of his birthday, I propose as keynoter to dwell

a while on a longtime friendship. It began in the spring
of 1961. Ronald and Nancy Reagan, whom I hadn't met,
were seated at one end of the restaurant, my sister-in-law
and I at the other end. We were out of sight of one another.
Both parties were headed, after dinner, across the street to
an auditorium in a public high school. There I would be
introduced as the evening's speaker, addressing an assembly of doctors and their wives, by Ronald Reagan, a well-
known actor and currently the host of a television series
sponsored by General Electric; moreover, a public figure
who had taken an interest in conservatives and conservative writings.

We bumped into each other going out the door. Ronald
Reagan introduced himself and Nancy, and said he had just
finished reading my book *Up from Liberalism*. He quoted a
crack from it, done at the expense of Mrs. Roosevelt, which
he relished. I requited his courtesy by relishing him and
Nancy for life.

He distinguished himself that night—and dismayed
Mrs. Reagan—by what he proceeded to do after discovering that the microphone hadn't been turned on. He had
tried, raising his voice, to tell a few stories. But the audience was progressively impatient. Waiting in vain for the
superintendent to unlock the door to the tight little office
at the other end of the hall, in which the control box lay,
he sized up the problem and, having surveyed all possible
avenues of approach, climbed out the window at stage level
and, one story above the busy traffic below, cat-walked,
Cary Grant style, twenty or thirty yards to the window of
the control room. This he penetrated by breaking the window with a thrust of his elbow; he climbed in, turned on
the light, flipped on the microphone, unlocked the office

door, and emerged with that competent relaxed smile of his, which we came to know after Grenada, Libya, Reykjavik, and Moscow; proceeding with the introduction of the speaker. And all that was thirty years before bringing peace in our time!

In later years I thought his movements that night a nifty allegory of his approach to foreign policy, the calm appraisal of a situation, the willingness to take risks, and then the decisive moment: leading to lights and sound—and music, the music of the spheres.

We stayed friends.

Twenty years later he was running for President of the United States. Early that winter the Soviet military had charged into Afghanistan, beginning a long, costly, brutal exercise. A week or two after he was nominated in Detroit, I wrote him. I told him I thought he would be elected. And told him then that, on the assumption that on reaching the White House he might wish to tender me an office, I wished him to know that I aspired to no government job of any kind.

He wrote back that he was disappointed. "I had in mind," he said, "to appoint you ambassador to Afghanistan." Over the next eight years, in all my communications with him, I would report fleetingly on my secret mission in Kabul, the capital of Afghanistan, where, in our fiction, I lived and worked. In his letters to me he would always address me as Mr. Ambassador. The show must go on, where Ronald Reagan was involved.

Soon after his election I was asked by the Philadelphia Society to speak on the theme, "Is President Reagan doing all that can be done?" It was a coincidence that my wife, Pat, and I had spent the weekend before the Philadelphia

speech as guests of the President and Mrs. Reagan in Bar-
bados. I recalled with delight an exchange I had with my
host on the presidential helicopter. We were flying to our
villa the first evening, before the two days on Easter weekend reserved for bacchanalian sunning and swimming on
the beach in front of Claudette Colbert's house. I leaned
over and told him I had heard the rumor that the Secret
Service was going to deny him permission to swim on that
beach on the grounds that it was insufficiently secure. I
asked him whether that were so, that he wouldn't be allowed in the water.

Helicopters, even Air Force One helicopters, are pretty
noisy, but I was able to make out what he said. It was, "Well,
Bill, Nancy here tells me I'm the most powerful man in the
Free World. If she's right, then I will swim tomorrow with
you."

Which indeed he did.

I recall also that during one of our swims I said to him,
"Mr. President, would you like to earn the *National Review*
Medal of Freedom?" He confessed to being curious as to
how he would qualify to do this. I explained: "I will pro-
ceed to almost drown, and you will rescue me." We went
through the motions, and that evening I conferred that
medal on him, *in pectore.*

I remember telling the Philadelphia Society that the most
powerful man in the Free World is not powerful enough
to do everything that needs to be done. Retrospectively,
I have speculated on what I continue to believe was the
conclusive factor in the matter of American security
against any threat of Soviet aggression. It was the character of the occupant of the White House; the character

of Ronald Reagan. The reason this is so, I have argued, is that the Soviet Union, for all that from time to time it miscalculated tactically, never miscalculated in respect of matters apocalyptic in dimension. And the policymakers of the Soviet Union knew that the ambiguists with whom they so dearly loved to deal were not in power during those critical years. So that if ever the Soviet leaders were tempted to such suicidal foolishness as to launch a strike against us, suicidal is exactly what it would have proven to be. The primary obstacle to the ultimate act of Soviet imperialism was the resolute U.S. determination to value what we have, over against what they, under Soviet dominion, had; value it sufficiently to defend it with all our resources.

Ronald Reagan, in my judgment, animated his foreign policy by his occasional diplomatic indiscretions: because of course it was a diplomatic indiscretion to label the Soviet Union an "evil empire." But then, quite correctly, he would switch gears when wearing diplomatic top hat and tails. He did not on those occasions talk the language of John Wayne—or of Thomas Aquinas.

But how reassuring it was for us, you remember, every now and then ("Mr. Gorbachev, tear down this wall"), to vibrate to the music of the very heartstrings of the Leader of the Free World who, to qualify convincingly as such, had after all to *feel* a total commitment to the Free World. When in formal circumstances the President ventured out to exercise conviviality with the leaders of the Soviet Union, the scene was by its nature wonderful, piquant: What would he say that was agreeable, congenial, to the head of the evil empire? The summit conferences brought to mind the Russian who, on discovering that his pet parrot was missing, rushed out to the KGB office to report that his parrot's political opinions were entirely unrelated to his own.

The Reagan years accustomed us to a mood about life and about government. There were always the interruptions, the potholes of life. But Ronald Reagan had strategic visions. He told us that most of our civic problems were problems brought on or exacerbated by government, not problems that could be solved by government.

That, of course, is enduringly true. Only government can cause inflation, preserve monopoly, and punish enterprise. On the other hand, it is only a government leader who can critically affect a national mood or put his stamp on a historical period. One refers not to the period of Shakespeare, but to the period of Elizabeth. Reagan's period was brief, but he did indeed put his stamp on it. He did this in part because he was scornful of the claims of omnipotent government, in part because he felt, and expressed, the buoyancy of the American Republic.

It is fine that the Ronald Reagan Library, Museum, and Center for Public Affairs, which serves as our host, will collect his papers and ambient literature, permitting generations of students and scholars to explore and linger over those happy years which augured the end of the Soviet threat, the revitalization of our economy, and a great draft of pride in our country. To the library I'll convey in years ahead my own collection of letters from Ronald Reagan. The very last one written from the White House, the day the Soviet Union announced that it would withdraw from Afghanistan, began:

Dear Mr. Ambassador:

Congratulations!
The Soviets are moving out of Afghanistan. I knew you
could do it if I only left you there long enough, and you did it
without leaving Kabul for a minute.

He closed by saying, "Nancy sends her love to you and
Pat."

That was eleven years ago, and we cherish it today, and
through her, convey our own love and gratitude to the
President, on his 88th birthday.

FAMILY

Patricia Taylor Buckley

—◆—

(1926–2007)

"I'm just a simple country girl from the woods of British Columbia,"
Pat Buckley liked to say, but everyone who knew *la grande dame*
knew how given she was to untruths—the more outrageous and
amusing, the better. As WFB's wife of fifty-seven years, Pat was
every inch the equal of her famous husband and essential, in her way,
to his engagement with presidents and intellectuals. "Pat looks like a
queen, acts like a queen, and is just the match for Billy," WFB's sister
Trish Buckley wrote home in 1948. Trish's Vassar suite mate, Patricia
Aldyen Austin Taylor, a debutante from one of Canada's wealthiest
families, sported a fabulous figure, nearly six feet tall, her fine features framed by lustrous brown hair. "She came into Buckley's room
with a mink coat on," remembered Francis Donahue, faculty adviser
to the *Yale Daily News,* "and she just let it fall off her shoulders onto
the floor. All the students were in love with her." "She didn't enter
a room," agreed Schuyler Chapin, the Metropolitan Opera executive, "she took possession of it." Over the July Fourth weekend in

1949, seventy-two hours into their first extended time together, Bill resolved to propose. The setting was Shannon, the Taylor home in Vancouver: an enclave of English gardens surrounding a Georgian mansion. Bill asked Pat's sister, Kathleen, to fetch her from a canasta game. Told her new boyfriend wanted to see her and was acting strangely, Pat set down her cards and strode to the library. There she found Bill pacing and smoking. "Bill, what do you want?"

"Patricia, would you consider marriage with me?"

"Bill," she replied, "I've been asked this question many times. To the others I've said no. To you I say yes. Now may I please get back and finish my hand?"

Over the next six decades—in locales as far-flung as New Haven, Mexico City, Manhattan, Stamford, and Gstaad—Pat provided ballast to WFB's frenetic life, most significantly in the gift of their one "miracle" child, Christopher Taylor Buckley, in September 1952. A pair of ectopic pregnancies surrounding Christopher's birth precluded any more children, let alone the kind of extended family Bill had cherished as a child. "It was a terrible blow," Bill said. As Christopher matured, and with WFB frequently traveling, Pat threw herself into philanthropy. Her prime beneficiaries were the Costume Institute of the Metropolitan Museum, the Museum of Modern Art, and the Memorial Sloan-Kettering Cancer Center. For the last, Pat helped raise an estimated $75 million over thirty years.

In all they did together and much of what Bill did on his own, Pat tirelessly supported her husband. Where this loyalty was most severely tested was in Bill's love of sailing. Eulogizing his father, Christopher Buckley said: "Some of my earliest memories are of my mother, shrieking at him as the water broke over the cockpit and the boat pitched furiously in boiling seas, 'Bill—*Bill!* Why are you trying to kill us?'"

As in any marriage, there was strain; Christopher's *Losing Mum and Pup* (2009) recorded that Pat and Bill, who addressed each other as "Ducky," quarreled so frequently as to have been on non-speaking terms for "about a third" of their marriage. No one else could more swiftly defenestrate WFB, chop the champion debater down to size, with a tart one-liner—or a look. "The wrath of Pat Buckley," Christopher wrote, "could instill fear in an advancing column of mechanized infantry." No less outsized a figure than Henry Kissinger recalled Pat's "rather overpowering personality," remembering that she exhibited "no hesitancy in interrupting me in midparagraph, saying, 'You're making no sense at all.'" When Pat's acerbic wit or penchant for The Whopper created awkward moments—usually, Christopher noted, "after the supernumerary glass of wine"—the famously articulate WFB would freeze into an expression "somewhere between a Jack Benny stare and the stoic grimace of a thirteenth-century saint being burned alive at the stake." At times, of course, WFB gave it right back. The British filmmaker Peter Glenville remembered an occasion when Pat, still seething from a spat, admonished Bill not to address her as Ducky. "Oh, why not?"

"I'm not going to go into it. Just don't call me Ducky."

"Then what would you like me to call you?" Bill asked. "Shit-face?"

All of it—the full Buckley complement of fame and intellectual engagement, high society and haute couture, adventures literary, snowy, and nautical, the grand style that helped make WFB so persuasive in the controversial arts—was made possible by Pat: She captained the ship of their *lives*. As Christopher, supreme witness to the Buckley marriage, observed, "Deep in her DNA was something that I think she had learned from her mother: you take care of your men." Pat Buckley's own summation of her life was as reliable, perhaps, as the description of her as a simple country girl. "I'm just an Arab wife," she said. "When Bill says, 'Strike the tent,' I do."

"*Patricia Taylor Buckley, R.I.P.*"

National Review, May 14, 2007.
[Christopher's memoir notes that both he and WFB prepared eulogies
for Pat's funeral but "neither Pup nor I trusted ourselves to get through
a eulogy." Bill wrote the foregoing for the program, then published it in
NR; Christopher's tribute became the service, an ornate and beautifully
executed affair at the Metropolitan Museum's Temple of Dendur.]

By any standard, at near six feet tall, she was extraordinary. She shared a suite with my sister Trish and two other students at Vassar, and on that spring evening in 1949 I was the blind date she had never met. When I walked into the drawing room the four girls shared, I found her hard pressed. She was mostly ready for the prom but was now vexed by attendant responsibilities. I offered to paint her fingernails, and she immediately extended her hand, using the other one on the telephone. The day before, she had given the sad news to her roommates that she would not be returning to Vassar for junior and senior years. She was needed at home, in Vancouver, to help her mother care for a dying family member. My own parents had gone to their place in South Carolina for the winter and the house in Sharon, Conn., was closed. But I would dart over from Yale for an occasional weekend in the huge empty house, and Trish brought her there once, and we laughed all weekend long, and Trish promised to visit her in Vancouver during the summer.

I had a summer job in Calgary working for my father in the oil business, and from there happily flew over to Vancouver to join Trish and Pat for a weekend. Her father's vast house occupied an entire city block, but did not dampen

our spirits. On the contrary, the tempo of our congenial-
ity heightened, and on the third day I asked if she would
marry me. She rushed upstairs to tell her mother, and I
waited at the bottom of the huge staircase hoping to get
the temper of her proud mother's reaction (her father was
out of town), and soon I heard peals of laughter. I waited
apprehensively for Pat to advise me what that was all about.
The laughter, she revealed, was generated by her mother's
taking the occasion to recall that eight times in the past,
Pat had reported her betrothal.

One year later, in the company of about a thousand
guests, we exchanged vows. Two months after that, we
rented a modest house in a suburb of New Haven. Pat resolved to learn how to cook. Her taste was advanced and
her ambitions exigent, so she commuted to New York City
and learned cooking from experts, becoming one herself.
Meanwhile, I taught a class in Spanish to undergraduates
and wrote *God and Man at Yale*.

Primarily to avoid exposure to further duty as an infantry officer, I joined the CIA and we went to live in Mexico
City, buying and decorating a lovely house in the district of
San Angel Inn. Pat was radiant and hyperactive in maintaining the house and its little garden. She resolutely failed
to learn the language, even though, until the end, the staff
was Spanish-speaking, but intercommunication was electri-
cally effective.

Her solicitude was such that she opposed any venture
by me which she thought might adversely affect me. She opposed the founding of *National Review*, my signing up with
a lecture agency, my nonfiction books and then my fiction
books, my contract to write a syndicated column, the projected winter in Switzerland, my decision to run for mayor

of New York. Yet once these enterprises were undertaken, she participated enthusiastically. It was she who located the exquisite house, every inch of which she decorated, that we shared for 55 years. We had only one child, Christopher, of whom she was understandably proud. And it was she—all but uniquely she—who brought to this house the legion of guests, of all ages, professions, and interests, whose company made up her lively life.

Her infirmities dated back to a skiing accident in 1965. She went through four hip replacements over the years. She went into the hospital a fortnight ago, but there was no thought of any terminal problem. Yet following an infection, on the seventh day, she died, in the arms of her son.

Friends from everywhere were quick to record their grief. One of them was especially expressive. "Allow a mere acquaintance of your wife to sense the magnitude of your loss. As surely as she physically towered over her surroundings, she must have mentally, spiritually, and luminously surpassed ordinary mortals. She certainly was in every sense of the term *une grande dame,* a distinction she wore as lightly as a T-shirt—not that one can imagine her in anything so plebeian. The only consolation one may offer is that the greatness of a loss is the measure of its antecedent gain. And perhaps also that Pat's memory will be second only to her presence. For as long as you live, people will share with you happy reminiscences that, in their profusion, you may have forgotten or not even known.

"I am a confirmed nonbeliever, but for once I would like to be mistaken, and hope that, for you, this is not goodbye, but *hasta luego.*"

No alternative thought would make continuing in life, for me, tolerable. —WFB

William F. Buckley, Sr.

◆━◆

(1881–1958)

In *Losing Mum and Pup,* Christopher drew on one of his earliest childhood memories, from the age of five, to chronicle a pivotal moment in his father's adult life. Christopher was sleeping with his parents in their bed when the clanging of the telephone jolted them all awake. "A great commotion of grown-ups followed," he wrote,

> Mum going down to make coffee, Pup hunched over the phone, speaking in grave, urgent tones. Of course, I found it all exciting and eventful and hoped it would involve—with any luck— a reprieve from school that day. "What is it?" I asked Mum. "Pup's father has died, darling."

The death of William F. Buckley, Sr., weighed heavily on all ten of his children, of course, and naturally on Aloise, his wife of forty-one years and the mother of those children, but those who knew the Buckleys during the children's formative years, in Connecticut, had always observed in Bill a singular desire to please his father and in WFB Sr. a corresponding delight in the combination of moral devoutness, intellectual rigor, and performing ability so markedly on display in his sixth child. None of the Buckley children did more than Bill to internalize, or spread, the gospel bequeathed to them by their accomplished, exacting, and sometimes forbidding father. Born in Washington, Texas, in 1881, William Frank Buckley was one of five brothers and sisters raised in tiny San Diego, Texas, ninety minutes from the Mexican border. Their Irish-Protestant father had emigrated from County Cork to Canada and then to Texas in the 1840s. While Will's accounts of John Buckley emphasized their indigence, records show that John, a sheep farmer turned sheriff, also sold insurance and paid for Will's education at the University of Texas. Under the influence of his mother, an Irish-Catholic whose family had emigrated from County Limerick, young Will was raised a Catholic and tutored in Latin. After completing his undergraduate and law degrees in five years, Will spent two desultory years at the General Land Office in Austin before heading south of the border in 1908 to practice law. Within a few years, he and his brothers had established the premier law firm in Mexico for oil companies, leading Will to become a speculator himself. Those were years of revolution and counterrevolution for Mexico, and for a time, affecting studied neutrality, Will navigated the political upheaval. But he often felt as buffeted by the U.S. government.

> MR. KEARFUL: Have you made a study of Mexican conditions during the time that you were in Mexico and during the last few months in this country?

> WILLIAM F. BUCKLEY, SR.: Yes.... To understand the Mexican situation it must be understood in the beginning that the present is more or less the normal condition of Mexico; the era of peace during the Diaz regime from 1876 to 1910 was an

abnormal period in the history of that country. All revolutions in Mexico work along conventional lines and the present series of revolutions are in no material sense different from those that beset the country from 1810 to 1876; the abnormal element of the present series of revolutions is the active participation in them by the American Government.

—Testimony before the House Committee on Foreign Relations Subcommittee on Mexican Affairs, Washington, D.C., December 6, 1919

On a business trip to New Orleans in 1917, Will was introduced to Aloise Steiner, the sister of a girl he had met the previous year in Mexico City. After several days, WFB Sr. proposed; they were married on Christmas Day and moved to Mexico, where Will returned, *con mucho gusto,* to the intrigues of Mexican politics. He actively plotted a counterrevolution against the Obregon regime, including an abortive effort at gunrunning, and courted danger. "He'd talked Pancho Villa out of shooting a train conductor," Christopher Buckley reported, with another occasion finding Will "kidnapped by thugs . . . and taken into a forest to be killed." By 1921, when Obregon ordered Will Buckley expelled from the country, confiscating his assets and fortune, the native Texan was lucky to get out alive. The experience simultaneously reinforced Will's Catholicism and his opposition to communism and all other revolutionary movements. He, Aloise, and their three children retreated to Great Elm: a large house on ample property in Sharon, Connecticut. There the ten Buckley children were raised, during Will's absences, by Aloise and a rotating cast of nannies, governesses, teachers, and tutors. Ceaselessly the children shuttled between classes, activities, and lessons on the property, with Great Elm forming its own Catholic community: a privileged and mannered space, "elite and self-isolating," whose inhabitants, driven hard by their father, came to see the world outside with some skepticism. "There was nothing complicated about Father's theory of child-rearing," wrote eldest daughter Aloise Buckley Heath. "He brought up his sons and daughters to be absolutely perfect."

> To this end his children were, at one time or another, given pro-
> fessional instructions in: apologetics, art, ballroom dancing, banjo,
> bird-watching, building boats in bottles, calligraphy, canoeing, car-
> pentry, cooking, driving trotting horses, French, folk-dancing,
> golf, guitar (Hawaiian and Spanish), harmony, herb-gardening,
> horsemanship, history of architecture, ice-skating, mandolin, ma-
> rimba, music appreciation, organ, painting, piano, playing popular
> music, rumba, sailing, skiing, singing, Spanish, speech, stenogra-
> phy, swimming, tap-dancing, tennis, typing and woodcarving.

"If his children ended up as captains of their college football teams (they didn't), or editors of the school yearbook or presidents of the class (they occasionally did), it was all well and good, and he was very proud," wrote Priscilla Buckley, an editor of *National Review* for four decades. "But it was far more important to William Buckley that his children be courteous, industrious and God-fearing." John Buckley, the eldest son, described the atmosphere Will created in less benign terms: "My father played it two ways—either I am going to be alone with my wife and nobody is going to disturb me, includ-ing you children—or he would have a dinner party for forty-eight people." When Will's company struck oil in Venezuela, he rebuilt the fortune seized from him in Mexico and shuttled the family to different locales—France, England, Camden, South Carolina—all while maintaining his high standards for the children and an exhor-tative, if occasionally puckish, correspondence with them:

> *Memorandum to the Buckley Children:*
>   *I have been much concerned of late with the apparent*
> *inability of any of you, at any time to go anywhere on foot,*
> *although I am sure your Mother would have informed me if any*

*of you had been born without the walking capacity of a normal
human being. [. . .]*

> *Affectionately,*
> *Father*

From Will's writings and Senate testimony, one can discern traces
of the rhetorical style—marked by circumlocution and sarcasm—
that Bill later would make famous. Sister Jane recognized that of all
the Buckley children, Billy emerged as "the apple of his father's eye."
"Father had a very special love of Bill," agreed brother Reid. When
WFB Jr. was fifteen, a sophomore at Millbrook, Will wrote him:

> *My dear Billy,*
> *In thinking over my letter to you it may have appeared very
> critical and I hope you did not take it that way. Your mother
> and I like very much your attitude of having strong convictions
> and of not being too bashful to express them. What I meant
> was that you would have to learn to be more moderate in the
> expression of your views and try to express them in a way that
> would give as little offense as possible to your friends.*

Bill's veneration for his father was total. When a professor suggested the study of metaphysics, Bill replied: "I have God and my
father. That's all I need." "I don't know if you were aware of this
while I was in Millbrook," Bill wrote Will at twenty, "but I was not
very popular with boys."

> *After a good deal of self-analysis, I determined that
> the principal reason for this revolved around my extreme
> dogmatism—principally in matters involving politics and the
> Catholic Church. I could not understand another point of view;
> it seemed to me that anyone who was not an isolationist or a*

*Catholic was simply stupid. Instead of keeping these sentiments
to myself, I blurted them out and supported them upon the
slightest provocation. I was intolerant about all kinds of things.
I would not sit in on sex conversations or trivial gossip because
I considered them wrong. . . . The result of this was that my
company was very little sought for except by a close few friends.*

*When I went into the Army, I learned the importance
of tolerance, and the importance of a sense of proportion
about all matters—even in regard to religion, morality
etc. . . . I found that there were actually very few prerequisites
to the good friend: he had to have a good sense of humor,
a pleasant personality and a certain number of common
interests.*

WFB Sr. did not live to see WFB Jr. achieve his greatest fame or
influence, the eventual triumph of the ideals Will had labored to instill in his children; he died shortly before *National Review,* launched
with a $100,000 "loan" from him, marked its third anniversary. But
Will saw his son marry Pat, witnessed the publication of *God and Man
at Yale* (1951) and *McCarthy and His Enemies* (1954), and supported his
son's early career as *l'enfant terrible* of American commentary.

ROSEN: I'm wondering if there's anything you've done since
you became a so-called public person of which you think your
father would have disapproved.

WFB: Well, there's a—there's a certain looseness of language,
which is pretty conventional today, not to say profligate, which
would have been very shocking to somebody in my father's generation. My father died in 1958. [laughs] And I remember when
he read the galleys of my book on Joe McCarthy. I used the
word—intending exactly to use it—a "damned son-of-a-bitch."

And he was really offended by that. He put a big cross mark in the margins, suggesting that it should be eliminated. I suppose he would have gotten used to the vernacular, because every-body has to; otherwise, they can't watch television. That's your fault!... But beyond that, no, I don't think there's any position that I have taken that would have surprised or disappointed him.

The first piece below is the eulogy that ran in *National Review* in October 1958. Then follows a short treatment of Will's final days from the privately published *W.F.B.—An Appreciation by His Family and Friends* (1959) and a reminiscence, published forty years after Will's death, about an "affair of the heart" and a final communication from the grave.

"William Frank Buckley, 1881–1958"

National Review, October 25, 1958.

The vital statistics are that he grew up in Texas and, as the oldest son, undertook, upon the premature death of his father, to look after the health and welfare of his mother and the education of his three brothers and two sisters. He did this, and educated himself at the University of Texas by teaching Spanish, which he had mastered by living as a boy on the frontier. He went to Mexico to practice law, and saw the revolution against the benevolent and autocratic Porfirio Diaz and what followed in its wake, and learned, and never forgot, his distrust of the revolutionary ideology.

There are not many alive who knew him then, but those who did remember keenly the intelligence, the wit, the largeheartedness, and—always—the high principle, which brought him a singular eminence in the community. That eminence the American government repeatedly acknowledged, as when three successive Secretaries of State called on him for guidance; as when the Wilson administration offered him the civil governorship of Veracruz (he refused indignantly); as when the Mexican government appointed him counsel at the ABC Conference in Niagara; as when he was called by the Senate Foreign Relations Committee as the premier American expert on the tangled affairs of Mexico. And in 1921, the end of the line: exile from Mexico. At that, he was lucky. For he had indeed materially aided a counterrevolutionary movement. The fact that the counter-revolutionists were decent men, and those in power barbarians, does not alter the political reality, which is that it is a very dangerous business indeed to back an unsuccessful insurrection, and he knew it and barely escaped with his skin.

He had married, and had three children, and would have seven more, all ten of whom survive him. He launched a business in Venezuela, and his fortunes fluctuated. But as children, we were never aware of his tribulations. We knew only that the world revolved about him and that whether what we needed was a bicycle, or an excuse to stay away from school for a day, or the answer to an anguished personal problem, he was there to fill the need, and when he thought the need exorbitant or improper, he would, by a word, bring us gently to earth. He worshipped three earthly things: learning, beauty, and his family. He satisfied his lust for the first by reading widely and by imposing on his lawless brood an unusual pedagogic regimen. The second impulse he gratified by a meticulous attention to every shrub, every stick of furniture that composed his two incomparable homes. The third he served by a constant, inexplicit tenderness to his wife and children of which the many who have witnessed it have not, they say, often seen the like.

In his anxiety for the well-being of his country his three passions fused. Here in America was the beauty, the abundance, that he revered; here in the political order was the fruit of centuries of learning; here his wife, and his ten children, and his thirty-one grandchildren, would live, as long as he lived and years after. So he encouraged us to stand by our country and our principles. To his encouragement, moral and material, *National Review* owes its birth and early life. It was only two weeks ago that, crippled and convalescent in Austria, he registered, in turn, joy, and indignation, and amusement, and sadness, as his wife read aloud to him from the latest issue of this chronicle of America's glories and misadventures.

My father died last week at seventy-seven, and we take leave of him in the pages of the journal which had become his principal enthusiasm. We pray God his spirited soul to keep.

"The Last Days"

In Buckley, Priscilla L., and Buckley, William F., Jr. (Eds.), *W.F.B.—An Appreciation by His Family and Friends* (privately published, 1979).
[At bottom, Buckley listed the "honorary pallbearers": Cecilio Velasco, Van Zandt Wheeler, Joseph H. Himes, Warren W. Smith, George S. Montgomery, Jr., J. MacMillan Harding, Dr. M. D. Touart, John deLoach, and John Villepigue.]

Father and Mother spent the late summer of 1958 at Bad Gastein in Austria, as they had two of the preceding three summers. Bad Gastein was one of the few places in which Father found refuge in his lifelong flight from hay fever. Reid and Betsy and their children joined them there and spent several weeks with them. They met again in Paris. From there, Reid and Betsy returned to Spain where they were living; and Mother and Father took the train to Le Havre, and boarded the S.S. *United States.*

Father had been in high spirits. He was feeling well, and had enjoyed and profited from the daily baths at Bad Gastein. He spent hours every day playing with Hunt and Job; he read voraciously letters from his children, and kept abreast of developments in the office. And Mother, as always, was at his side. But by the time he reached Paris he was eagerly looking forward to the return trip, and reunion with his children. The night before he left Paris, he was suddenly nauseated. That was the beginning, the doctors later deduced, of his fatal brain hemorrhage.

But the disturbance was not prolonged, and they left on schedule for Le Havre; again, Father was feeling well, and had a hearty dinner on boarding the liner Thursday evening.

On Monday afternoon, the day before the ship was due in New York, the office at 103 East 37th Street received a cable from Mother addressed to John. The cable was read to Bill, because John was in Canada hunting, and Jimmy was in the Philippines. Father had become ill, Mother cabled, giving no details, and we should request Dr. Touart to meet the boat when it docked the next morning. Bill telephoned the S.S. *United States.* He reached Mother, who told him that during the preceding day and a half Father had been losing consciousness. The ship's doctor, and an internist who was among the passengers and had been consulted, diagnosed the trouble as probably due to a stroke. By Monday afternoon, Father was only intermittently conscious.

At eight that night, Mother called again and spoke with Maureen. Father had been moved to the ship's infirmary, she reported, at the suggestion of the doctor. Arrangements had been made for Mother to spend the night with him in the adjacent bed. Fearing the worst, Mother had called in a priest, who administered the last rites. Father remained unconscious except for an occasional intelligible remark addressed to Mother.

(Four years earlier, gravely ill after his first stroke, Father lay seemingly unconscious on his hospital bed at Charlotte, N.C. Mother opened his bible and began to read aloud from the psalms in the Old Testament. Father's voice rang out for the first time in four days: "Boy, could those Jews write!" And, having paid tribute to good prose, which he always admired, he relapsed immediately into his coma.)

We lost touch with the boat after nine. The ship-to-shore Transatlantic telephone service is suspended at that hour, until eight the next morning. The entire night was consumed by devoted friends of the family, notably Bill Shields and Austin Taylor [Pat Buckley's father], in attempting to arrange for Bill to go out to The Narrows the next morning on the Coast Guard cutter that takes out customs officials, reporters, and persons whose presence is indispensable to the serenity of very important passengers. The bureaucratic logjam was finally broken the next morning, thanks to Ralph de Toledano, and permission was secured a bare ten minutes before the cutter set out at ten in the morning. Mother meanwhile had been reached by telephone. There was no change in Father's condition. Bill reached the S.S.

United States at eleven. Father was unconscious; Mother had not slept.

The boat docked at one and Father was taken immediately to the Lenox Hill Hospital by ambulance.

Dr. Touart took immediate charge. A spinal tap confirmed his suspicion that there was, or had been, bleeding within the skull. They would wait to see whether the blood vessel would mend itself, and whether the brain had been damaged. By Wednesday, Father had not recovered consciousness, and an exploratory brain operation was indicated, to repair the blood vessel and examine the damage that had been done. The hemorrhage was located by X-ray, and the operation performed on Thursday, by Dr. Juan Negrin.

Except for Reid who was in Spain, and Jimmy who was in Manila, the entire family had come to New York (John was reached in Canada and returned immediately), including Father's youngest sister, Aunt Eleanor. We hoped the operation would reveal the point of pressure against the brain which was causing the unconsciousness, and that, relief having been effected, Father would revive, and recover. Meanwhile, he was not in pain, or so the doctors assured us; and there is no reason to believe that he was ever aware of what went on during that week. After Monday, the last day aboard the S.S. *United States,* he did not have a moment of consciousness; or a moment's apprehension. There had been plenty, in the last four years, against which to exercise his enormous reserves of courage: a paralyzed left side, the treatment—and the inevitable condescension— that is meted out to all cripples; yet he was never heard by any living soul, including the woman in whom he confided everything, and reposed all his trust, to utter a single word

of complaint—against the pain, the boredom, the humili-
ations, the immobility. But at the end, he was not called
upon to suffer more.

Twenty-four hours after the operation, he had not re-
vived, and his blood pressure was alarmingly low. But on
Saturday, it began to rise, and danger of postsurgical shock
appeared to have been surmounted. Priscilla and Jane
drove to Sharon to pick up a fresh set of clothes. Mother
had dinner on Saturday night, after leaving the hospital, with Aloise, Patricia, Gerry, Maureen, and Carol. She
talked after dinner with the nurse in attendance, who reported that Father was sleeping peacefully.

At ten minutes to three in the next morning, on Sunday, October 5, the telephone rang. Mother picked up the
phone. The nurse told her to hurry to the hospital, that
Father had taken a turn for the worse. Within fifteen minutes she and Aloise and Patricia and Carol arrived at Lenox
Hill. Father was dead.

That afternoon the family met at the Church of Our
Savior at 38th Street and Park Avenue where a priest read
the rosary. The word had got out quickly, and many of his
friends and associates, from his office and elsewhere, appeared at the church, and joined the family in prayer.

Mother decided to bury Father in Camden, having in-
ferred from a casual remark he once made that this was
Father's preference. Monday evening, the family, including
Aunt Eleanor, boarded a private car at Pennsylvania Sta-
tion. We reached Camden at 11:30 the morning of October 7th, a bright and beautiful day. Father was taken to
the funeral home, which was a sea of flowers. At 4:00 P.M.
the pallbearers, Austin Sheheen, Carleton Burdick, Cyril
Harrison, Thomas A. Ancrum, David R. Williams, John

Whitaker, Henry Carrison, Sr., Ross Buckley, and Edmund Buckley, Jr., brought the casket into the crowded church, and Father Jeffords performed a funeral service that lasted about ten minutes. The procession to the cemetery included about a hundred cars. We took a circuitous route, to avoid a parade which the mayor of Camden had postponed a half hour to make it possible for us to cut through the town to the cemetery. Six months before, the mayor had called on Father with a delegation, to present him with a silver bowl, a token of Camden's gratitude for Father's generosities over the years. As we drove by, the policemen saluted the hearse.

Father's tombstone, which is on the northern side of the Quaker Cemetery, and is shaded by a magnolia tree, bears the inscription "W.F.B., 1881–1958." —W.F.B., Jr.

"Wine in the Blood"

Wine Enthusiast, June 1998.

At age 40, my father had *never* (he said so, and he never lied) tasted an alcoholic drink. But that year his doctor, after fishing around with whatever doctors fish around with to examine the heart, recommended that he drink red wine every day. It became an affair of the heart.

He tended to take on his enterprises in a big way. I have an early memory of my father doing a single thing with his own hand (he was inept in manual pursuits). He was in the large wine cellar he had built during the '20s, in his house in Connecticut, engaged now in the painstaking job of pouring wine from the barrels he had bought in France into appropriate bottles, which he then labeled. I remember that it was a very protracted project, lasting several evenings. In those days serious purchasers brought their wine in barrels to America and let the wine rest for five or six years before decanting it. But that has changed—I suppose, as a result of cork technology. And I assume there are additives now that accelerate the wine's development, even as they short-change its longevity. In any event, my memory of it is that by the end of the '30s Father was buying his wine already bottled, wherein lay a tale that greatly amused his ten children during the war years.

In 1939, Father augmented his collection by ordering a great many splendid French wines. It is difficult, at my age, to imagine such practices in wine-collecting as my father engaged in, which was quite simple and direct: He would order the best wines (of contemporary vintage) that could be bought. Today we spend our lives tasting hundreds of wines and swooping down on the bargains. My father—and who knows how many others—simply bought, having tested them, the best wines. In the '30s, these were moderately priced. But the large shipment he ordered in 1939 was held up because, of course, freight was suspended during the war.

But the mails were not suspended, and every year or so the wine broker would write from Lyon reporting that my father's wine was still securely stored at a repository in the countryside, safe from bombs bursting in air and other wartime distractions. But then the terrible letter came in 1943—the Nazis had discovered the hidden wine in the château and consumed it! My father was stoical about these things, but he was, not unexpectedly, saddened at the loss of thousands of bottles of lovely Bordeaux and Burgundies.

The second letter on the subject was a happy surprise. In fact, the German soldiers had fled and the merchant learned that they had not discovered the wine, which rested contentedly in its storing place. That was good news, but sadly interrupted by the next letter, some time soon after the Normandy landing in 1944. The American invading force had chased out the Germans—but, *"en cherchant partout,"* they had come upon the wine and, presumably toasting to the Allied cause, had consumed it.

Gloom set in. But a year later, after the German surrender, the wine broker's jubilant letter came: In fact, the wine survived and would be shipped in a matter of weeks; which indeed it was.

A few years later, for the purposes of insurance, my father brought in to his house in Connecticut, to assess his cellar, a Frenchman whose English was insecure. The enologist spent a half hour surveying the wines, taking notes. After he was done he came up to my father's study and said solemnly, "Your wine is valueless."

"Oh?" my father said. "I had thought it very fine wine." "That's what I said," the expert said. *"Valueless!"* It was with some relief that it dawned on us what a Frenchman can do in search of the English word "invaluable."

Father was devoted to his 10 children and every year distributed what he could of his material belongings. Doing that, you can move quickly toward self-liquidation, if you have 10 children. Some months after he died, each of us received a notice, with an accompanying check, of our share of his probated estate. The checks were for $62. The jolt came when, a few months after that, a revenue agent appeared. He wanted to look at the deceased's wine cellar. My father had absentmindedly forgotten to list it as an asset, or to give it away to his children.

But our consolation, year after year, for more than 20 years, was prolonged. Whenever any of us visited the lovely house in northwest Connecticut, we would be served the wines Father had accumulated, those lovely things that had slept peacefully, gaining flavor and enhancing their power to delight, through a world war and several occupations. It is a wonderful way to remember one's benefactors, isn't it? To drink wine in their memory?

Aloise Steiner Buckley

(1895–1985)

A portrait survives, from 1898, of Aloise Steiner at three: an angel with brown hair, heavy-lidded blue eyes twinkling with surprise, and a perfect little nose above a downturned mouth, slightly agape. Her head is tilted up, leaning rightward, her fist perched thoughtfully under her right ear; all that's missing, really, for the little girl to be hosting *Firing Line* is a clipboard and Bach's *Brandenburg Concerto No. 2 in F Major*.

DENIS BRIAN: Apart from being a language purist and a conservative, how else are you like your father?

WFB: I'm decisive. I'm very fond of my family, but that's hardly a unique quality.

DENIS BRIAN: [...] And your mother? Have you any similar traits?

WFB: Since she's absolutely perfect, anything I said would be self-serving. [laughs]

—Denis Brian, *Murderers and Other Friendly People: The Public and Private Worlds of Interviewers* (1973)

By all accounts Aloise Steiner Buckley provided, in the family's busy households at Great Elm and Kamschatka, the Buckleys' summer home in Camden, South Carolina, the indispensable counterpoint of sweetness and light to Will Buckley's sternness. "If Father was in an authoritarian mood," said Patricia Buckley, "Mother would try to soften it." "It was Mother who was with us day in and day out," recalled James Buckley, renowned today as a former U.S. senator and federal appellate judge. "Hers was the dominant influence when it came to such essentials as faith, love of country, and consideration for others." Buckley biographer John Judis characterized Aloise's marriage to Will as "happy and fruitful."

It would survive more than forty years, the first half of which Will scrambled, often with little success, to recoup the fortune that he had lost in Mexico City, leaving Aloise alone—sometimes without money to pay the bills—to manage the affairs of their growing and demanding family. In 1918, they had their first child, Aloise, then six others in quick succession—John in 1920, Priscilla in 1921, James in 1923, Jane in 1924, Bill in 1925, and Patricia in 1927. Reid would come in 1930 and Maureen in 1933, when the Buckleys were living abroad, and Carol in 1938.

Aloise was the more outwardly demonstrative Catholic, apt to pray spontaneously, to invoke the Lord in conversation or in the short stories she wrote and told her brood at bedtime. From this rooted faith came endless good cheer. Aloise loved it when young

Bill, rejecting pagan myths, hid the family's Santa costume, and she sometimes could be seen bowling in three-inch heels. "God," Reid would say, "was that woman fun."

"Aloise Steiner Buckley, RIP"

National Review, April 19, 1985.

She bore ten children, nine of whom have written for this journal, or worked for it, or both, and that earns her, I think, this half-acre of space normally devoted to those whose contributions are in the public mode. Hers were not. If ever she wrote a letter to a newspaper, we don't remember it, and if she wrote to a congressman or senator, it was probably to say that she wished him well, and would pray for him as she did regularly for her country. If she had lived one day more, she'd have reached her ninetieth birthday. Perhaps somewhere else one woman has walked through so many years charming so many people by her warmth and diffidence and humor and faith. I wish I might have known her.

ASB was born in New Orleans, her ancestors having come there from Switzerland some time before the Civil War. She attended [H.] Sophie Newcomb College but left after her second year in order to become a nurse, her intention being to go spiritedly to the front. Over there. Over there. But when the young aspiring nurses were given a test to ascertain whether they could cope with the sight of blood and mayhem, she fainted, and was disqualified. A year later she married a prominent 36-year-old Texas-born attorney who lived and practiced in Mexico City, with which she had had ties because her aunt lived there.

She never lived again in New Orleans, her husband taking her, after his exile from Mexico (for backing an unsuccessful revolution that sought to restore religious liberty), to Europe, where his business led him. They had bought a house in Sharon, Connecticut, and in due course returned there. The great house where she brought us up still stands, condominiums now. But the call of the South was strong, and in the mid-Thirties they restored an ante-bellum house in Camden, South Carolina. There she was wonderfully content, making others happy by her vivacity, her delicate beauty, her habit of seeing the best in everyone, the humorous spark in her eye. She never lost a Southern innocence in which her sisters even more conspicuously shared. One of her daughters was delighted on overhearing an exchange between her and her freshly widowed sister who had for fifty years been married to a New Orleans doctor and was this morning, seated on the porch, completing a medical questionnaire, checking this query, exxing the other. She turned to Mother and asked, "Darling, as girls did we have gonorrhea?"

Her cosmopolitanism was unmistakably Made-in-America. She spoke fluent French and Spanish with undiluted inaccuracy. My father, who loved her more even than he loved to tease her, and whose knowledge of Spanish was faultless, once remarked that in forty years she had never once placed a masculine article in front of a masculine noun, or a feminine article in front of a feminine noun, except on one occasion when she accidentally stumbled on the correct sequence, whereupon she stopped—unheard of in her case, so fluently did she aggress against the language—and corrected herself by changing the article: the result being that she spoke, in Spanish, of the latest encyclical of Pius XII, the Potato of Rome (*"Pio XII, la Papa*

de Roma"). She would smile, and laugh compassionately, as
though the joke had been at someone else's expense, and
perhaps play a little with her pearls, just above the piece of
lace she always wore in the V of the soft dresses that covered her diminutive frame.

There were rules she lived by, chief among them those
she understood God to have specified, though she outdid
Him in her accent on good cheer. And although Father
was the unchallenged source of authority at home, she was
unchallengeably in charge of arrangements in a house
crowded with ten children and as many tutors, servants,
and assistants. In the very late Thirties her children ranged
in age from one to 21, and an in-built sense of the appropriate parietal arrangements governed the hour at which
each of us should be back from wherever we were—away
at the movies, or at a dance, or hearing Frank Sinatra sing
in Pawling. The convention was inflexible. On returning,
each of us would push, on one of the house's intercoms, the
button that said, "ASB." The conversation, whether at ten
when she was still awake, or at two when she had been two
hours asleep, was always the same: "It's me, Mother." "Good
night, darling." If—as hardly ever happened—it became
truly late, and her mind had not recorded the repatriation
of all ten of us, she would rise, and walk to the room of the
missing child. If there, she would return to sleep, and re-
monstrate the next day on the forgotten telephone call. If
not there, she would wait up, and demand an explanation.

Her anxiety to do the will of God was more than rit-
ual. I wrote to her once early in 1963. Much of our youth
had been spent in South Carolina, and the cultural coor-
dinates of our household were Southern. But the times
required that we look Southern conventions like Jim
Crow hard in the face, and so I asked her how she could

reconcile Christian fraternity with the separation of the races, a convention as natural in the South for a hundred years after the Civil War as women's suffrage became natural after their emancipation, and she wrote, "My darling Bill: This is not an answer to your letter, for I cannot answer it too quickly. It came this morning, and, of course, I went as soon as possible to the Blessed Sacrament in our quiet, beautiful little church here. And, dear Bill, I prayed *so* hard for *humility* and for wisdom and for guidance from the Holy Spirit. I know He will help me to answer your questions as He thinks they should be answered. I must pray longer before I do this."

A few years earlier she had raised her glass on my father's 75th birthday, to say: "Darling, here's to 15 more years together, and then we'll both go." But my father died three years later. Her grief was profound, and she emerged from it through the solvent of prayer, her belief in submission to a divine order, and her irrepressible delight in her family, and friends. A few years later her daughter Maureen died at age 31, and she struggled to fight her desolation, though not with complete success. Her oldest daughter, Aloise, died three years later. And then, three months ago, her son John.

She was by then in a comfortable retirement home, totally absent-minded; she knew us all, but was vague about when last she had seen us, or where, and was given to making references, every now and then, to her husband, "Will," and the trip they planned next week to Paris, or Mexico.

But she sensed what had happened, and instructed her nurse (she was endearingly under the impression that she owned the establishment in which she had a suite) to drive her to the cemetery, and there, unknown to us until later that afternoon, she saw from her car, at the edge of an assembly of cars, her oldest son lowered into the earth. He had been visiting her every day, often taking her to a local restaurant for lunch, and her grief was, by her standards, convulsive; but she did not break her record—she never broke it—which was never, ever to complain, because, she explained, she could never repay God the favors He had done her, no matter what tribulations she might need to suffer.

Ten years ago, my wife and I arrived in Sharon from New York much later than we had expected, and Mother had given up waiting for us, so we went directly up to the guest room. There was a little slip of blue paper on the bed lamp, another on the door to the bathroom, a third on the mirror. They were: lovely notes on her 3 x 5 notepaper, inscribed "Mrs. William F. Buckley." Little valentines of welcome, as though we had circled the globe. There was no sensation to match the timbre of her pleasure on hearing from you when you called her on the telephone, or the vibration of her embrace when she laid eyes on you. Some things truly are unique.

Five days before she died—one week having gone by without her having said anything, though she clutched the hands of her children and grandchildren as they came to visit, came to say good-bye—the nurse brought her from the bathroom to the armchair and—inflexible rule—put on her lipstick, and the touch of rouge, and the pearls. Suddenly, and for the first time since the terminal descent began a fortnight earlier, she reached out for her mirror. With effort she raised it in front of her face, and then said, a teasing smile on her face as she turned to the nurse, "Isn't it amazing that anyone so old can be so beautiful?" The answer, clearly, was, Yes, it was amazing that anyone could be so beautiful. —WFB

L. Brent Bozell, Jr.

(1926–1997)

When they more or less took over the Yale debating team, L. Brent Bozell, Jr., was undeniably Bill Buckley's better: a lanky, red-haired Omaha native and merchant marine who outpointed Buckley for the Ten Eyck Award for oratory. The two were inseparable friends and destined to be linked forever. In 1949, still in school, Bozell married Buckley's sister Patricia (Trish). Five years later, while the Bozells were on their way to having ten children, and with Trish having introduced Bill to Patricia Taylor, whom he would marry, WFB and Bozell teamed up once again: this time as coauthors of the controversial *McCarthy and His Enemies: The Record and Its Meaning,* a pointillist defense of the anticommunist senator who was soon to self-destruct. It has been suggested that Bozell's admiration for WFB in these early days led him to abandon some liberal ideas and even to convert to Catholicism. As early as 1958, however, Buckley biographer John Judis has written, hints of strain began to show, as when WFB rebuked his brother-in-law in a note: "It makes sense, I feel, not to be sarcastic in a serious communication

for consideration by a board of high-strung editors...." Bozell's influence in the conservative orbit reached its high point when he ghost-
authored Barry Goldwater's best-selling manifesto *The Conscience of a
Conservative* (1960). By the mid-1960s, Bozell had moved his family to
Spain and founded *Triumph,* a Catholic journal. WFB was supportive,
but Bozell's tone changed—he angrily accused *NR* and conservatives
of exalting the Constitution over Catholicism—and the two men's
correspondence grew barbed before falling silent. Marvin Liebman
told Judis that the feud was "very traumatic" for Buckley; Pat Buckley thought her husband's celebrity had stirred resentment; in reality,
Bozell was descending into mental illness. Although it references this
"creeping invalidism," WFB's eulogy is unusual for how much of it he
gives over to someone else's eulogy: that of his nephew, L. Brent Bozell III, a notable conservative activist in his own right. It seems the
elder Bozell's dissolution, at first mistaken for stubbornness, remained
so painful to WFB that he scarcely could bring himself to write about
it. Even after the many years of estrangement, Bill called the son, as his
father lay dying, with strict instructions that he was to be notified the
very instant the inevitable came. When Brent called WFB two days
later and told him, "Dad's gone," Buckley responded with an unrec-
ognizable noise on the other end of the line—a despairing cry, almost
animal in nature—and hung up.

"L. Brent Bozell, RIP"

National Review, May 19, 1997.

Brent Bozell was a seminal figure in the early days of
National Review. As an undergraduate at Yale he was re-
nowned as a debater and orator (he had won the National
American Legion Oratory award in 1944, and at Yale was

president of the Political Union). His postcollege years (as an undergraduate he was my closest friend; he married my sister Patricia in our senior year) were crowded and exciting. He graduated from the Yale Law School in 1953 and moved to California anticipating a career in the law. During his law-school days he collaborated with me in writing *McCarthy and His Enemies,* a study of McCarthy's activities up through the Tydings hearings in 1953. Soon after the book's publication, Edward Bennett Williams, serving as attorney for Joe McCarthy, persuaded Brent to detach himself from Pillsbury Madison & Sutro in San Francisco and help defend McCarthy against censure by the Senate.

The defense failed, but Brent and McCarthy had become friends, and McCarthy asked Brent to stay in Washington and write speeches for him part time. Brent did, and in the years ahead became close to Sen. Barry Goldwater. Retired Notre Dame dean Clarence Manion had set up a small publishing company and commissioned Brent to write a short book for Sen. Goldwater. In nine days. Brent (normally slow) wrote *The Conscience of a Conservative.* It had the largest sale of any polemic in American history. Its popularity contributed to Goldwater's nomination for president in 1964.

While working for McCarthy and for Goldwater, Brent served as Washington correspondent for *National Review* and as a Senior Editor. He competed twice for public office, once for the House of Delegates in Maryland, once for Congress. In 1960, he moved his family to Spain, intending to write a thorough examination of the Supreme Court under Earl Warren (*The Warren Revolution* was published in 1966 by Arlington House). While in Spain he felt the need to found a magazine devoted to Catholic thought. In 1965, the monthly *Triumph* was first published. It was a profound venture, theocratical in orientation, in one sense another expression of the totalist tendencies of the culture of the 1960s. In 1975 it discontinued, Brent Bozell's creeping invalidism a factor in its demise, as also the gradual reconsolidation, during that decade, of conventions cast off during the abandon of the earlier decade. *Triumph* was in a sense the counterpart of Woodstock. The one argued the imperative of the licentious, self-indulgent lifestyle; the other, the ultimate satisfactions of faith, duty, and fidelity.

The personal story was searingly and poignantly told at Our Lady of Mount Carmel, the Dominican church close by Catholic University in Washington, D.C., where eight priests, including the priest who had married the Bozells in 1949, concelebrated a funeral Mass presided over by Father Michael Bozell, a Benedictine monk who was ordained a priest at Solesmes in France in 1994. The eulogists were two of Brent's six sons. The story was told by Brent Bozell III, well known as president of the Media Research Center and as a syndicated columnist.

Young Brent spoke of receiving a letter while at college from "Pop," as he was known to his children, saying lightheartedly that he hoped never to be a burden to them. "Shortly after that letter arrived, Pop's behavior became erratic, nonsensical, and when finally he was hospitalized came the shattering diagnosis: manic depression.

"Dozens of times over the next 25 years the attacks would come, and with each bout, yet another blow, yet another public humiliation. He would lose Montejurra, the home in the foothills of the Shenandoah mountains which he loved so much. He could only watch helplessly as *Triumph* magazine, to whose survival he had given every ounce of energy, collapsed. There were the seemingly end-less searches around the country just to locate him; in fact, around the world, as he brought on one crisis after another. There were arrests and forced hospitalizations, escapes and rearrests and recommitments. There was the never-ending parade of lawyers, police, doctors, and, yes, from time to time the State Department was on the line to brief us on yet another prospective international upheaval caused by this very unpredictable man."

The mourners in the packed church listened attentively. Some hadn't known how ill Brent was. "Manic depression by itself is enough to break the spirit of any man, but Pop was no ordinary man. He suffered from peripheral neu-ropathy, sleep apnea, osteoporosis, degenerative disk dis-ease, asthma, and Alzheimer's. One by one they came, and when it seemed that no part of his body had been left un-touched yet a new illness was diagnosed. We wondered how he could endure so much, accept this torture with such nobility, with never one word of complaint."

The eulogist, searching for an explanation, came up with a passage from his father's book *Mustard Seeds*. "There is no greater paradox in the cosmos," the deceased had written, "than the apparent contradiction of our helpless-ness ('without me, you can do nothing') alongside God's 'helplessness.' Oh, I know, God is all-powerful, and so on; but he cannot undo what he has done, and what he once did was to make men free. This means that he 'needs' us in order to get us to Heaven as his lovers, and in order to do his will in the world. All we have to do in order to frustrate those wishes—to render God 'helpless'—is to say No. But God is not helpless, really, because he has mercy—himself. And what mercy does is convert, change our hearts. Which

God never stops trying to do until we are dead. This means continued suffering for him, which is what Christ is all about."

Young Brent headed home with his eulogy. "Love, mercy, suffering. Those became the three pillars in a remarkable spiritual journey that would transform Pop from a good man to a truly holy man in his final days. It is said that a saint never aspires to that status except by abandoning himself completely to Christ and his suffering; if so, then Pop was saintly. Ask his friends, his brother and sister, his nephews and nieces, his extended family, so many of them here today, how that man could pierce the soul with such beauty, such warmth, such dignity, such friendship. Ask his ten children, who undertook that 'burden' he prophesied, a small price to pay to savor one more hour his wisdom and disarming wit. Ask his queen, his Juliet. No two ever loved more fiercely. Mom, your heart is heavy now, but let it also be joyful. He is where he is meant to be, and that is good. And just as you whispered in his ear, in those final days, that he would never be alone, he now whispers back in yours that he's still with you, will always be with you."

"Little Brent," as the eulogist is referred to by the senior members of the family, was in the room with his father when he died. Indeed all ten children were there. Little Brent closed by saying that his father was now "finally to be placed at the feet of his Creator, who will beckon him forward with his Song of Songs,

Arise, my beloved, my beautiful one, and come!
For see, the winter is past,
the rains are over and gone.

The flowers appear on the earth,
the time of pruning the vines has come,
and the song of the dove is heard in our land. . . .
Arise, my beloved, my beautiful one, and come!"

—WFB

ARTS AND
LETTERS

Truman Capote

＞‿＜

(1924–1984)

On the evening of November 28, 1966, Pat and Bill Buckley were among the elite New Yorkers who bounded up the steps of the Plaza Hotel to attend the masked Black and White Ball thrown, with unprecedented fanfare, by Truman Capote. Tuxedo-clad, hands in pockets, WFB sported an outsized robber's mask; Pat dazzled, as ever, in a Catwoman-like getup. Heralded as the party of the century, the Black and White Ball brought together Frank Sinatra and Andy Warhol, Alice Roosevelt Longworth and Candice Bergen, McGeorge Bundy and Norman Mailer, and cemented Capote's status as a central figure of artistic and intellectual life in the mid-1960s. He had just published *In Cold Blood,* his "nonfiction novel," previously serialized in *The New Yorker,* about the gruesome 1959 slayings of a Kansas family. A best-seller made into a movie, *In Cold Blood* helped usher in the "New Journalism," in which writers such as Capote and Mailer, Jimmy Breslin, Joan Didion, Gay Talese, Hunter Thompson, and Tom Wolfe dazzlingly applied the techniques of fiction to nonfiction subjects. To many, WFB's books—particularly the more personal works, such as *The Unmaking of a Mayor* (1966), *Cruising Speed* (1971), *United Nations Journal* (1974), and the sailing volumes—made Buckley one of the most prolific and commercially successful New Journalists. That literary affinity and the mutual habitat of Manhattan's Upper East Side accounted for the unlikely friendship between Capote and the Buckleys—until 1976, when the latter performed, in the pages of *Esquire,* the spectacular act of social hara-kiri WFB records below. Unusually, WFB wrote two eulogies for Capote: the first, for the syndicated column, the second, published in *National Review,* shorter—and more unforgiving. "What are the politics of Truman Capote?" Buckley had asked in *Esquire* in 1967. "In the liberal-conservative sense, there were no discernible politics, except insofar as the social Zeitgeist says that liberals are more beautiful than conservatives."

"Truman Capote, RIP"

Syndicated column, September 1–2, 1984.

The only time I was ever at a movie set was in 1976 when I went to the designated studio to pick up David Niven for lunch. But the scene being shot was not yet finished, and so I found myself waiting, at the camera end of the dining room set in which Lionel Twain was so foully murdered in Neil Simon's *Murder by Death.* Three times, before the shot was over, Truman Capote, playing Twain, came into the room, leaned forward over the table, stumbled, was caught by a dozen hands in one of which was a bare bodkin plunged into Truman Capote's back. Question: In whose hands was the dagger that killed him?

At lunch David Niven commented that at that particular

moment, everyone was suspect. Everyone seemed to have a motive to kill poor Truman Capote: "It's like *Murder on the Orient Express*." The background was *Esquire* magazine's publication, a month or two before, of "Unspoiled Monsters," the first part of Capote's "novel," *Answered Prayers*. That work finished Truman Capote's social life as decisively as a hangman's trapdoor. It collected brilliantly and with relish related every ugly fact and rumor about New York's glitterati that Truman Capote, in years of knowing and mixing with them, had assembled.

He seemed astonished, at first, that old friends hung up the telephone when he called, and that others took trouble to avoid him. And so he took refuge in booze and pills, pills and booze. And then one day, on television, in a high pitch of wrath, he lashed out by name at Lee Radziwill and a few others. Then there was word he was submitting to treatment. And then there was word he was not submitting to treatment. And then there was word that he had died.

It was a most awful fall from the dizzy heights he had achieved in 1966, when all the world contended to receive an invitation to his famous Black & White Ball at New York's Plaza Hotel. Some men left for Europe rather than risk the suspicion that they had not been invited. One woman hired a huge public relations firm, first to bring pressure on Capote to invite her, second, in the event that it failed, to elaborate ennobling reasons why she had not been invited.

Oh, those were the days for Truman Capote, fresh from the literary victory of *In Cold Blood*, which incorporated nothing less than the discovery of a new art form, he told the world, basking in self-contentment, some of it earned by his formidable talent, that included an ear wonderfully acute for detail, irony, and speech. His big new novel would secure him in the pantheon of American literature, he confidently predicted. But for many years he had begun to lean progressively on his social life rather than his professional life to sustain him, so that when the former collapsed, his remaining crutch became booze. And there was, really, not time enough, or clearheadedness enough, to resume serious production.

One day he called and asked to be introduced to Gov. Ronald Reagan, because Capote was doing an hour's documentary on capital punishment and needed access to the Death House in California. An unlikely, yet enduring, friendship was struck up between the Reagans and Capote. It had its own theatrical life when Capote ran afoul of a contempt citation and was sentenced to several days in jail, from which only a pardon by Governor Reagan could save him: It was all handled with dignity.

"He's quite a guy, and very interesting," Reagan once said. "But you know, when you first meet him, it is kind of a shock." The reference was to the exaggeratedly effeminate voice. A few weeks before they met, Reagan's office was scandalized by the discovery of Reagan's top aide in a homosexual spa off in the mountains. After Capote left the governor's office, Reagan was seen to lean out of the door and bellow out, "Troll that feller in and out of the hall here a couple of times, let's see if there are any left." Capote would probably have put that line into his next book.

The doctors have not told us what Truman Capote died from, but it was not old age. "Forsooth," the Rabelaisian character says to his reproachful physician, "I do believe I know more old drunkards than I do old doctors." But not this time around. And so, once again (in our day, in our country: Hemingway, Faulkner, Fitzgerald, Steinbeck, Cozzens) the reading world lost a half-dozen breakfasts at Tiffany that sat, ungestated, in the mind of a brilliant and essentially likable man, sat there smothered by booze, the consumption of which proved terminal. The same imbalance that created "Unspoiled Monsters" acquiesced in that fateful, sad exchange.

"Truman Capote"

National Review, September 21, 1984.

In Cold Blood, a nonfiction "novel" about two murderers, was probably Truman Capote's best book. Here he was able to apply his literary talents to the presentation of material derived from the external world, which excused him from having to imagine it. He did not have a powerful novelistic imagination, and in this, at least, he resembled Norman Mailer, whose *In Cold Blood* was *The Executioner's Song* [1979], Mailer's best book.

Capote emerged at 23 with *Other Voices, Other Rooms* [1948], emerged as a writer and as a personality. The photograph on the dust-jacket, depicting a tiny androgynous dandy, reclining, with a blond doe's stare, established the identity. His prose style, which some admired and for which he himself claimed a great deal, reinforced that idea. It was offbeat in its focus on odd details, consistently alienated, and "fragrant"—music for chameleons indeed.

In his later years he had calamitous drug and alcohol

problems, not so unusual for writers, and it is useless to try to diagnose his state of mind. Perhaps he had stretched his minor talent as far as it could go; perhaps, in his social life, he was, in Barbara Gordon's phrase, dancing as fast as he could. He died last week in Los Angeles, at the age of 59.

Johnny Carson

⁕

(1925–2005)

Johnny Carson was a comedian and the host of *The Tonight Show* on NBC for thirty years, starting in 1962. In an age before the Internet and social media, when the three television networks were Americans' primary sources for entertainment, Carson's program reigned supreme among talk shows, with Johnny himself emerging over time as a kind of national father figure who helped see Americans through the upheavals and calamities of the 1960s and 1970s. His witty nightly monologues reflected, like the work of no other entertainer of his time, the collective mood of the country. Although Buckley could be critical of Carson for oversimplifying national issues and slighting conservatism, WFB wrote frequently about Carson and appeared on *The Tonight Show* a half dozen times over a quarter-century span. In 1971, questioned about his often ridiculed patrician accent—Carson himself once did a sketch called "Monday Night Football with William F. Buckley"—Buckley told the *Tonight Show* audience: "There are certain kinds of accents that strike people as somehow stilted. I don't think mine is, because it's the only one I know." In a 1985 appearance, Carson drew laughs by asking WFB why his arrival on set always made Carson feel like he was back in the principal's office.

"Johnny Carson, R.I.P."

National Review, February 14, 2005.

If Johnny Carson could have managed it, no doubt his death would have been a private affair. Who would have been invited to his memorial service? We don't know. That is the measure of his integrity as a private man. We don't even know how many of his ex-wives would have been invited, or would have come.

I was his guest a half-dozen times, and was always handled with great courtesy. He once confided to a critic that I was the only guest he had ever been frightened of. I don't know what the circumstances of that odd situation were, and the critic didn't pause to ask, and Johnny didn't elaborate. As far as I know.

As I write these words a memory flashes up.

Scene: *The Tonight Show.* Guests: David Susskind and me (WFB).

David Susskind is widely forgotten, but he was a singular presence on television for about 20 years. He staked out the ultimate talk show (he called it *Open End*) by the simple expedient of making it endless. He would start out at 9 P.M., on Channel 13 in New York (this was before it had become a part of the educational network), with one or more guests, and just talk on & on into the night, sometimes not closing down the program until after midnight.

I was sometimes his guest, and he developed over several years an uncontainable sense of indignation . . . that I, and my views as expressed in *National Review,* should exist. At all. The hostility had come to something of a boil when Johnny Carson convened us for a joint appearance on *The Tonight Show.*

Susskind began with a minute-long prewritten, memorized excoriation, and Johnny asked me to reply. I remember that Susskind had misused two words, so I thought to concentrate my reply on his solecisms, rather than on his political views. Carson was hugely amused and beckoned Susskind back into the fray, whereupon Susskind denounced my "noxious" views. I said to Carson that Susskind didn't know the proper meaning of that word, Susskind shot back indignantly, "What is the proper meaning?" and I said, "I won't tell you." Johnny Carson was amused by everything, but I think he was especially amused that night, and on succeeding occasions when I was his guest, he would come into the Green Room before the program began to chat for a moment or two.

Never about politics, at least not directly. But since I was always there to try to bring attention to a book I had written, he would touch on the subject of the book, being careful not to suggest to me that he had actually read it. It was unprofessional for any guest to suppose that Johnny had actually plowed through the books written by his guests.

But there was an exception, and it taught me enduringly. The book was about a sailing trip I had taken across the Pacific Ocean. At the end of our eight to ten minute session he turned to the audience and said, "Now you people know there isn't any way I can read every word of every book I mention. But I want to show you how thoroughly I read this book." He opened his copy to the cameras and pointed out his own annotations on specimen pages. He told his ten million viewers: Go and buy this wonderful book.

I was not about to let the viewers get ahead of me and rushed from the studio to a pay telephone, dialing my publisher: He must order a mass printing, in anticipation of the avalanche of demand for the book the following day.

But Johnny's audience, unlike Oprah's, wasn't tuning in to decide what books to buy. They wanted entertainment, and they got it, not from the contents of books being promoted on *The Tonight Show,* but from conversation by Johnny, and incidentally his guests.

The last time around he said to me, "I'd like to schedule an entire hour with you." I dined that night with a friend, who brought along *Tonight*'s producer. I mentioned the suggestion. He replied, "The last thing Johnny Carson needs is you on his show for an entire hour."

He was almost certainly right, but it was a nice thought, and I thought Johnny Carson a nice man, and if it doesn't interrupt his privacy, I'll say it in public. —WFB

Alistair Cooke

—◆—

(1908–2004)

To his fellow Americans, Alistair Cooke was best known as the erudite host, from 1971 to 1992, of the award-winning PBS drama series *Masterpiece Theatre*. In his native Britain—he emigrated to America in 1937 and became a U.S. citizen four years later—Cooke was famous as the host of the weekly BBC Radio series *Letter from America,* in which the expatriate reported on events and personalities in the former colonies. *Letter* ran from March 1946 to February 2004—a span of nearly fifty-eight years—making it the longest-running program of its kind in the history of broadcasting. Cooke also authored two dozen books, including the runaway best-seller *The Americans* (1979). WFB's friendship with Cooke—*what a match!*—began when the latter favorably reviewed one of Buckley's books; fifteen years later, Cooke penned the introduction to *On the Firing Line: The Public Life of Our Public Figures* (1989), the anthology of *Firing Line* transcripts. A lifelong liberal, Cooke made only one appearance on the program, in November 1968, but the Manchester native was an avid viewer,

reveling in WFB's assumption all at once of the roles of "district attorney, mocker, lover of the last word, and—it must be admitted—
confessor of grievous sins." Buckley, in his acknowledgments, replied
in kind: "There is no figure in television I admire more; and there are
few writers who match the eloquence and shrewdness of his written
work." WFB's eulogy for Cooke was unique: He wrote it in advance
and sent it to the rapidly declining subject, then ninety-five; Cooke declined to read it. It is also the only eulogy of WFB's that carried three
sign-offs, and appears below in the semi-epistolary form in which it
was published in *National Review*. Also below is a shorter appreciation
WFB had published four years earlier, when Cooke was still alive.

Wm. F. Buckley Jr. * 215 Lexington Avenue
New York, NY 10016

March 10, 2004

Dear Alistair:
   I brooded over the news you gave me, trying to think how
I might express myself. I decided on a device I have never
used before, and will never use again: I have written the
short obituary I will publish in NATIONAL REVIEW at the
appropriate time. I confide it to you. And look forward to our
visit on Monday. XB

————

Alistair Cooke was, in England, the best-known living Amer-
ican except for the president. That meant, during his ca-
reer, excepting Presidents Roosevelt, Truman, Eisenhower,
Kennedy, Johnson, Nixon, Ford, Carter—correction!
Cooke was probably better known than Carter—Reagan,
Bush, Clinton, and . . . Bush. He coexisted with all these

chiefs of state over all those years in several capacities, most
prominently as author of a weekly BBC "letter" in which he
recounted what was going on in his adopted country with
a poise and understanding unequaled by any other expatriate, and unsurpassed by any native-born observer. He
called an end to his *Letter from America* in March; his last letter was Number 2,869. One commentator in London said
that news of Cooke's ending his broadcasts to England was
on the order of news that the Queen had died.

He did everything with that wry, amiable, but firm-
handed assurance that made him the ideal host on large-
scale television enterprises. He was master of ceremonies
for *Masterpiece Theater*, and proved irreplaceable when he
gave up that commission. His book on America was a startling bestseller. When published it sold out almost immediately, reaching #1 on the *New York Times*'s list. He was
dismayed to learn that the intricately designed volume
would take three months to reproduce in a second printing. Three months later it reappeared in the bookstores
and leaped once more to the #1 spot.

My experience of his friendship was, if not unique, at
least ever so unusual. The narrative of it goes back to 1974,
when he reviewed one of my collections for the *Washington Post*. I was unsurprised by its acuity, but moved by its
courtesy and indeed geniality. (AC was a political liberal.)
I wrote to him and he proposed that we lunch, which we
proceeded to do in what became a lunch every quarter for
nearly thirty years. His copious memory and Scots background always supplied, at the end of lunch, the answer to
the question, Is it your turn to pay the bill, or mine?

A few years ago the doctors told him he would need
to stay home, so that our quarterly lunches became fortnightly glasses of wine, with his beautiful ninety-year-old

wife, the artist. These visits were at his apartment on the eleventh floor overlooking Central Park. Eight floors closer to the ground was the apartment of *New Yorker* legend William Shawn, who declined to visit at the penthouse because he was afraid of heights.

No visitor was ever afraid that conversation would flag, or that niches of American history or English literature would be ignored, let alone that listlessness would creep into the room. Cooke's animation was boundless, his pointed memory infinite. He remembered everything, including the history of the world and amusing encounters with kings and writers and his true heroes, the great golfers. He would sit, his head slightly bent, and observe his lifelong rule, which was to entertain and to charm and to inform.

He called me the week after he announced the end of his BBC program to give me a confidence. His doctor, after examining his lungs, had pronounced a death sentence. When that is told you by someone aged ninety-five, expressions of hope are limited. What can one say, except to curse the necessary ending even of lives of such singular men, after so many years of enchanting the public and his friends? Nothing, beyond expressing quiet gratitude for the promise of eternal life in the hereafter. —WFB

"Alistair Cooke, R.I.P."

National Review, April 19, 2004.

We met, as we habitually did, on the Monday afternoon, at six. He was seated in the usual chair, in a dressing gown, and didn't take my hand—"Nobody is permitted to touch me! Infection, they say." And he was off, touching in the hour on a hundred points of interest, if not of concern, including the career of the German whose King Lear he had so much admired, and who had fled Hitler for America, ending his career playing butler parts in Hollywood. "I received yesterday," Cooke said, an impish grin on his face, "a letter from Churchill College in Cambridge. It read, 'Mr. Cooke, now that you have ended your BBC broadcasts, you will have time to relax and put your feet on the desk. This will, we hope, give you time to act as a trustee of Churchill College.'" He laughed. "I wrote back: 'Thank you for your invitation. In about two months, I will put my feet up on the desk permanently.'" Cooke thought this very funny, which indeed it was, very nearly, though not quite, dispelling the gloom in his visitor's heart. His animation was at par, and I told him good night and said I'd be with him the following Monday.

That next Monday—yesterday—I called and learned that he was not feeling well; I'd best postpone my visit. This morning the news came to me that he had died at midnight. I called his secretary, who I knew from prolonged contact was so intelligently and affectionately involved in his life. She told me that on reading my covering letter, he had instructed her to reinsert my obituary into the envelope: He declined to read it.

He would certainly have corrected my mistaken reference to him as a Scotsman—he was raised in Manchester. And he might have suggested that I give the name of the beautiful lady he was married to, Jane White Hawkes. His declining a look at the obituary was understandable, though I regret he did not have from me this record of my affection and admiration for him. —WFB

Excerpted from "10 Friends," *Forbes FYI,* September 2000.

The first time was lunch.

Nothing pleases the author more than a fine book review, especially from an unexpected source. My book was a collection, and I stared with dumb gratitude at a marvelously hospitable review by the great, discerning Alistair Cooke in the *Washington Post.* I characterize as "discerning" any complimentary book reviewer! But it was welcome, from so august a figure, more widely known in his native England than any American with the exception of the president. Moreover, Cooke—I had gathered, from his writing, and from certain intimations in his famous introductions on *Masterpiece Theater*—was something of a liberal, so that the surprise was especially great. I expressed my gratitude in a letter. He wrote back immediately and said let's lunch.

That was in 1971, and the wonder of it is that at the end of the lunch we made another lunch date for three months later. There was the usual reaching-for-the-check, but soon we agreed to alternate. And then that was followed by a date for another lunch—three months later. The schedule is unbroken, though interrupted by his recent illness.

What's it like, lunching with Alistair Cooke?

For one thing, there's his memory. He's 91 and I'd be surprised if he has forgotten anything. I amuse myself every now and then by asking, when the check comes: "I forget, Alistair, is it your turn to pay or mine?" He remembers instantly. He is a resolute Scot [*sic*].

His memory extends to improvisational powers. He

doesn't tell of his accomplishments, but by probing I learned how he did his famous introductions of *Masterpiece Theater* on PBS. He would concentrate on the play or the drama and its author and the circumstances of its writing, then he would arrive at the studio, sit down in his armchair, and the perfectly phrased 90-second introductions would flow from his lips. He'd speak the improvised lines as confidently as if called upon to give the Lord's Prayer—which I've never asked him to do. Next lunch I'll try to remember.

His cachet, beginning many years before PBS, has been his weekly 15-minute report on America for the BBC. In America, we know him for his television work; among the cognoscenti, he is celebrated for his fine writing style and memorable portraits. His friends know him for his humor and geniality.

"Is there anybody you *haven't* known?" He pauses, his white hair framing the famous face, the eyebrows that lift for a moment, the smile. He is thinking.

"Not really, I guess I'd have to say." I make it a point not to ask him who out there among the thousand public figures he didn't like. He'll get to that, if he wants to; one doesn't press.

Though I did nag him about his legs. For Cooke, golf comes in just after good reading and writing. But the anxiety ended. At one memorable lunch (we meet at the Carlyle Hotel) he surprised me on arrival by saying: "Ask me to dance around the buffet."

"To what?"

"Watch." He did a jig around the collection of trays and sat down with a triumphant smile. "That's what the operation has done for me." He had had two knee replacements, and now could go back to his golf without pain.

Alistair Cooke has never sounded old-fashioned, let alone out of date, but certain ways of doing things are unalterable, including his love of jazz (he was a fine pianist) and his devotion to an old typewriter, with its distinctive, falling-apart-old font. "A young grandson came to see me the other day. He's 17. He said, 'Grandfather, is it *true* you have a typewriter?' Yes, I said. 'Could I see it?'"

He loved that: genuine innocence. It had better be genuine, because Alistair Cooke sees through everything and everybody. His geniality and bounce are always there, but his light blue eyes are penetrating. What a piece of luck, lunching with Alistair Cooke for 30 years.

Milton Friedman

(1912–2006)

Upon his death at the age of ninety-four, the *New York Times* hailed Milton Friedman as "the grandmaster of free-market economic theory in the postwar era and a prime force in the movement of nations toward less government and greater reliance on individual responsibility." Ranked among the greatest intellectuals of his era, Friedman received every honor that can be bestowed on an economist, including the Nobel Prize and the Presidential Medal of Freedom. His best-selling 1978 book *Freedom to Choose,* coauthored with his wife, Rose, receives an early nod in WFB's eulogy, which begins with meditations on the propriety of lamenting the death of nonagenarians and on the different ways in which personal friends and the nation at large will mourn an individual. Buckley's friendship with Friedman spanned five decades. It extended—once annually for nearly twenty years—to the ski slopes and, of course, to the set of *Firing Line.* Their most memorable televised encounter came in December 1990, two months after the publication of WFB's *Gratitude: Reflections on What We Owe to*

Our Country, in which the founder of *National Review* argued that
government incentives—and sanctions—should be deployed to en-
courage young people to devote a year of service to America. "You,
of all people," Friedman scolded, "somebody who's spent his life trying to fight the overgrown government, who's spent his life defending the virtues of individual freedom, of the free market—and here
you come up with a program that's the opposite of everything you've
stood for all your life." "We live in a society in which young people
and older people don't give any evidence of gratitude for what it is
that we inherit," Buckley countered, "and I'm looking for the redevel-
opment of an ethos that causes people to show that they are willing
to reciprocate." Friedman was not persuaded: "The question is: Why
is it that we have had so much of a reduction in the sense of gratitude? In my opinion it's primarily because we've been doing so much
through government . . . and as a result we have destroyed a sense of
individual responsibility and responsibility to one another."

"Milton Friedman, R.I.P."

National Review, December 18, 2006.

It isn't right to rail against fortune when death comes to a
friend, or a hero—in this case, both—at the high age of
94. Still, we are free to choose, and there was grief when
word came to us of the death of Milton Friedman. We were
on board a large ship, where a week of seminars at sea was
being guided by a dozen celebrants of conservative doctrine. One was to have been Friedman himself, but when
the boat pulled away from San Diego, bound for Mexico,
Friedman was in a hospital in San Francisco.

What struck the band of brothers who came together

last Friday afternoon to devise an impromptu tribute to our missing seminarist was in fact exactly that—grief, never mind that he had lived 94 years. Although Professor Friedman engaged himself to the end, in tandem with his brilliant wife, Rose, in academic and philosophical work, it was not the discontinuation of this that caused the pang aboard the S.S. *Oosterdam*. If the word had come that Friedman would never again write an academic paper, or a book or column, we'd have tightened our belts, and perhaps reminded ourselves of the million words that are there in print, and will always be there, to reread and to ponder. But what we felt was not so much the discontinuation of that great wellspring of liberal and penetrating thought. It was grief for the loss of a person.

It is inevitably so that the end of life of a central intellectual or political or indeed theatrical figure can be felt personally only by a comparative few, because only a few can have known any historical figure. The legion of admirers at a remove—those who felt for him, without ever having met him, admiration, devotion, even love—is something different, more detached. But there was also the impact of his person on individual students and friends and coadjutors, and on Thursday, November 16, we felt a wholly personal loss.

The next day we put together an afternoon seminar at the hands of confederates on board. John O'Sullivan spoke of the international impact Friedman had had during five decades, from the Sixties until the end. Robert Conquest, the scholar of Russia, poet, and, along with Friedman, fellow at the Hoover Institution, remarked the cultural impact of the great economist. Rich Lowry and Ramesh Ponnuru spoke of his influence on undergraduates. Arnold

Beichman, also a fellow at the Hoover Institution, an author and public intellectual—and nonagenarian—had known the deceased as long as anyone present, and did not attempt to hide his tears. Jay Nordlinger presided, weaving together, for the benefit of the 400 guests, the highlights of the life so mourned.

This author and friend had been struck down by an overnight illness. Had I spoken, I'd have stressed Milton's capacity for friendship and fine company. We met, along with another friend, every year for nineteen years for a long weekend of skiing and conviviality, interrupted, finally, by illness. "When I undertook the operation," he wrote me in 1994, "I did it very much in the hope that it would enable me to go skiing in January, but I am afraid the recovery isn't going to be fast enough for me to do so. I have already told Lawry [Chickering] about it. I cannot tell you how much I regret having to do this. With all my love, Milton." A year later: "I do not believe in miracles, and that is what I believe it would take to enable me to be on skis in six months' time." A year later: "Those many years we spent three days together at Alta are among my happiest memories." And after I published a piece about our skiing life, "You captured beautifully our joint satisfaction with our sessions at Alta. The fluency and sensitivity of your writing always astound me. Your generosity of spirit is remarkable and I am most grateful for having been a major beneficiary."

That is how true friends can address each other, and it was the impact of an end to the expression of such sentiments that struck me so hard on learning of the death of this Nobel Prize winner, the dominant economic and libertarian voice of the 20th century, my sometime skiing buddy. —WFB

Jerry Garcia

—◦—

(1942–1995)

WFB's eulogy for Jerry Garcia, lead singer and guitarist for the Grateful Dead, offers insight into the way Buckley processed news events about individuals with whose work or legacy he enjoyed only passing familiarity—or, as he admits here, none at all. Still, Buckley's commentary on the hippie mentality and its outward expressions was earnest and cultivated in the sense that he engaged the subject for decades; one thinks of the scene, recounted in *Cruising Speed* (1971), in which WFB and Pat, joined by Peter Glenville and a friend, ducked into a Manhattan theater to see the Rolling Stones documentary *Gimme Shelter*. (Pat objected: "I saw *Woodstock* and hated it!") In polemical terms, WFB's critique of the Deadheads is strictly inductive—perhaps *inductio ad absurdum*.

"Jerry Garcia, RIP"

Syndicated column, August 18, 1995; published in *National Review,*
September 25, 1995.

If I ever heard a song played by the Grateful Dead I wasn't aware of it. If I had been, I'd have pricked up my ears and listened real hard because I have a memory. It is of a young man who came to work at my shop. He had just graduated from Harvard, wanted to do some opinion journalism, and qualified for a summer internship that stretched into two or three years.

It was toward the end of the decade of the Sixties that he drew me aside one day, after we had gone to press. He said that he had been to a concert by the Grateful Dead and that it was a wonderful experience, and that he would go again whenever the group was in reach, and he invited me to join him at one of the concerts, which I wish I had done.

I have to suppose that, like so many others, I would have survived the experience without such harm as finally came to Jerry Garcia and, 25 years before Garcia, to our young intern. He did his work, but with progressive listlessness. His editorial paragraphs had never been razor sharp but they had been trenchant and readable, and now they were murky.

Things got worse, and now came the trappings, which were conventional. It began with sandals, then went in the usual direction, though I don't remember that he ran a ring through his ear. When an anniversary issue was planned for the magazine he suddenly demanded that his "generation" be represented, so I told him to go ahead and write what he thought would be a useful essay.

I don't remember seeing it myself, but I was told not that it was unsuitable, or unfinished, or unprofessional, but that its meaning was impenetrable. At about that time an associate ten years older reported his (informed) opinion that our intern was going off the deep end. At a collegial staff lunch he once excused himself so abruptly as to provoke the melancholy conclusion that he had needed a quick jolt of whatever drug he was taking. One day he announced that he would be married, and soon brought in an addled flower child dressed as he dressed. One weekend they just faded away. A few years later we received formal invitations to a second marriage, to a South American. He went with his new bride to her country and taught English. In due course he sent us an article submission. It was potentially publishable but needed work, and the managing editor sent it back to him with recommended changes. We did not hear from him again, except after another interval of five years or so, when we learned he had married yet again, this time to a native, and gone off to live in the hills. Question before the house: Is Jerry Garcia in some way responsible for this?

The issue of *Newsweek* that put Garcia on the cover quoted in huge type the words of a 21-year-old college student. "It's a free life when you're at a show. It's all about happiness. I'd just take my watch off and want time to stop." It isn't easy to rail against anyone who brings happiness, and one has to assume that many, perhaps the majority, of those who heard "shows" by the Grateful Dead achieved their highs without the use of intoxicants. But something unusual accounted for the young Americans, pictures of them reproduced in the days just gone by, exhibiting Dionysiac pleasure in their role as Deadheads. Exuberance finds its forms throughout the world and concentrates its energies on the young. But is the joy unconfined? Ought it to be?

Jerry Garcia died only a week after leaving the Betty Ford Center. He is quoted as having said two years ago that, really, he needed to do something to restore his health, otherwise he would be dead, like "two years from now." He went on schedule, and is said to have died with a smile on his face, no doubt because he was a happy man but also because he made so many others happy. But he also killed, if that's the right word for such as our intern, a lot of people. And although he had a pulsating forum world wide for thirty years and knew from his own experience what his habits were doing to him, he never went public on it, not really. One has to suppose, sadly, that in his case, going public on his problem, extending a truly firm handshake to his legions, would have required the dramatic gesture of retiring from the stage. If he had done so, it would not have been wounding to those of us who were never exposed to Jerry Garcia's special intoxicant, but, if he had done so, how many would have had better prospects for health, love, and longer lives?

Vladimir Horowitz

(1903–1989)

Vladimir Horowitz was the greatest pianist of the twentieth century. Born in Kiev, he debuted at Carnegie Hall in 1928, demonstrating a thunderous virtuosity, particularly in the Romantic repertoire, that excited audiences around the world and made him one of the best-selling recording artists in the history of classical music. Reportedly a closeted homosexual—which he denied—Horowitz married Wanda Toscanini, daughter of the world-renowned Italian conductor Arturo Toscanini; their lone child, a daughter, died from a drug overdose at age forty-one. Notoriously volatile and difficult, a reported recipient of electroshock therapy, Horowitz punctuated his six decades on the world stage with numerous retirements, retreats, and cancellations, but he returned to form in his eighties, when he recaptured critical acclaim, and the top spot on the classical music charts, with a series of performances in his native Soviet Union, which at that time was experiencing glasnost under Gorbachev. WFB's eulogy displays his love of classical music, his incurable "worship" of his idols, and his deft comedic gifts, including his ear for foreign accents.

"Vladimir Horowitz, R.I.P."

Syndicated column, November 9, 1989; published in *National Review,*
December 22, 1989.

Everybody knows that Vladimir Horowitz was (a) a great musician, and (b) a temperamental human being. He was different from his father-in-law Arturo Toscanini (I gather; I did not know Toscanini, though I worshiped him) in that he could be surprisingly affable, even unpredictably so. I met him under the most unexpected circumstances: on the Eastern Shuttle coming up from Washington 15 years ago. He came over and introduced himself and his wife, smiles lighting up the whole of his volatile countenance.

For a while we were friends. I remember especially an evening at his home in Connecticut when another guest and I conspired (ahead of time, over the telephone) to devise ways to bring him to the keyboard. I mean, why have supper with perhaps the greatest pianist in the world and not get him to play for you?

What, I asked him, would be his program the following month, when he would appear at the Metropolitan Opera House as the first one-man performer in the history of the house? Well, he said, maybe begin with something by Scarlatti. Then perhaps a sonata by Clementi—I grabbed my cue and gave the eye to my coconspirator.

"Clementi? You are going to waste your time with Clementi?"

"Why Clementi?" my friend, his brows furrowed, chimed in provocatively.

We earned the national actors award, because if we had rehearsed it, it could not have gone better:

Vladimir Horowitz rose. His voice and countenance were now grave. "You doan lahk Clementi? Clementi wass a JEE-nee-us! Clementi is as goot as the middle Beethoven!"

"Come on," I said condescendingly, pushing my luck.

And he marched to the piano, lifted the lid—and we heard not only Clementi, but the entire, historic two-hour concert he would give two weeks later. He and his wife were redoing the living room in their country house at the time and there was a third guest, their interior decorator, who during an interval while our host was walking his cat and our hostess was off in the kitchen somewhere, confided to us in whispers the great happening of the week before, when the local Italian curtain-maker had come in to quote the cost of the new set of curtains. "It will come to $278," he said to the decorator. Pause. "Or—for nothing! If Mr. Horowitz will play next Sunday for me and my wife."

This was on the order of suggesting in the presence of Cleopatra that, rather than pay to repair her gondola, she might extend her favors to the shipwright. Horowitz froze, and there was a moment of most awful tension. Horowitz then stood up, bowed his head slightly, and said: "I would be honored to play for you and your wife on Sunday." This was noblesse oblige in marble. It would be either that— Horowitz would accept the alternative—or else Horowitz would pull out a shotgun and end two careers, one musical, the other having to do with curtains.

He was also a man of considerable polemical shrewd-ness. Mike Wallace and his cameras were at Horowitz's New York apartment doing a *60 Minutes* segment and Wallace graveled out in his interrogatory-accusatory voice, "Is it true that for 13 years you stayed here without going out?" Horowitz looked at Mike Wallace, the disappointment of a child on his face. "Vot? Vot you mean? You doan like my room here?" The camera did a little tour of the comfort-able living room. "Vot you doan like about my room?"

Poor Mike. What can you say to someone who suggests that questioning his self-enclosure in an apartment for 13 years is the equivalent of finding his living room unattrac-tive?

Ah, but the time came when the Maestro wrote me off, wrote me off without a cent. The circumstances were: An-other invitation by Horowitz to dinner, which we accepted. After dinner, the Great Man disappeared, to walk his cat or whatever. It had been a most awfully long day, and after a half-hour or so, I beckoned to my wife, rose, and bade goodnight to Mrs. Horowitz, who was clearly startled at guests leaving before they were invited to do so. He was a stickler for decorum. Once he showed me a letter from the first lady, the first sentence of which had shocked him. "Jimmy and I are so pleased that you are coming to play for us at the White House on. . . ." The date followed, and the time. "Imagine! She sess 'Jee-mee' when she mean zee pressident off the United States! And she says nothink— NOTHINK!—about Wanda comink with me to the White House!" I clucked my grave Republican shock at Jacksonian manners.

I never heard from him (or her) again. He was a very great musician, and as long as music is bought and sold, presidents of the United States and curtain-hangers in Ridgefield, Conn., will ask for "the Horowitz recording."

Russell Kirk

—◆ ◆—

(1918–1994)

In the young WFB's eyes, Russell Kirk was an idol, a famous man approached with trepidation; in his seventies, WFB looked upon Kirk as the "neglected prince of conservative thought." With his publication of *The Conservative Mind: From Burke to Santayana* (1953), Kirk presented the scholarly tablets of modern conservatism: an academically rigorous work, acclaimed across the ideological spectrum, that rooted conservatism in Enlightenment traditions and linked it to some of America's most revered figures. At WFB's invitation—an event recounted with cinematic hilarity in the eulogy below—Kirk recruited to write a column for *National Review*, commencing with the inaugural issue in 1955 and ending with the magazine's silver anniversary. Along the way and beyond, Kirk published several dozen learned works of social history (*The Roots of American Order* [1974]), biography (*Edmund Burke: A Genius Reconsidered* [1967]), and literary criticism (*Eliot and His Age: T. S. Eliot's Moral Imagination in the Twentieth Century* [1971]) while also indulging a sweet tooth for fiction and ghost stories. Short, burly, balding, and bespectacled, Kirk made an unlikely Moses and was given to acts of heresy (e.g., voting for Gene McCarthy). Rancor between him and another founding figure of *NR*, Frank Meyer, who negatively reviewed one of Kirk's books, was mitigated by the fact that neither reported to the magazine's New York office, with Kirk remaining in his native Michigan, yet the friction was felt sufficiently for WFB to lament that "one-half of such diplomatic talents as I dispose of were regularly exhausted in editing a magazine that regularly published Frank Meyer *and* Russell Kirk." It was a price worth paying. "Russell," WFB declared in 1980, "I considered indispensable to the health and prestige of *National Review,* and his name is indissolubly linked to the journal."

"Russell Kirk, RIP"

National Review, May 30, 1994.

In the next issue of *National Review* we will pay appropriate tribute to a figure whose death on April 29 left the conservative community desolate. He was omnipresent, coming at us from every direction. He wrote a seminal book and, for many years, a syndicated column. He lectured, gave speeches, wrote ghost stories and histories, and edited anthologies. Through it all he maintained a special presence as ever so faintly bohemian, the orthodox husband of a beautiful wife, father of four daughters, obdurately professorial in demeanor, yet those who noticed never needed to wait too long before catching the wink, in what he said, and did.

Much of all this in the issue to come, so that here, we pause merely to remark his loss, reach out our hands to one another, expressing our shared grief.

Our own association with him—and I clutch in here to the personal mode—is older than the life of *National Review*. I had of course read his important book, but I had not met Russell Kirk. The publication of *National Review* was now anticipated, to begin about a year later, and the time had come to meet him.

It was in the fall of 1954; I made the date, and flew to Michigan. I had a single objective, and I greatly feared that I would fail in it. I desired that Professor Kirk would consent, beginning with the opening issue, to contribute a regular column to *National Review* on doings in the academic world.

I confess I was very nervous. Although Russell was only a few years older, at 28 I felt that an entire world lay between us, the wide gulf between his learning, and my own. He was then a bachelor, and shortly after I arrived to stay as a guest at his house, Piety Hill, he took me to dinner at a neighborhood restaurant, where he promptly ordered two Tom Collinses. Emboldened by that warm aloofness which was his trademark, I put it to him directly, and his reply was instantaneous: Yes, he would write a regular column for my prospective magazine.

I was so elated by his spontaneous and generous willingness to associate his august name with that of a wizened ex-schoolboy known mostly for an iconoclastic screed directed at his alma mater, that I took to ordering more Tom Collinses, but in every case, one for each of us. The evening proceeded toward a pitch of such hilarity that, at midnight, I was barely able to drive the car back to Russell's house. On arriving, he led me to my bedroom, bade me goodnight only one second before I collapsed into my bed, to rise seven hours later and bump into Russell Kirk—only then emerging from his study. He had, in the interval since dinner, written a chapter of his history of St. Andrews University, and would catch a little sleep after he served me breakfast.

In the ensuing 25 years he never missed a deadline. At his wedding to the woman his readers resigned themselves finally to acknowledging as "the beauteous Annette," I thought that possibly the most useful gift I might give him would be a honeymoon's-length moratorium from his column, since he was off to Scotland. I stammered out the proposal to him moments before he ascended to the altar. He acknowledged it by reaching into the pocket of his morning coat and presenting me with—four columns. Perfectly typed. Perfectly edited. Perfectly executed. Not many had more direct, week-by-week knowledge of the extraordinary professionalism of Russell Kirk, which matched that of Samuel Johnson and G. K. Chesterton.

He served us notice, a few months before our 25th anniversary in 1980, that he would discontinue his column at that point. He gave no reason for doing so, and questions weren't asked. A. J. Nock had recalled that Thoreau abandoned his pencil factory after he had achieved the exemplary pencil. What was there left to do?

In the ensuing 14 years Russell Kirk wrote many books and a hundred essays, gave a thousand speeches, and influenced the lives of another half-generation. His last day, he rose, breakfasted, sat down in his armchair, exchanged words with his wife and two of his daughters, closed his eyes, and died. Few have repaid their debt to their family, their country, and their faith so extravagantly. —WFB

John Lennon

(1940–1980)

In the quasi-religious movement that was Beatlemania, WFB was an apostate. It wasn't, he pleaded, that he hated rock 'n' roll: "When Elvis Presley came along I was consigned to hopeless vulgarity by my discerning friends for suggesting that he was, somehow, worth listening to." With the Beatles, however, Buckley drew a line—one of his sharpest. "The Beatles are not merely awful," he declared in a September 1964 column titled "Yeah Yeah Yeah, They Stink":

> I would consider it sacrilegious to say anything less than that they are godawful. They are so unbelievably horrible, so appallingly unmusical, so dogmatically insensitive to the magic of the art, that they qualify as crowned heads of antimusic, even as the imposter popes went down in history as "antipopes."

That column drew more than 500 letters of protest—"a hundred times as many" as anything else WFB wrote—and is still routinely quoted as a jewel of early philistinism about the band. When John Lennon generated a firestorm by saying the Beatles were "more popular than Jesus," WFB chastised Lennon for his "coarse ejaculation" and "nonmusic"—but otherwise agreed that the Beatles' founder had spoken "the plain truth."

> The reaction appears to be based on the assumption that Mr. Lennon was comparing not the relative popularity of himself and Jesus, but their related virtues. And this is of course to miscomprehend what Mr. Lennon said, which was certainly untactful, and indubitably accurate.... The Beatles...are, however inadvertently, self-anointed substitutes for rather more meaningful objects of adulation.

Seeing the Beatles retreat to Rishikesh to meditate with the Maharishi, WFB, from London, quipped that the youth of the sixties "will go anywhere to experience spirituality—except next door." Yet that year also marked one of the greatest reversals in Buckley's career. "I mean, how can one prevail against them?" WFB wrote in a column titled "How I Came to Rock." "The answer is: One cannot. And even if they are hard to listen to, there is an exuberance there that is quite unmatched anywhere else in the world."

After Lennon's murder, Buckley protested his deification. Yoko Ono's request that the world mark the tenth anniversary of the grim event by singing "Imagine" led to a WFB column dissecting, and rejecting, the song's lyrics, which envisioned a world without religion, borders, or possessions ("No, thanks, I don't want to imagine a world in which Yoko doesn't possess the goods that John left her"). But in December 1980, when a deranged fan leaped from the shadows of the Dakota building and pumped five bullets into Lennon's body, with Yoko looking on in horror, and the world responded with displays of grief redolent of the Kennedy assassination, WFB set aside his philosophical disagreements.

"John Lennon"

Syndicated column, December 18, 1980.

My son (age 28) said to me the day after, "Imagine how you would have felt if Arturo Toscanini had been killed?" He didn't have to say more, having fingered my own boyhood hero. I can't clearly remember whether, in the '30s, Toscanini was exactly a cult figure. But he was a formidable presence—charismatic, an acknowledged genius, above all a perfectionist. He liked Broadway music.

My guess is that he would not have been taken by the Beatles; and the general disorder of the Beatles' audience would not have been tolerated by the conductor who, when he played his famous series for NBC, requested that the programs be made out of silk, lest he be distracted by the noise of paper-flutter. When Toscanini died he was mourned, and they played Verdi's Requiem and broadcast it. But he was old, and Lennon was young; and Toscanini died of a conventional old man's disease, and Lennon died of a bullet wound.

Why was the grief so intense? Those of us who mourned his death without any marked sense of privation (i.e., those of us who did not feel the call of his music or of his words, did not purchase his albums, nor looked to him for sumptuary or moral guidance) mourned for two reasons. The first and obvious being that his killing was one of those grotesqueries so common in this century, about which we can only say in defense of ourselves that we have not quite got used to them, though this year alone, we have suffered Allard Lowenstein, Sarai Ribicoff, and Michael Halberstam. Beyond this, our grief is derivative. It is saddening to experience so deep a sadness in others. It isn't very often that people gather together in Central Park in order to weep. And one wonders whether it is even seemly to ask exactly what it was that caused that special bereavement.

I have a notion about this, and it is based on an entire half day devoted in the winter of 1973 [*sic*; 1971] to reading a two-part profile on John Lennon published in *Rolling Stone*. I cannot remember a worse reading experience. In 1971 John Lennon was a convinced egomaniac (his word). He could not utter a sentence without obscenity. His animadversions on his old companions, in particular Paul McCartney, were quite simply unpleasant (Paul was jealous of him, the Beatles' music was arid and formalistic). His autobiography was right out of Olympia Press: he had been stoned "thousands of times." His sex orgies had cloyed. The fakir in India to whom he had committed himself turned out to be a commercial old lecher. Everyone was jealous of him. Yoko Ono's least song was better than the best of the Beatles. At the time, I wrote, "Lennon is greatly talented as a musician. As a philosopher, he is as interesting as Jelly Roll Morton, less so, as a matter of fact. He is interesting only to an anthologist of pieces on 'How I Wrecked My Own Life and Can Help Wreck Yours.'"

But there followed, not long after, the five years of seclusion. He is said to have spent most of the time with his wife and son. And, unless I am deluded by the pervasive sadness, he achieved something of a nobility of feature. The pictures of him showed: gravitas. No one's face had more aspects than John Lennon's. He was the mischievous, theatrical, erotic, iconoclastic playboy.

Then suddenly he seemed to walk tall. And it was in this posture that he was shot down. And perhaps his own experiences—with drugs, with joyless sex, with enervating solipsism—shrived him, and the generation that turned out to weep for him experienced something of that spiritual emancipation that comes to people who come to see things philosophically. They find this (I take their word for it) in his music and in his lyrics. And they found it in him, for reasons no one at Central Park interviewed by the ubiquitous cameras could quite explain, for the best of reasons, namely that it was unexplainable; is unexplainable, but the grief was real.

Norman Mailer

(1923–2007)

Norman Mailer was one of the most celebrated and vilified writers of the twentieth century. Although he was acclaimed as a novelist, two of his nonfiction works—*Armies of the Night* (1968), about the Vietnam War, and *The Executioner's Song* (1980), about the life and death of a convicted murderer—won the Pulitzer Prize. Brilliant, reckless, and pugnacious—literally: he liked to box and fight and stabbed the second of his six wives—the far-left Mailer made an unlikely friend to WFB. Yet they *were* friends, starting with a sold-out debate at the Medinah Temple in Chicago in September 1962 before a crowd of 4,000 people. In his opening statement, Buckley declared: "I do not know of anyone whose dismay I personally covet more; because it is clear from reading the works of Mr. Mailer that only demonstrations of human swinishness are truly pleasing to him. . . . Pleasant people, like those of us on the right wing, drive him mad, and leech his genius." Influenced by WFB's 1965 run for mayor of New York City, Mailer followed suit four years later. He appeared on *Firing Line* three times, first in May 1968 to promote *Armies,* which Buckley called "an extremely interesting and enjoyable book, if that's the right word for it." "I wish someone on the right wing would write a book that would be as good," Mailer replied, "because it would be a great help to us on the Left." "You wouldn't notice it if it were written," WFB shot back. When the historian Kevin M. Schultz published *Buckley and Mailer: The Difficult Friendship That Shaped the Sixties* (2015), many critics—this one included—contended that WFB would not have regarded his friendship with Mailer as definitive either in WFB's own life or in the upheavals of the sixties; however, it is true that WFB, writing near the end of his life, devoted a large effort—more than 1,200 words—to Mailer's eulogy, noting at the outset that their dealings, years earlier, had been "extensive" and characterizing his departed friend as "a towering figure in American literary life."

"Norman Mailer, R.I.P."

National Review, December 3, 2007.

In conversation with the book editor of *National Review* the subject of Norman Mailer of course came up. Passing by the event (he had died on Saturday) as if it were inconsequential was one alternative, ruled out. The most obvious reason being that Mailer was consequential, as a writer and as a human being. The next question was, Ought I to write about him? A commanding reason for this is, I suppose, that I am, so to speak, the principal obituarist at *National Review.* Another reason is that years ago I had pretty extensive dealings with Norman Mailer.

And so here I am, and I begin by acknowledging the truth of much that is being said about him, that he was a towering figure in American literary life for 60 years, almost unique in his search for notoriety and absolutely unrivaled in his coexistence with it. Roger Kimball of *The New Criterion* has written that Mailer "epitomized a certain species of macho, adolescent radicalism that helped to inure the wider public to displays of violence, anti-American tirades, and sexual braggadocio."

But to delve into one's own little portfolio, Mailer's career sliced by my own when in September 1962 two entrepreneurs rented the Medinah Temple in Chicago, which held over 4,000 people, having engaged Mailer and me to debate on the nature of the right wing in American politics. They found the hall all but sold out for the affair.

It happened that everyone in the world who was sportsminded was in Chicago that week—to view the title match between world heavyweight champion Floyd Patterson and challenger Sonny Liston. Pugnacity reigned for those two or three days, and it pleased Mailer, who was complaining widely about his poverty, that *Playboy* magazine immediately contracted to publish his and my opening statements in their next issue.

A few years later I had Mailer as a guest on *Firing Line*. "Seeing Buckley and Mailer on the tube yesterday I can't get over it," one critic wrote in the *New York Avatar*, which was briefly the court circular of the underground press. "The greatest representation of the two extremes I've seen in a long time. Conservative meets liberal, right meets left, before meets after. Buckley didn't know what the f*** Mailer was talking about, it just jammed his computer, he even had to resort to childish insults to try and keep up his end." ("Norman Mailer decocts matters of the first philosophical magnitude from an examination of his own ordure, and I am not talking about his books," I had said.)

"Mailer's steady stream of reject material," Mel Lyman went on, "was just too much for Buckley's computer to take, it started smoking. Computers don't get mad, they just smoke when they're overloaded. Buckley is a computer, Mailer is a man. A man can only be categorized and computerized to a certain extent, the greater part of him lies out of definition. Greatness can be recognized only. That is why Buckley went all to pieces when Mailer spoke of the 'greatness' he saw in Castro. Buckley could only see the un-American activities accredited to the man, Castro. He could only see him as far as he could define his actions. Mailer could look right at him, like a child, and see a great force, an inner strength, a fearlessness that had nothing to do with right or wrong. This is the sadness of Buckley and all that he represents, it cannot possibly recognize anything greater than itself for it takes all that it sees and reduces it to a lifeless, sterile set of rules and regulations. . . .

"[Buckley] truly believes he has an open mind," this disciple of Mailer wrote. "He is open, you can say anything to him, but he has only one thing to say to you, and he is a master at finding ways to say it. I love Buckley, but he makes me very sad, he's completely mastered the art of living in prison but Mailer's mastered the art of what you do after you get out, and Buckley doesn't even know there is an out."

"It didn't start out that way," Roger Kimball wrote. "Mailer was brought up in Brooklyn, 'a nice Jewish boy' as he once put it, from a middle-class family of first-generation immigrants. It was a background from which he had long endeavored to escape." Norman Podhoretz, in his memoir *Ex-Friends,* observed that "Mailer would spend the rest of his life overcoming the stigma of this reputation as a 'nice Jewish boy' by doing as an adult all the hooliganish things he had failed to do in childhood and adolescence." There was a hint of this struggle in his appearance on *Firing Line,* where I failed to absorb what the underground press was so eager for me to discover.

Mailer took two practical steps that bounced off our Chicago exchange. The first was to sue *Playboy*—on the grounds that, manifestly, his essay was worth more than the $5,000 paid to us. That done, he said he wished to explore with me a string of Buckley-Mailer debates throughout the country, "beginning in Carnegie Hall."

This initiative brought him and his wife to our house in Stamford, Conn., and I took him out on my 36-foot sailboat. He could not believe it when I turned the wheel over to him, pointing out a course to the end of the harbor. It was very cold by the time we had finished dinner, but he ordered his wife Jeannie to the back of his motorcycle, and they zoomed off to Brooklyn.

There were other episodes. There was the night in New York when, after dinner, I said I needed to file a column, but he wasn't ready to go home, pursuing us to our apartment nearby. Wobbling up the steps, his then-current wife passed out and was placed by my wife in a spare bedroom. Norman climbed upstairs with me to my study, and spoke disparagingly of the column as, paragraph after paragraph, I gave it to him to read. Finally he said it was time to go home, and we walked down the stairs to where his wife had been taken. But rousing her from that sleep defied any resource we were willing to deploy, so Norman announced fatalistically that, never mind, she would eventually rise, go out the street door, and get a cab. "Me, I'm going home, Slugger," as he called my wife. I helped him find a cab.

But Norman Mailer is a towering writer! So why this small talk? Perhaps because it no longer seems so very small. I said about Mailer a few years ago that he created the most beautiful metaphors in the language. I reiterate that. But I go further, wondering out loud whether the obituaries are, finally, drawing attention to the phenomenon of Norman Mailer from the appropriate perspective. The newspaper of record says of him, as though such a profile were routine, that he was married six times, that he nearly killed one wife with a penknife, and that he had nine children. What if he had had seven wives, the seventh of them abandoned there in somebody's bedroom, waiting for a taxi to take her home, any home? Would that have claimed the obituarists' attention? —WFB

Vladimir Nabokov

——◆——

(1899–1977)

As if his life weren't charmed enough, Buckley counted among his fans and regular lunch companions Vladimir Nabokov. Born in Russia and educated at Cambridge, Nabokov vaulted to greatness with *Lolita* (1957), a satirical novel about the erotic relationship between a twelve-year-old nymphet—a term Nabokov created—and a middle-aged professor. A resident of the United States for two decades before settling down for the last eighteen years of his life in Switzerland, Nabokov was an ardent reader of *National Review* and carried on a lengthy correspondence with Buckley. When WFB sent Nabokov an Ezra Pound anthology edited by WFB's dear friend Hugh Kenner, Nabokov replied: "Though I detest Pound and the costume jewelry of his verse, I must say Kenner's approach is very interesting." "The *National Review* has always been a joy to read," Nabokov wrote WFB on March 26, 1973, from Montreux, "and your articles in the *Herald Tribune* counteract wonderfully the evil and trash of its general politics." Spurred by the vastness of the talent he was seeking to capture in portraiture, WFB's eulogy for Nabokov is one of Buckley's most literary: Note the seamless shifting back and forth of point of view ("Isn't that right, Vera?") and the allusive depiction of Vera Nabokov as a brooding, authoritative presence in her husband's life and mind.

"VN—RIP"

National Review, July 22, 1977.
[brackets and ellipses in original]

The cover of this magazine had gone to press when word came in that Vladimir Nabokov was dead. I am sorry—not for the impiety; sorry that VN will not see the cover, or read the verse, which he'd have enjoyed. He'd have seen this issue days ahead of most Americans, because he received *National Review* by airmail, and had done so for several years. And when we would meet, which was every year, for lunch or dinner, he never failed to express pleasure with the magazine. In February, when I last saw him, he came down in the elevator, big, hunched, with his cane, carefully observed by Vera, white-haired, with the ivory skin and delicate features and beautiful face. VN was carrying a book, which he tendered me with some embarrassment— because it was inscribed. In one of his books, a collection of interviews and random fare, given over not insubstantially to the celebration of his favorite crotchets, he had said that one of the things he *never* did was inscribe books. Last year, called back unexpectedly to New York, I missed our annual reunion. Since then I had sent him my two most recent books, and about these he now expressed hospitable enthusiasm as we sat down at his table in the corner of the

elegant dining room of the most adamantly unchanged
hotel in Europe: I cannot imagine, for all its recent architectural modernization, that the Montreux-Palace was any
different before the Russian revolution.

He had been very ill, he said, and was saved by the
dogged intervention of his son, Dmitri, who at the hospital
ordered ministrations the poor doctors had not thought
of—isn't that right, Vera? Almost right—Vera is a stickler for
precision. But he was writing again, back to the old schedule. What was that schedule? (I knew, but knew he liked to
tell it.) Up in the morning about six, read the papers and
a few journals, then cook breakfast for Vera in the warren of little rooms where they had lived for 17 years. After
that he would begin writing, and would write all morning
long, usually standing, on the cards he had specially cut to
a size that suited him (he wrote on both sides, and collated
them finally into books). Then a light lunch, then a walk,
then a nap, and, in nimbler days, a little butterfly-chasing
or tennis, then back to his writing until dinner time. Seven
hours of writing, and he would produce 175 words. [What
words!] Then dinner, and book-reading, perhaps a game
of Scrabble in Russian. A very dull life, he said chortling
with pleasure, and then asking questions about America,
deploring the infelicitous Russian prose of Solzhenitsyn,
assuring me that I was wrong in saying he had attended
the inaugural meeting of the Congress for Cultural
Freedom—he had never attended any organizational meeting of anything—isn't that right, Vera? This time she nods
her head and tells him to get on with the business of ordering from the menu. He describes with a fluent synoptic virtuosity the literary scene, the political scene, inflation, bad
French, cupiditous publishers, the exciting breakthrough
in his son's operatic career, and what am I working on now?

A novel, and you're in it.

What was that?

You and Vera are in it. You have a daughter, and she becomes a Communist agent.

He is more amused by this than Vera, but not all *that* amused. Of course I'll send it to you, I beam. He laughs— much of the time he is laughing. How long will it take you to drive to the airport in Geneva?

My taxi told me it takes *"un petit heure."*

Une petite heure [he is the professor]: that means fifty minutes. We shall have to eat quickly. He reminisces about his declination of my bid to go on *Firing Line*. It would have taken me *two weeks* of preparation, he says almost proudly, reminding me of his well known rule against improvising. Every word he ever spoke before an audience had been written out and memorized, he assured me—isn't that right, Vera? Well no, he would answer questions in class extemporaneously. Well *obviously*! He laughed. He could hardly program his students to ask questions to which he had the answers prepared! I demur: His extemporaneous style is fine, just fine; ah, he says, but before an audience, or before one of those . . . television . . . cameras, he would freeze. He ordered a brandy, and in a few minutes we rose, and he and Vera and I walked ever so slowly to the doors. "As long as Western civilization survives," Christopher Lehmann-Haupt wrote in the *Times* last Tuesday, "his reputation is safe. Indeed, he will probably emerge as one of the greatest artists our century has produced." I said goodbye warmly, embracing Vera, taking his hand, knowing that probably I would never see again—never mind the artist—this wonderful human being. —WFB

Elvis Presley

—◆—

(1935–1977)

National Review greeted the death of Elvis Presley with a harsh un-signed editorial, two paragraphs long, allowing that he might rate "a footnote or two" in showbiz history. "Presley's music, even at its best, was obscured by side issues like hair and hips; and the best lasted only a few short years before being overwhelmed by commercialism, white jumpsuits, and avoirdupois." WFB must have been sailing dur-ing that editorial meeting, for he was an Elvis man! Something in Bill Buckley—the romantic subversive, perhaps—identified, very early on, in the fifties, with Elvis Presley and his (televised) revolution. He ad-mired professionally Presley the performer, electrifying and dynamic, while judging his "the most beautiful singing voice of any human being on earth." This enduring fascination culminated in *Elvis in the Morning* (2001), a novel that explored an alternative scenario by which Pris-cilla Beaulieu might have entered the singer's life. Buckley never wrote a proper eulogy for Elvis, but in the column below, written after he made the pilgrimage to Graceland in 2000, he revealed the roots of his fascination with the Boy from Tupelo whose stage act threw open the doors of race and sex. WFB loved Elvis's voice—but as a Catholic, he marveled at the divinity that modernity conferred on a secular King.

"Elvis's Bad Break"

Syndicated column, May 22, 2000.

If you think you were hurt by the market, think what happened to Elvis Presley. So you don't care what happened to Elvis Presley? You would care if you stopped by at Graceland, which 700,000 people do every year, one-quarter of them foreign-born. So that's all very interesting, but why the economic blues? Did they cause him to sing a song or whatever about how lonesome he became one day after his market went down?

Even if you care not at all about Elvis Presley, never listened to one of his songs or, if you did, certainly didn't intend to listen to another, he was an important musical figure. But he blanked out in the mid-Seventies from drug bloat, so why can't we get on with somebody else?

We can and do, but how to account for almost 1 million people going to Graceland every year? And here's something else. He died on August 16 (1977), and a year after that, a few fans began to congregate on the eve of the anniversary of his death, carrying, each one, just one candle. They would walk up and down in front of Graceland. But in 1981 the property was opened to guided tours, so beginning then, the candlelight vigil makes its way in and around the Graceland preserve, passing by the little graveyard where Elvis is buried.

Mr. Jack Soden, who is the chief executive officer of the Graceland operation, tried trimming the crowd down, but after a few years had no alternative than to permit the earliest arrivers to begin their walking vigil at five in the afternoon. By dawn the succeeding day the pathways were drenched from the wax of the memorial candles. Are they older people? After all, Elvis was born in 1935, became famous in 1954—are these old baby boomers who come to Graceland? No. There are still many teenagers who come every day. Graceland doesn't anticipate ending its operation when contemporaries of Elvis die off, which will begin to happen about ten years from now.

But what was his economic crash, that could distract attention from our own free-fall? The man who managed Elvis's affairs was a mysterious, assertive marketer who called himself "Colonel" Parker. He was a libidinous patron of the casinos. The speculation is that when he made the proposal to Elvis in 1975, the Colonel terribly needed some cash. He persuaded (or simply instructed) Elvis to sell to RCA all of his recording royalties as of that moment. The deal was $5 million and the Colonel got his customary 50 percent. Well, those royalties now earn $25 million per year. The bummest deal in musical history.

The same curiosity that brings visitors to Graceland inevitably prompts them to ask to see the second floor, where Elvis lived and died in grisly stupor. The answer is a flat, ingratiating no. That is the deal, imposed unsparingly by Lisa Marie, the daughter and heir. Why should anybody want to visit those quarters and ogle at the seven-foot diameter shower in the bathroom and the voluptuous bedroom, an extension of Elvis's resoundingly vulgar tastes?

A silly question: Why do people want to poke into the

spot in the warehouse where the killer waited for President Kennedy? Why the allure of the balcony on which Martin Luther King strolled, awaiting the fatal bullet? Elvis Presley is something of a legend, and it is in very full display at Graceland. There is his pink Cadillac, and his motorcycles, and his big jet airplane and his little jet airplane, and the costumes he wore, which would have dazzled the Pharaohs, and the tractors he bought having zero use for them. But there also, in dazzling numbers, are the gold records he won from the industry, authentic memorabilia of a voice and manner and style that dumbfounded, enthralled, and repelled the largest musical audience ever got together by a single musical artist.

What are they there at Graceland to venerate? An aspect, perhaps, of the spiritual inclination of the American people, who do not require that the memory being venerated should have been a martyr or a prophet. Just someone truly singular and mythogenic, who contributed to his own legend his suicidal ending as a victim of the drugs he inveighed against with the strange, disquieting, appealing innocence that marked his entire life.

A. M. Rosenthal

~

(1922–2006)

A. M. ("Abe") Rosenthal was a Pulitzer Prize–winning foreign correspondent for the *New York Times* who ascended to become managing and executive editor of the paper during its headiest and most tumultuous years, from 1969 to 1986: the era of the Pentagon Papers and Watergate and of the *Times*'s dramatic expansion in editorial scope, circulation, and profitability. After reaching the mandatory retirement age, he became a columnist. As the *Times*'s own obituary noted, Rosenthal was a notoriously volatile man who assumed leadership of the paper at a time when mass media began devoting greater scrutiny to the top executives of mass media. "Perhaps more than those of any editor in modern times, Mr. Rosenthal's life and career were chronicled closely," wrote *Times* reporter Robert D. McFadden, "and his personal traits and private and professional conduct were dissected and analyzed with fascination in gossip and press columns, in magazines and books, and in the newsrooms and bars where those who had worked for or against him told their tales of admiration and woe." WFB first became friendly with Rosenthal in New York in the early sixties. While recounting the lone instance in which he felt the lash of Rosenthal's famous temper, Buckley likened his friend, in historical impact, to William Randolph Hearst and Henry Luce, calling Rosenthal "the commanding figure in the evolution of serious daily journalism." Here is another example of one of WFB's "transideological" friendships—and evidence that the founder of *National Review* saw no contradiction in being a conservative and loving the *New York Times*. Indeed, in a 1996 column, Buckley declared the *Times* "the greatest news institution in the history of the world, in the absence of which many of us would stumble about as if without arms or legs" even as he lamented how often the paper's editorial board, and venerated *Times*men from Walter Duranty to James Reston, had acted as apologists for the totalitarian regimes in China and the Soviet Union.

"A. M. Rosenthal, R.I.P."

National Review, June 5, 2006.

Only one in a thousand Americans brushes up against such foreign bodies as newspaper writers and editors. Some bylines become recognizable, but unless the reporters have a life on television, they are sheer palimpsest, and this is the reason for the surprise, here and there registered, at the huge attention given to A. M. Rosenthal, who died on May 10 in New York, age 84. Notwithstanding that his name was not known to the many, what he did touched the lives of everyone who reads newspapers. He was the commanding figure in the evolution of serious daily journalism, which he influenced as decisively as William Randolph Hearst influenced the tabloids, and Henry Luce the weekly newsmagazines.

Abe Rosenthal did it through the *New York Times,* where he worked for fifty-five years, rising from stringer at his college campus to executive editor.

In twenty years he altered journalism by hugely increasing the range of public notice—everything interested the Canadian-born journalist whose father, an immigrant from Byelorussia, was an indigent fur trapper and house painter. By the time Abe was named executive editor of the most influential newspaper in the world, he had changed not only the purview of the daily press but also the idiom in which it was written. The *Times,* by general acknowledgment, had become a model for journalists, and Abe did that.

His obituaries tell that he was often an angry man, that his tempers were violent, his manners often oppressive. We were friends from the time he returned home from Japan, after nine years as a prize-winning correspondent, to begin his administrative career at the *Times.* He was cofounder of a little club. The reasons for its formation are not chronicled and not known, but the alluvium was a half-dozen New Yorkers, some of them decisive voices in American journalism, meeting for lunch five or six times every year. Only once, that I remember, did we have the flavor of Rosenthal Anger. I myself had it once for a blistering five minutes on the telephone when he accused me of misrepresenting the *New York Times* in a news story. But that mode of A. M. Rosenthal was all but unknown to most who experienced him as a friend.

He thought of accredited journalists as something of a priestly order, their incorruptibility to be taken for granted. We met often, at his home and mine, and I once posed a hypothetical question. What would be the discipline, at the *New York Times* back when he was its boss, against a delinquent reporter? He seemed mystified by the question. He thought he was answering it when he said that no reporter at the *Times* would be guilty of such an offense as I described—"They are all professionals." He spoke in such accents as a cardinal might use in referring to men of the cloth. His respect for his profession activated the fury with which he dealt with imperfect performances by postulants.

When he wrote, he seldom displayed his hot flushes, but he could write scathingly on human rights. He was kicked out of Poland by Gomulka during the Cold War because he filed dispatch after dispatch on Communist-directed censorship and oppression. When he retired as executive editor he undertook to do a column for the *Times* twice a week. After some years, this was reduced to just once a week, and this saddened many because of his fidelity to the cause of human freedom. Cardinal John O'Connor mourned the revised schedule. The Chinese Communists were at that point bearing down hard on Tibet, bringing on a public reproach by President George H. W. Bush. This the cardinal applauded, adding, "Mr. Rosenthal, however, was writing about the plight of Tibet before many people could even find it on the map. It would not surprise me in the slightest if presidential speechwriters were avid readers of the Rosenthal column."

A very sad day was not long off, and I had the news of it from him on my cellphone. Abe was communicating to a few friends that he had been told his column would be discontinued. He had been summoned, he said, by the new young publisher ("maybe the second or third time I ever laid eyes on him") and told simply, "It's time."

This wasn't arrant cruelty: Publishers make up their own minds, and the decisions they arrive at are sometimes done without due regard for the sensibilities even of great princes, whose time has now gone. Abe Rosenthal went on and wrote elsewhere, but a few years ago he stopped completely, and spent his time reading books and magazines and lightening the days of his friends. A month ago, at lunch, he chuckled that he had lost track of the conversation in which we were engaged. He smiled with the sweetness that marked his affection for his family and friends. We were to have dined, with our wives, two days before his dialogue with all worldly matters finally ended. We profit, endlessly, from his ingenuity and perspective. —WFB

William Shawn

❧

(1907–1992)

In today's media environment, in which the most prestigious outlets struggle to lure clicks from cat videos, younger readers probably cannot grasp how vaunted, how powerful, was the editor in chief of *The New Yorker,* William Shawn. The *New York Times* called the mild-mannered, bald-headed Shawn a "gentle despot" of the magazine, where, across a thirty-five-year reign, he edited and catapulted to fame countless literary giants, from J. D. Salinger to Truman Capote to Hannah Arendt. It was three years into the Shawn era when *National Review* debuted, and as editor of his own fledgling magazine, Buckley revered *The New Yorker* and understood the special place its editor held in American letters. In the great literary contretemps of 1965, when Tom Wolfe published "TINY MUMMIES! The True Story of the Ruler of 43rd Street's Land of the Walking Dead!" in the *New York Herald-Tribune*—a savage, often hilarious attack on Shawn as a craven and tyrannical creature, so constrained by antiquated proprieties as to have become mummified—WFB, who also admired Wolfe, remained neutral; only cursorily did he treat the affair in *The Unmaking of a Mayor* (1966), noting Shawn's refusal to speak to Wolfe as one strategy for dealing with "the tendentious journalist." In later years, Buckley lamented the arrival of profanity at *The New Yorker;* Tina Brown, he said, had "let little time go by before pushing to one side the taboos observed by the august William Shawn." As Shawn had published Buckley's work so often, WFB wanted this eulogy to be special. It appears here as it did in *National Review*, uniquely crafted as a letter to WFB's successor and illustrated by a handwritten note from Shawn, quoted herein.

"William Shawn, RIP"

National Review, January 18, 1993.

MR. JOHN O'SULLIVAN
National Review

Dear John:

You asked me to do an obit on William Shawn, and I replied that I could not write a formal piece about him because of the odd intimacy of my experiences with him. I speak of a man on whom I laid eyes twice in my life. The day the newspapers carried the news of his death a letter from him arrived at the office. It was handwritten and had been mailed the day before he died. I quote it in full:

Dear Mr. Buckley:

Thank you for sending me copies of *WindFall* and *In Search of Anti-Semitism.* Since you are the author of both books, I am confident that I will not be disappointed. I have not yet read *Anti-Semitism,* but I've read enough of

WindFall to see that I can read the rest with confidence.
The Buckley style, thank goodness, is Intact, and the
humor is undiminished. I'll go on reading. Meanwhile,
I send you warmest regards,

> William Shawn

Obviously, he was "Mr. Shawn" to me, as he was Mr.
Shawn even to authors older than I, who had much closer experiences with him than I. But from the beginning he was in
his own way so very courteous to me that I took extravagant
pains never to suggest that I was urging on him a familiarity
he might have found uncomfortable. With almost anyone
else with whom I have fairly extensive personal dealings, as
you know, I'd have got around pretty early on, never mind
how I addressed him/her, to signing off as "Bill." Never with
Mr. Shawn. Always, "Wm. F. Buckley, Jr." I can't help believing that he knew what I was up to, and liked it.

I don't recall what it was that prompted me to send my
manuscript, *Cruising Speed,* to him in 1970. The chances
against *The New Yorker's* running an intensely personal
journal of a single week in the life of a youngish (I was 45)
right-wing journalist were overwhelming. We all remember
the usual things, the day Kennedy was killed, V-J Day; I
remember the afternoon I reached Camden, South Carolina, to visit with my mother. Frances Bronson had left
word to call her at the office. I did, of course, and she told
me breathlessly that Mr. Shawn had *called her up* and told
her that he very definitely wished to publish "Mr. Buckley's" book, which, he told her, was "beautifully written and
witty" and that he would himself be editing the excerpts
run by *The New Yorker.* No other professional experience in
my lifetime has so buoyant a place in my memory.

He had assigned himself, I gather from reading about him and talking with a few *New Yorker* professionals, the job of personally editing one book manuscript every year, I think it was, and whether he selected me because, by lot, my manuscript came up at the time his turn had come to serve, or whether, for whatever reason, he selected mine as the book he wished to edit I don't know. But the experience was unique, a word he would frown upon unless it was used with great precision.

I use it with great precision. Others have written about it, but it is ever so hard to believe, even having lived through the experience, that the part of your book Mr. Shawn has elected to reproduce arrives one day in galley form. A single column, two inches wide, running down the middle of a long sheet of paper, clipped to the next galley. The appearance is identical to cutting out a column from *The New York Times* and pasting it on a long sheet of paper eight inches wide. There was no apparent reason at all for the extraordinary extravagance of the procedure: Why did it not come to you typewritten and double-spaced, cheaper to execute (these were the days of Linotype, when any alteration meant replacing an entire line of metal type), and easier to edit? One did not ask.

In the roomy spaces to the right and to the left appeared Mr. Shawn's handwritten "queries." He wondered whether this was the correct spelling of a name, whether, on reflection, one wished to say exactly this, worded exactly so, about that phenomenon, or that statement, by that man or woman. He questioned the use of a comma there, of a paragraph marking somewhere else. The author confronted also the queries of the "fact checker." No "fact" was ever taken for granted, if it could be independently verified.

I remember that in one passage in my book I made a reference to the speech given by Tom Clark, with whom I was debating before the annual conference of the Chamber of Commerce. I had written that Clark's opening speech was "a half-hour" long. On the side, a tiny note from the fact-checker. "Listened to tape. He spoke for 22 minutes."

But this was the first of three drafts of the 30,000 words *The New Yorker* published in two installments. The second and the third drafts were completely reset at the printer, assimilating edited alterations; and they arrived with fresh queries, and suggestions. But the great moment came when Frances told me that Mr. Shawn had called her to ask if I would lunch with him at the Plaza Oak Room, He liked to talk to your secretary, much preferred doing this to talking to you; or in any event, that was so in my own case. For every conversation I had with him over the telephone, Frances had a half-dozen. I acknowledge that this probably says something about Mr. Shawn, but conceivably says something about the relative advantages of talking to Frances Bronson instead of to me.

I went to the Plaza, of course, and we sat behind a small screen. I don't remember what he ate, but do remember that the waiter knew what to bring him, and I think I read somewhere that he pretty much always ate the same thing. He was genial only in the sense that his courtesy was absolute. There was only the barest amount of small talk. He wished to talk about the book he was editing, and to ask me a question or two concerning this point or the other. In particular I remember his telling me, in the most mild-mannered tones, that on reading the proofs I had returned—in most cases I had stuck by the punctuation I had originally used, rejecting the proffered alternatives—he had concluded that I was given to rather . . . eccentric uses of the comma. He said this by way of imparting information. It was not a reproach, or, rather, not exactly a reproach: but I could feel the tug of his great prestige, and so told him I would go back and look again at my footloose commas. The lunch ended fairly quickly and most agreeably, and a week or two later he called me, as he did four or five times before the manuscript finally appeared in print, to tell me, "Mr. Buckley, I really do not think that you know the correct use of the comma." I can't remember what it was that I replied, but do recall that I resolved not to fight *à outrance* over the remaining commas in the essay.

It is not everywhere known that, under Mr. Shawn, the author was given the final say as to what parts of his book would run, subject to the limitations of the space designated for that book. On some points Mr. Shawn would not give way—animadversions, for instance, which he thought for whatever reason unfair or unjustified. "Mr. Buckley, I do wish you would eliminate that paragraph about Mr. [Jones]. You see, we do not run a letters page, and it isn't quite fair to leave him without an opportunity to defend himself. . . ." I don't know how other authors handled him, but in almost every case, I yielded. His style was to cause the author to acquiesce in the change, rather than to dictate the change. With me this worked, though I remember a few cases in which, through an intermediary editor, I pleaded my case, and in all but one of these, Mr. Shawn yielded.

Two years later, I sent him the first of my sailing books, *Airborne,* once again thinking the possibility remote that he would himself read it, let alone publish it. But he did, passing along, through Frances, some nice words about my prose. A year or two later I wrote him to say that I had completed a book about the United Nations, but doubted he would wish to read it because United Nations life was intolerably boring. He replied instantly by mail asking to see it and one week later wrote to say he wished to publish my United Nations book. I made the dreadful mistake of declining, finally, to release it to *The New Yorker* because of its ruling that no book published in the magazine could appear in the trade press until six months had gone by. My publisher didn't want to let six months go by, and so I hurried out with it, only to discover that not more than 16 people in the entire world are willing to read any book about the United Nations. I was pleased to hear from Mr. Shawn that I had written the only book about the United Nations that was both "literate and readable." I appreciated the compliment even though it was not hard to make, inasmuch as at the time there were no books about the United Nations, literate or illiterate, except an odd Brazilian memoir and a kind of coffee-table book by Conor Cruise O'Brien, designed to promote some artist.

A year or two later I wrote him to say that I had cruised again across the Atlantic, and did not suppose that he would wish to consider yet another book on yet another Transatlantic sail. Oh but he would; and he proceeded to publish *Atlantic High*. Five years later I told him that only out of courtesy was I mentioning to him my manuscript, *Racing Through Paradise*, as it was inconceivable that *The New Yorker* would wish a third book by me with an ocean cruise as background. Inside of one week he advised me he wished to publish it. The last book of mine that he published was *Overdrive*, a sequel of sorts to *Cruising Speed*, in that it too was the journal of one week in my life. It was greeted as a most provocative, outrageous book, and was bitterly criticized by many reviewers. I winced at one reviewer, who wrote that perhaps Mr. Shawn's imminent departure from *The New Yorker* had something to do with the manifest deterioration of his literary judgment, as witness his publication of *Overdrive*. When a few months later I wrote the introduction to the soft-cover edition of the book, a long (glorious!) essay examining the criticisms of the book, I sent him a copy. He called me to say, in gentle accents but without running any risk of my misunderstanding him on the subject, that the critics of my book had had other things in mind than the quality of the book, which he was pleased to have sponsored.

I mentioned that he liked to speak to Frances. When a *New Yorker* check arrived for *Overdrive,* she called me in San Francisco to report jubilantly that the check was for $40,000. But later in the afternoon she called and said with some dismay that Mr. Shawn had telephoned her. "What he said was, 'Oh, Miss Bronson, our bookkeepers have made a most embarrassing mistake on the check for Mr. Buckley, and I would be grateful if you would simply mail it back to us, and we will mail the correct check tomorrow.'" That could only mean, we both reasoned, that I had been overpaid. The following day a check arrived for $55,000. Mr. Shawn had his own way of twinkling at the world he treated so formally.

An interesting postscript. When he had retired from *The New Yorker,* as you know, there were great protests from his adamantly loyal staff. About nine months later I said to myself: Should I write and invite him to lunch with me? I'd never have done any such thing while he was still the editor of his magazine, with powers of life and death over

you. Such an overture might have been thought a venture
in self-ingratiation. So I put it very carefully in my little note
to him, saying merely that it would give me great pleasure to
lunch with him but I recognized that he didn't go out very
much and that when he did he almost certainly had on his
mind a professional objective. He called Frances a day or
so later and said he would be most pleased to lunch, and a
week or so later we met at the Carlyle, and talked together
animatedly. He had read that week's issue of *National Review*.
I can't believe that he (a hardy political liberal) read *NR* as
a matter of habit, but could easily persuade myself that he
had made it a point to read the current issue in order to
prepare for our lunch. (He read, by the way, with the speed
of light. Everything that appeared in *The New Yorker* he had
himself read, some of it two and, as with my books, three or
even four times.) The hour went quickly and pleasantly and
there was a total absence of ambient pressure, I thought.

The difficult decision came one year later. What went
through my mind was this, that if I did not invite him one
more time to lunch, he might think that the first invitation
was done out of a sense of duty to a retired editor who had
acted generously to me, and that now that he was so far
away from the scene, I had no further interest in him. I
decided to invite him again to lunch. He replied to Frances
that he would like very much to have lunch, and suggested
that perhaps some time in the fall would be good. That
was in 1991. In the fall, he called Frances, to say that he
still looked forward to our lunch but would rather not set a
date for it right away, would this be agreeable? I wrote back
that of course that would be agreeable; any time would do.
I did not hear again from him until the letter I received the
day he died.

He was a mythogenic character, a man totally taken by his muse and by his determination to hold to the standards he respected. I hope someone, perhaps one of his talented sons, will one day produce if not exactly a "life" of William Shawn, a book about his priorities, his literary manners, his immense effect on our culture, and his enormous impact on his devoted admirers. —Bill

Rosalyn Tureck

—◆—

(1914–2003)

A classical pianist and harpsichordist, Rosalyn Tureck was Bill Buckley's favorite performer—in any artistic medium, any genre. That was because she had been, as he put it in her eulogy, "the greatest living interpreter" of the works of the composer whom Buckley termed, in a note he dispatched to Tureck's deathbed, "the greatest genius of all time": Johann Sebastian Bach. WFB's boundless adoration of Bach and by extension his enthusiasm for Tureck—a Chicago native and five-time guest on *Firing Line,* usually at the piano—offer a window into one of the many childlike attributes Buckley determinedly carried into adulthood and, ultimately, old age. Hero worship on this scale bespeaks—I know from experience—a stubborn refusal to part with that facet of the childhood imagination that idealizes athletes, entertainers, and others who perform feats we know we could never replicate, on stages we know we could never ascend. Having debuted at Carnegie Hall in 1932, Tureck devoted her life almost entirely to playing, recording, and evangelizing on behalf of the works of Bach and other classical giants.

She married at fifty, only to see her new husband, an architect, die that same year, and never remarried. WFB's friendship with Tureck spanned decades, and she made special recordings, and even the pianist's version of house calls, for him and Pat. Though his eulogy focuses on her art, Buckley makes a point of recalling Tureck's eccentricities. "Rosalyn could sometimes be attracted," he writes, "to personal drama."

———•———

She died (finally) on July 17. As it happened, only a few minutes after a Tureck tribute at the Mannes School in New York at which the audience—more accurately, the congregants—heard her playing on video and tapes, listened to a lecture or two about her accomplishments, and on to two young pianists who tried to communicate her authoritative style. They played, of course, J. S. Bach. She and Bach devoted their lives to each other.

I approached her in the late Sixties, inviting her to appear on *Firing Line* to discuss a recent jab at Bach by a young protester in Los Angeles who had raged at a public rally that Bach had nothing to say to modern life. I knew her, as everyone who listened to Bach did, as the greatest living interpreter of his works. She had played the whole piano repertory, old and new—David Diamond wrote a piano sonata for her. Her first public performance in Chicago was done at age nine, and after intensive studies with fine artists in Chicago and at the Juilliard School, she began her exhaustive career, giving, gradually, only all-Bach programs. She played in every part of the world, earning, always, standing ovations, and taught music and musicology at Oxford, Yale, and Cal Tech.

We became friends, and she appeared five times on *Firing Line* programs, on one of them defending the role of the performing artist against the claim that technology had anachronized the live recital, a claim flamboyantly advanced by Glenn Gould. There was nothing here to be confused with fuddy-duddyism: She was receptive to explorations at every level, even mastering the (New Age) Theremin after some years of study with its developer. She performed on the harpsichord and, indeed, on the clavichord and organ, but was supreme on the piano, writing, collaterally, technical papers and books on performance and musical structure.

In 1977, she undertook at Carnegie Hall to play the *Goldberg Variations* before dinner on the harpsichord, and to play them after dinner on the piano, intending to display the strengths and individuality of the two instruments, at her singular hands. To do that one thinks of singing Tristan in the afternoon and Siegfried in the evening. At a reception—held at our quarters after the event—she declined to shake hands (dear Rosalyn could sometimes be attracted to personal drama). The *Goldbergs* are thought of as her signature piece. When she was 17, she undertook to learn this formidable work (I once timed her in it—118 minutes). After seven weeks she agreed to perform it for fellow students at Juilliard. Her teacher simply assumed that she would rely on the music, but she didn't even bring it to the piano, tucking away only a few three-by-five cards giving the beginning bar of each of the 32 variations. "I never actually looked at them," she told me.

But playing the *Goldbergs* at my house (for the second time), seven or eight years ago, she told me she would want the music in front of her, in the event she wished to consult the score on one or two variations; though she never in fact did. She was then 80, so it was for over 60 years that she carried the music in her head, that and 35 hours of other music of Bach. That performance was the last of seven she gave for me. The first, in 1975, was "a birthday present." It was recorded, and, with two later recitals at home in Connecticut, combined to produce two CDs, "great works of J. S. Bach," which still circulate. But the surprise came when in 1995 she called to ask whether I would like her to play for me and my wife and guests the program of Romantic music she would perform a week later in Buenos Aires. Her audience was flabbergasted as she went through without music an hour of Mendelssohn, Brahms, Schumann, and Debussy, music she hadn't played for 40 years, playing it now faultlessly and masterfully, from that huge repertory she carried in her head.

Four weeks ago I had a telephone call from a friend of Mme Tureck. He spoke from the hospital to tell me that she was dying and probably would live only another day, in the event I wanted to send her a farewell note, which he would take her from his e-mail. "She has just finished her autobiography and will have the manuscript sent to you before the weekend. But if you want to write to her you need to do it in the next half hour, because I have to go out, and she isn't expected to survive." I completed a hasty note, which, via her attentive friend, she acknowledged warmly.

"I don't know the details of your incarceration," I wrote, "not even whether there is any music at your bedside. There is, if you are interested to know, music at my bedside: the 48 [Preludes and Fugues] performed by Rosalyn Tureck. The recordings are truly sublime, and every time I experience any of it I am reminded of your incomparability. How fine to know that you have been of service to the greatest genius of all time, and how proud he'd have been to hear you perform."

She lived another eight weeks—not, really, a welcome extension of life—with the assertive cancer that killed her.

Meanwhile, I had got to the last page of her 600-page book. It ends, "I gave a talk on my eightieth birthday to the North American nations which was aired from Washington, D.C., telephoned from London, in which I spoke of my musical development, and ended with the words, 'I am still growing.' Today, almost eight years later, I still can say, with equal conviction, I am still growing." I, a mere listener, know what she meant by that, while doubting there is anywhere to grow in the art she developed in playing Sebastian Bach.

GENERALS, SPIES, AND STATESMEN

Winston Churchill

◆—◆

(1874–1965)

When Neville Chamberlain descended from an airplane in London to announce, fresh from meeting with Hitler, that "peace in our time" had been secured, young WFB, then attending boarding school, witnessed the historic moment firsthand. A decade—and a world war—later, in 1949, WFB, by then a junior at Yale, traveled to Cambridge to see Winston Churchill speak at the Massachusetts Institute of Technology. "He was shorter than I envisioned, less rotund," Buckley observed. Churchill struggled to the lectern, but then, as WFB recalled, "the hypnotizing voice boomed in, and our attention was on tiptoe." "Are we winning the Cold War?" Churchill asked on that occasion. "This cannot be decided by looking at Europe alone. We must also look to Asia." Like most Americans, Buckley viewed Churchill with awe—"the genius of Churchill was his union of affinities of the heart and of the mind, the total fusion of animal and spiritual energy"—but not uncritically. As WFB wrote in 1996:

> Mr. Churchill had struggled to diminish totalitarian rule in Europe, which, however, increased. He fought to save the empire,

which dissolved. He fought socialism, which prevailed. He struggled to defeat Hitler—and he won. It is not, I think, the significance of that victory, mighty and glorious though it was, that causes the name of Churchill to make the blood run a little faster. He later spoke diffidently about his role in the war, saying that the lion was the people of England, that he had served merely to provide the roar. But it is the roar that we hear, when we pronounce his name.

WFB recognized Churchill as a titanic figure in the struggle of civilizations, a fellow inheritor of the patrimony—he approvingly quoted Churchill as having remarked, after Chamberlain announced his devil's pact with Hitler, that "all wisdom is not new wisdom"—but he insisted that our consideration of Churchill could not end at Yalta.

"Churchill in the Balance"

National Review, February 23, 1965.

For as long as heroes are written about, Winston Churchill will be written about. The proportions are all abundantly there. He was everything. The soldier who loved poetry. The historian who loved to paint. The diplomat who thrived on indiscretion. The patriot with international vision. The orderly man given to electric spontaneities.

The man who flunked everything at school and then kept a generation of scholars busy interpreting his work and his words. The loyal party man who could cross the aisle and join the opposition when principle called. The Tory traditionalist revered in his old age by the neoteric levelers.

He was a very great man, and it is the crowning pity under the circumstances that he did not have that final ounce of strength to deliver Europe from the mess in which he left it after the great war to which he, as much as anyone else, committed the entire world. It is ungrateful to say of the dead, particularly of those few among the dead who were so distinguished in their lifetime, that they owed us more than they gave us. But Churchill is as much responsible as anyone else in our time for calling forth exacting judgments. The nobility of his utterances galvanized us to believe in the final possibilities of individual human beings, of statesmen, and of nations. His great orations during the war which he told us he was waging, and believed that he waged, in behalf of righteousness, require the observer to apply the highest standards to his life and goals.

All those men who were moved by the martial rhetoric of Winston Churchill to go out and die also figure in any obituary notice of Winston Churchill, and they are not appeased by glossing over the final imperfection of Churchill's life.

It was Churchill who pledged a restored Europe, indeed a restored world order after the great war. He did not deliver us such a world. No one else could so have stirred the world's imagination as he, at that critical point in world history, to press for the final goal the war was fought to achieve—the elimination of the source of aggressive evil that finds us today, on Churchill's death, not only living in a world in which more people are slaves than were slaves in the darkest hours of the Battle of Britain, but in a world that cares infinitely less about the wretchedness of these peoples than cared about such things even during the lackadaisical, disorganized thirties. At least during that period Churchill was there to bellow his indignation at the depravities of Adolf Hitler. Now, a generation later, it has become uncouth, dislocative, warmongering, to bellow against injustice even on a vastly magnified scale.

Churchill suggested, in his autobiography, that after all he could not be held responsible for the incomplete peacemaking inasmuch as power was suddenly taken from him in the surprise election of 1945. But Churchill had been in power, was almost omnipotent, at Yalta, and at Teheran, where the great statesmen of the West took some steps, and failed to take others, that insured the consolidation of Stalin's power in the territories he had overrun during the war, and insured also the expansion of the Communist system over whole continents. During those days Churchill the diplomat overwhelmed Churchill the statesman, the practitioner of justice. During those days Churchill found himself in the House of Commons delivering eulogies on the person of the abominable Stalin—a man whose evil he had years before remarked, representative of an evil whom no one had better analyzed than Churchill in the twenties. During those days he stood still for such disastrous fatuities as Franklin Roosevelt's impetuous call for unconditional surrender, a rhetorical fillip which in the analysis of some military experts may have cost us the unnecessary death of several hundred thousand men, and which most certainly was responsible for the supine condition of much of Europe at the moment when Stalin's legions took the nations over.

Is Winston Churchill a hero to the Polish people who were betrayed by the West? To the Yugoslavs? To the Hungarians and Rumanians and Czechs, whose plight under Nazism Churchill had so effectively dramatized as to mobilize all the forces of moral concern the world over into a war that began as a war for their liberation from the evil Nazis, and ended as a war for their perpetual imprisonment by the evil Communists?

It is true that at Fulton, Missouri, in 1946, Churchill focused the attention of the world, as again only he had the power to do, on the deteriorating situation. But he seemed thereafter to have lost the great engine that fired him ten years earlier to force the recognition of reality. Thenceforward he seemed only concerned to complete his literary and historical masterpieces, to regain power from the Labor Party almost only for the sake of regaining power.

He turned over the leadership of the world to the faltering hands of Americans who were manifestly his inferiors in the understanding of history and the management of human affairs, and contented himself to write dramatically about decisive battles won for freedom on the soil of England centuries ago, battles whose victory he celebrated vicariously, having no appetite left to fight real enemies, enemies whose health he had, God save him, nourished by that fateful shortage of vision that, in the end, left him, and the world, incapable of seeing that everything he had said and fought for applied alike to the Russian, as well as the German, virus. May he sleep more peacefully than some of those who depended on him.

William Colby

(1920–1996)

There was no worse time to become director of central intelligence than when William Colby took the reins of the agency in the summer of 1973. With the daily metastasizing of the Watergate scandal, so many of whose key players were past or current CIA operatives, Langley suddenly found itself besieged as never before by explosive newspaper headlines, congressional investigations, subpoenas, Freedom of Information Act requests, all aimed at extracting the secrets of a spy service that, up to then, Colby, a mild-mannered child of the Midwest with a New England lineage, had served as director of covert operations. Amid that frenzied season of disclosure, during which calls for the abolition of CIA were common, Colby sought to stem the tide by compiling and sharing with lawmakers a previously unthinkable document: the so-called "family jewels," 700 pages recording illegal agency operations over the preceding two decades. Some in the intelligence community regarded Colby's triage as a monumental act of betrayal; from the sound of the eulogy below, WFB seems, belatedly, to have joined in that view. For when Gerald Ford announced Colby's dismissal at the end of 1975, to be succeeded by George H. W. Bush, Buckley wrote that the outgoing CIA director "has carried himself through these humiliating months with exemplary virtue and taste." Note: The eulogy below, which Buckley termed an "obituary," is unique for its playful ending, in which the author incorporated his signature ending, the use of his initials, into the closing sentence.

"William E. Colby, RIP"

National Review, June 3, 1996.

William Colby, who suffered a heart attack and, falling into the water from his canoe, drowned, served as Director of Central Intelligence from 1973 until 1975 [*sic*; Colby's term ended in January 1976]. Mr. Colby, a graduate of Princeton and of the Columbia Law School, was a war hero who had volunteered for the parachute corps, hiding the fact that he had one defective eye. He deserved the decorations he won.

His big mark on history was the testimony he gave in 1975, and arranged for others to give, to the Senate committee (headed by Frank Church) investigating the CIA. A sanguinary description of the CIA's activity, as given in the *New York Times:* ". . . The public learned of the agency's role in tapping the telephones and opening the mail of Americans, and compiling dossiers on them; plotting coups in foreign lands and planning to assassinate foreign leaders like Fidel Castro; using human guinea pigs for mind-control experiments involving LSD; and committing other offenses against its charter, the law, and common sense." Mr. Colby

explained his disclosures by rudimentary democratic arith-
metic: Congress and the people have a right to know.

Very different conclusions were reached by his predecessor, Richard Helms, memorialized in Thomas Powers's
book as *The Man Who Kept the Secrets.* Which man behaved
better?

I interrupt this obituary in deference to the protocol of
full disclosure. In my first cold-war novel (*Saving the Queen*)
and in my tenth (and last—*A Very Private Plot*) Blackford
Oakes declines to testify to Senate committees, in the first
instance, the Church committee. His grounds are that he
gave his word to people who collaborated with him in sundry CIA enterprises. That's all.

To be sure, Blackford Oakes was a subordinate; but so
was Richard Helms, a subordinate to the President. Democratic rectitude and abiding trust can and do conflict.
Mr. Helms's reading (like that of Blackford Oakes) of the
quandary is that an oath to secrecy having been given, it is
not cast aside, not under any circumstances. What the divi-
sion of opinion reminds us is that espionage is a moral art,
not subject to schematic arrangements. It is understandable, under the aspect of the heavens, that a president in
very special circumstances might order a particular action
executed, and deny that he had done so.

We learn that Mr. Colby had most recently embarked on
a marketing enterprise, "a computer CD-ROM game about
espionage and counter-terrorism." For some people, never
mind their own record of personal bravery, espionage is,
after all, a game. Ask Le Carré [*sic*; le Carré]. Don't ask
                                                    WFB

Princess Diana

~—~

(1961–1997)

Diana, Princess of Wales, strode the world as no figure of the British monarchy before her, mixing glamour and high fashion with an extraordinary compassion and commitment to charity. Her untimely death in a car crash in Paris while being stalked by paparazzi who lived parasitically off her fame and beauty seemed to epitomize the vulgarity of our times. Writing in his syndicated column two days later, WFB recalled having met Princess Di at the Reagan White House—in the company of John Travolta!—and mourned the passing of "the most beautiful woman alive."

"Princess Di, RIP"

National Review, September 29, 1997; originally published as WFB's
syndicated column of September 2, 1997.

People who get about bump into kings and queens here and there. A problem (in my limited experience) is that

the subject royalty is really most interesting on, in brief encounters, is—royalty. If you have five minutes with the king,
you are not really interested in his views on the Common
Market or even on Star Wars, but you wonder about such
things as, How many times in the course of a year does your
majesty have to talk about the weather? During my own encounter with Princess Di (at the Reagan White House, with
John Travolta), for all her reputation for informality, I took
the precaution, in seeking an inanimate subject of common interest, to speak to her about jet lag (she had crossed
the Atlantic that day). I gave her my son's prescription. On
hearing it she choked up with wonderfully expressive dis-
gust and drifted off, perhaps to talk about the weather.

My friend Bruce, working at the computer, spoke his
sorrow over the news. "It's like Cinderella in reverse." The
point is nicely made. Cinderella began poor and lonely
in shabby dress, was touched by the magic wand, and fell
into the royal ball, the prince enchanted by her youth and
beauty. At midnight she would flash back to indigence and
the torment of her stepmother and stepsisters, but the
princely levitation took over, and she lived happily ever
after.

In her celebrated interview, Diana spoke of her loneliness in the royal household. She told of her problems with
her health, admitted to an act of adultery, and spoke of
her passionate desire to regain her privacy and live happily,
superintending the education of her two sons. The divorce
was quick and, because it had been publicly discounted,
noiseless. The only rasp left in the proceedings was the
quiet but adamantine word: She would no longer be Her
Royal Highness. Indeed, even though she was no longer,
as a technical matter, the Princess of Wales, she was able

to continue to use that title. She spent much conspicuous time in good civic enterprise, and was inevitably the belle of the balls she attended with some regularity.

Her overnight dalliance with Dodi Fayed was accepted by most as an entirely extemporaneous romantic attraction by a lovelorn ex-princess. Others saw it as a personal act of irreverence—nice blonde princesses don't wander off with dark Muslim tycoons, not since Othello and Desdemona. Still others thought they were seeing strategic commercial planning. The union of Jackie Kennedy and Ari Onassis thirty years ago legitimized what in the public view would once have been thought of as on the order of miscegenation. But let it be, most people seemed to be saying.

The event itself is saturated with mythogenic detail. Was the driver really speeding into an underpass in the heart of Paris at over one hundred miles per hour? Did one or more of the paparazzi—was it possible?—touch off camera flashes that blinded the driver? Was he, at three times the legal alcohol limit, actually out of control? Why was the car speeding so? Had Dodi or the Princess called out to the driver to accelerate and escape the pursuing journalists? Will the bodyguard, when he wakes, shed light on these questions? Tell us what he heard said, saw done?

The Queen, we were reminded, is the final authority in specifying the shape of the funeral service. But within 36 hours we learned that just as the Supreme Court follows the election returns, so the Crown is guided by public opinion. It is known that the Queen loathed Diana (which doesn't challenge the sincerity of her grief and shock), assigning most of the blame for the marriage's break-up to her. There was reciprocal blame assigned—How could anyone young and tender live with someone brought up without that love of family that Charles's austere father deprived him of?

Yet we are reminded that the royal mandate stresses things other than fun living. The new biography of Prince Albert reminds us how successful an arranged marriage can be. The point is reinforced by the flood of books and movies featuring Jane Austen's young ladies and their methodical search for appropriate husbands. Princess Di charmed the whole world, but also reminded us, as the lives of her aunt and her brother-in-law and sister-in-law did, that the marriage bond is frailer even in royal circles than it used to be. It is an ironic masterstroke that the descendant of Henry VIII has been freed of an encumbrance by a midnight accident in an automobile.

How different it would have been if she had been ugly. The marriage, contracted under such circumstances, would probably have lasted, and the grief over a mortal accident would have been formalistic. We grieve the loss of a delicate fairy-tale princess, perhaps the most beautiful woman alive until that terrible moment on Saturday night.

Allen Dulles

(1893–1969)

As the grandson of a secretary of state, the nephew-in-law to another, and the brother of a third, Allen Dulles knew his way around the corridors of power. Educated at Princeton, a trained diplomat and lawyer, Dulles had met Hitler and Mussolini personally before joining the ranks of the Office of Strategic Services, the wartime predecessor of the Central Intelligence Agency. By 1953, with his brother John Foster Dulles serving as America's top diplomat, Allen Dulles was named by President Eisenhower as the first civilian director of the Central Intelligence Agency. Dulles would run the Agency for the next nine years—longer than any director since—and preside over a period of expansion and crisis for American intelligence. During Dulles's tenure, the Agency played a critical role in U.S.-backed coups in Iran and Guatemala and in the catastrophe at the Bay of Pigs. By late 1961, President Kennedy, displeased with his performance, pinned the National Security Medal to Dulles's chest in a ceremony at the Agency's Langley headquarters and then, the next day, announced Dulles's retirement. Two years later,

President Johnson appointed him to the Warren Commission that investigated Kennedy's assassination. In his eulogy—which notably did not carry the "R.I.P." heading—WFB struggles to find a kind word for an accomplished and patriotic man, one whose enemies WFB shared but whose legacy he regarded as injurious to national security.

"Thoughts on the Decease of Mr. Dulles"

National Review, February 25, 1969; originally published, with minor variations, as WFB's syndicated column of February 14, 1969.

During the last years of his life Mr. Allen Dulles was under relentless attack as the symbol of James Bond diplomacy, so gruesomely inappropriate, it is held, to the realities of modern politics, to such higher sophistication it makes heroes out of traitors, gods out of Kim Philby and the Rosenbergs. *Ramparts* magazine—it would be heartening to refer to the late *Ramparts,* except that it will no doubt be succeeded by something worse, the human imagination being capable nowadays of even that—made such reputation as it fleetingly had from exposing that the CIA under Mr. Dulles had done such outrageous things as subsidize *Encounter* magazine in London, the National Students Association in the United States, and a training program at a middlewestern university for area specialists headed for service in the CIA. For all of this, obloquy for Mr. Dulles. I do believe that he'd have been better treated in his late years by some of the press if it had transpired that he had been in collusion with the Communists, in pursuit of détente.

All of this left Mr. Dulles on the defensive, and the general clamor subdued a criticism of his strategy which sounds faintly perverse, but which is naggingly relevant now that we have, once again, a Republican Administration with critical decisions to make concerning such issues as faced Mr. Dulles. True, there were those who make the whole right-centered criticism of Mr. Dulles awkward by such surrealisms as that Mr. Dulles was a Communist agent (yes, that is among the contributions of Mr. Robert Welch). But the sane voices from the right wondered not that Mr. Dulles was involved in subsidizing social-political movements and journals around the globe, but that he selected for patronage the left-minded organizations, on the assumption that only people who occupy a position contiguous to that of the people you worry about are likely to be effective. Thus in Italy you deal with the Social Democrats in preference to the Christian Democrats. Or, if you deal with the latter, you deal with that branch within it which tends left. Ditto elsewhere.

The analogies abound. You deal with liberal Republicans in America, in order to try to satisfy Democrats. Rockefeller yes, Goldwater no. When time comes to send around subsidies, you send them around to journals of opinion like the *New Leader,* not to those like the *National Review.* I know one person who did service in Mexico for the CIA who happens to believe profoundly that what would most benefit the Mexican people would be a stiff dose of capitalism, so as to free the poor from the sclerosis of years and years of supergovernment. He found himself a dozen years ago serving as a paymaster, with a wad of money in an envelope destined for an organization whose principal slogan was "Ni Comunismo, Ni Capitalismo," that is to say: neither Communism nor Capitalism—leaving: well, leaving what Mexico has got.

The reasoning, as I say, is psychologically obvious. The mischief of it lay in the hesitation of Mr. Dulles and his superiors to adopt radical strategy, radical strategy being the defense of conservative institutions and ideas on the altogether reassuring assumption that they would result in radical relief for the wretched of this world. Shortly before he died, Henry Luce thought to formulate a similar position in addressing the National Council of Churches: Look (he intended to say) if you are genuinely concerned with the starving peoples of the world, which you no doubt are, are you not obliged to investigate the apparent corollary between agricultural plenty and the free marketplace, as also agricultural privation and socialism? In other words, could you not, even in the name of Christianity, bring yourself to say a good word for capitalism?

During the Dulles years, conservatives starved to death. Precisely those people who reasoned that you could not deal with the Soviet Union, that the politics of détente were doomed to suffer such deaths as Dubcek suffered last summer. It was a period during which the resoluteness of our anti-Communism was never in doubt, but a period during which the enemy gained vast continents, established themselves in power, developed their hydrogen bombs and missiles, and continued to hold us at missile-point.

It seems mean to observe at this point that Mr. Dulles should have been spared the criticisms of the Left, so as to expose himself to the criticisms of the Right. Let it be recorded, at least, that he sought to maneuver with the realpolitik of the postwar era, and that although he may have made bad strategic miscalculations, he was made to suffer at the hands of the wrong people. Because even if he did not know how finally to cope with the enemy, he knew at least who the enemy was, and that, these days, is practically a virtuoso performance.

Barry Goldwater

——~——

(1909–1998)

Barry Goldwater occupies a special place in the heart of modern conservatism and did in Bill Buckley's heart as well: The Arizona senator and 1964 Republican presidential nominee was one of only three friends—alongside Whittaker Chambers and Ronald Reagan—whom WFB treated, in nonfiction, at book length (in the posthumously published *Flying High: Remembering Barry Goldwater* [2008]). In addition to admiring Goldwater as a man and loving him as a friend, WFB understood that their advancement of conservative principles across the sixties—which laid the groundwork for the subsequent triumphs of Richard Nixon and Ronald Reagan—had been a collegial, even filial, effort, one in which he himself had played the seminal role. In October 2000, I asked Buckley if it was fair to say that he had been the first "telegenic" conservative. WFB demurred, citing Goldwater, but then acknowledged the impact he had had on the nominee:

> WFB: On the national scene, Goldwater was instantly and enormously appealing—obviously not to the majority of the voters,

but to a lot of them.... If you're asking the question, "Could Goldwater have been fielded if it hadn't been for the background work
done by *National Review*?" I would say, no, probably he wouldn't
have. The deep analytical reserves on which he relied—well, his
book was written by a *National Review* editor [L. Brent Bozell, Jr.,
WFB's brother-in-law] and that was the book that catapulted him
into fame, *The Conscience of a Conservative* [1960].

Goldwater's contributions to American life extended beyond his
monumental impact on electoral politics. To cite but two examples:
The senator's personal intervention after the release of the "smoking
gun" tape in Watergate, in August 1974, is widely credited with having persuaded President Nixon to resign from office, and Goldwater
sponsored the legislation, signed into law by President Reagan in 1986,
that restructured the Defense Department, including the removal of
the Joint Chiefs of Staff from the chain of command. Goldwater appeared on *Firing Line* three times between 1966 and 1989, the last
for a two-hour retrospective after his retirement from the Senate.
He remained every inch the stubbornly independent-minded champion of liberty, freedom, and decentralized government he had been
in 1964: "I voted against federal aid to education... because I don't
believe that some jackass sitting in Washington can tell my teachers
in Arizona how to teach our children.... You'd be amazed, sitting in
that body, if you listen to the amendments that are being offered that
just mean: Move a little more power, move a little more power."

"Barry Goldwater, RIP"

National Review, June 22, 1998.

In 1964 the fear & loathing of Barry Goldwater was startling. Martin Luther King, Jr., detected "dangerous signs

of Hitlerism in the Goldwater campaign." Joachim Prinz, president of the American Jewish Congress, warned that "a Jewish vote for Goldwater is a vote for Jewish suicide." And George Meany, head of the AFL-CIO, saw power falling into "the hands of union-hating extremists, racial bigots, woolly-minded seekers after visions of times long past." On Election Day Goldwater suffered a devastating defeat, winning only 41 electoral votes.

It was the judgment of the establishment that Goldwater's critique of American liberalism had been given its final exposure on the national political scene. Conservatives could now go back to their little lairs and sing to themselves their songs of nostalgia and fancy, and maybe gather together every few years to hold testimonial dinners in honor of Barry Goldwater, repatriated by Lyndon Johnson to the parched earth of Phoenix, where dwell only millionaires seeking dry air to breathe and the Indians Barry Goldwater could now resume photographing. But then of course 16 years later the world was made to stand on its head when Ronald Reagan was swept into office on a platform indistinguishable from what Barry had been preaching.

During the campaign of 1964, Goldwater was our incorruptible standard-bearer, disdainful of any inducements to bloc voting. He even gave the impression that his design was to alienate bloc voters. He didn't mean to do that; he was simply engaging in acts of full political disclosure in an attempt to display the architectural integrity of his views, at once simple in basic design, and individualistic and artful in ornamentation.

But by the end of last month the cumulus clouds had all gone. On the weekend of his death it was clear from the public commentary that Barry Goldwater was now the object of nostalgic curiosity and—even—of affection, here and there self-reproachful. When someone about whom such dire things had been said turns out to be as dangerous as your local postman, no meaner than a summer shower, the conscience is pricked.

What finally lodged in the memory of most Americans, to be sure, wasn't so much Goldwater the Conservative as Goldwater the individualist. He was never entirely imprisoned by ideology. In the last dozen years he had disappointed friends by declining to support constitutional amendments that would have reversed some of the decisions taken by the Supreme Court, decisions he once vigorously opposed. The public's final impression was of a thinker—or, better, a commentator—given primarily to home-grown attachments and individualized formulations. He said what he said because he was what he was. And then too there was his personal way of living and acting. He was venturesome, proud, determined, a bit of a daredevil.

In 1969 he flew me, my wife, and a friend from Phoenix for a tour of the Grand Canyon, acting as pilot and tour guide, moseying high in the air over territory he knew so well, Indian country, mining country. Over there—"See?" he pointed—is where he once crash-landed an Air coupe. Bits and pieces of the airplane are still cherished by the Navajos as amulets, and as eternal proof that flying over their territory is forbidden by their earth god, a reverence for whom prevents them even now from permitting wells to be drilled. "They need to go three miles for water," he explained. Seated on his right in the copilot's seat was a tiny old woman right out of Grandma Moses, wearing a shawl, and working on a piece of crochet. What was she doing there? She was (we learned) one of the important women fliers of the past forty years, a test pilot and instructor of legendary reputation. She was there that day—and every day thenceforth that Goldwater would fly—because the insurance company, now that Goldwater was sixty years old, required a qualified copilot when he flew his Bonanza. So he had picked out "Miss Ruth," who seemed about a hundred years old. She kept an eye on the instrument panel, even though the crocheting never stopped.

We were getting close to the airport and Captain Goldwater radioed ahead that he would be landing "in seven minutes." I stared out over the horizon: there was no airport in sight. I told him I thought his exact 7-minute estimate pure conceit. He gritted his famous jaw and ostentatiously activated the stopwatch. Six minutes and 45 seconds later we are within a few hundred feet of the runway. He throttles way down to stretch out those 15 seconds. But Miss Ruth calls his game. Without turning her head she says: "You want to reach the field or you want to stall?" ("Shut up, Ruth! Your job is to tell me when we are on the ground.") She parts her lips, a grandmotherly smile, and resumes her crocheting—she has made her point. Goldwater applies a little more throttle but arcs the airplane right and then left to consume the obtrusive seconds. At exactly seven minutes on the stopwatch the tires touch down. Miss Ruth continues with her crocheting as we taxi in. Goldwater looks back at his challenger, arches his brow, and says, "I told you seven minutes, didn't I?"

He would rise early, at Be-nun-i-kin, the Navajo name given to his home. That morning he had spent two hours, as he regularly did when at home in Phoenix, patching calls from Vietnam soldiers to family and friends via ham radio, a lifelong avocational interest. After that he went to his desk and greeted his houseguest. Though it was only 8 A.M. the doorbell rang—it often rang, tourists cruising by to take a picture of the home and grounds of the defeated presidential candidate and, with any luck, of its owner. Goldwater ignored the bell, continuing his conversation, but instinctively sliding his chair back, out of the line of sight from the door. That way when Mrs. Goldwater or the maid opened it, the tourist wouldn't spot Goldwater behind the desk. But this morning the large lady had her camera in hand and called out. "Senator Goldwater? Are you there? I want just one picture."

"Okay," Goldwater called out. "Just give me a minute so I can put on my pyjamas."

From that desk, his secretary told me, he had dictated 24,000 letters the year before. The voluminous correspondence went on year after year until his first stroke, three years ago. It didn't matter that he was no longer in the Senate, or contending for one more election. That, simply, was the way he lived, the way he reacted to people. The day after he died a stranger reached me. Did I know what charity Senator Goldwater had designated to receive gifts in his name? She wanted to do something, to give something, because thirty years ago, when she was desperate to hear from her husband in Vietnam, her phone rang early one morning. It was Senator Goldwater, patching in a call from her husband.

He was that way. He was the national figure, Mr. Conservative; but his private renown derived from his character, which even strangers coming to his door with a camera could instantly experience. He never changed, friendly but firm, a very grown-up man with a boyish streak. The guest who asked a provocative question could expect a very direct response, very different from weaving about in the air to postpone touching down.

He alarmed less and less, drew benevolent attention more and more. Even twenty years ago an old antagonist said it, with a nice turn—100 percent ADA liberal Senator Hubert Humphrey to 100 percent ACU conservative Senator Barry Goldwater: "Barry, you're one of the handsomest men in America. You ought to be in the movies. In fact, I've made just that proposal to Eighteenth Century Fox." I can guess Goldwater just smiled at the lovable, loquacious populist. But others, looking on, would venture that, back in the eighteenth century, Barry Goldwater would have been more at home at the Convention in Philadelphia than most modern liberals.

Richard Helms

—◆◆—

(1913–2002)

In the spy novels of the Cold War, the men of the executive ranks invariably resembled Richard Helms, director of central intelligence during the contentious period from 1966 to 1973. Helms epitomized the debonair spymaster: Tall, dapper, dry-witted, and patrician, he was educated abroad and spoke fluent French and German. The latter skill proved invaluable when, as a United Press reporter in Germany before World War II, Helms scored an interview with Adolf Hitler. A stint with the OSS led to a career at the top echelons of the Agency in Langley. Richard Nixon, who bristled at patricians, had disliked Helms since the early 1960s and could be heard on the so-called smoking gun tape in Watergate saying cryptically: "We protected Helms from one hell of a lot of things." Helms's refusal to involve CIA in the Watergate cover-up led Nixon to banish him by naming him ambassador to Iran. Returning to Washington amid a frenzy of revelations about past CIA misconduct, Helms wound up pleading guilty to two misdemeanor counts stemming from charges that he had improperly withheld information from Congress relating to CIA assassination plots and other matters. The opprobrium that attached to the Agency, and to Helms, in the post-Watergate era bothered Buckley both because WFB had briefly worked for the Agency in the 1950s and because he regarded a robust intelligence apparatus as essential to the preservation of American sovereignty and freedoms. When Helms's biographer Thomas Powers visited *Firing Line* in March 1980, WFB looked back with dismay on "the hang-it-all-out delirium of the mid-Seventies, when it became chic to reveal national secrets and criminal to conceal them."

"*Richard Helms, R.I.P.*"

National Review, November 25, 2002.

Some time after my first novel (*Saving the Queen* [1976]) was published, I had a handwritten note from Richard Helms. He had read the book, he said, and enjoyed it. I replied and, subsequently, we had one or two visits at lunch.

I was especially pleased inasmuch as he had been Director of Central Intelligence and would have been put off by any spy-time solecisms he'd bumped into. And he might have found a number of these, inasmuch as my protagonist, Blackford Oakes, was inducted into the CIA as an undergraduate, trained, and deployed in Great Britain where—as one might put it, in a trade in which one divulges nothing more than necessary—Oakes took on more than the CIA gave him to chew.

But what obviously caught the Director's eye was the predicament my protagonist was caught up in: He was asked to testify before a congressional committee about activity he had engaged in, and declined to answer questions.

The Senate committee asked Helms, in 1973, to disclose what he knew about the derailment of the Salvador Allende regime in Chile. Helms dissimulated. He had already left the CIA, Richard Nixon having replaced him when Helms refused to block the FBI's inquiry into Watergate. Nixon sent him off as ambassador to Iran, which was a shelter of sorts, but in 1976 he came home to Washington to face the music, pleading no contest to charges that he had lied to a congressional committee. He tried to explain his problem to the judge, as Blackford Oakes had tried to explain his silence to his own senatorial inquisitors. "I found myself," Helms told the court, "in a position of conflict. I had sworn my oath to protect certain secrets. I didn't want to lie, I didn't want to mislead the Senate. I was simply trying to find my way through a very difficult situation in which I found myself."

The judge had zero understanding of any such difficult situation. "You now stand before this court in disgrace and shame," he pronounced on this singular man of honor, sentencing Helms to two years in prison (suspended) and a $2,000 fine. An important book was generated. Thomas Powers's *The Man Who Kept the Secrets* [1979] told something of the unresolved conflict of the intelligence agent who promises to keep a secret, yet is questioned by an authorized investigator of government.

Richard Helms was impenitent, and at lunch spoke of the quandary, branching off to other of his encounters as DCI. As director of the CIA he attended, ex officio, the cabinet meetings of President Lyndon Johnson. "There was only one way to get the president's ear," he recalled. "It was to be the first to speak, and as CIA director I had this assignment, and to make the very first thing I said— interesting. The president gave you no second hearing."

He was relaxed, authoritative, a prominent figure in Washington, composed but not indifferent to damaging vicissitudes-of-state. He indulged a bitterness. "There are two men in the history of the time I served whom I truly despise. One was Frank Church, the other was William Colby." It was Senator Church who presided over the investigating committee that sought out the secrets, and it was William Colby, the incumbent director of the CIA, who gave away the secrets.

Dick Helms had a very full life, president of his class at Williams College, and editor of its newspaper; before that, two years of preparatory school in Switzerland, rendering him fluent in French and German, which helped when as a young journalist he had an exclusive interview with Adolf Hitler (Sieg Heil, Herr Shitface). He will need no evasive tactics where, R.I.P., we trust he finds himself. —WFB

E. Howard Hunt

~•~

(1918–2007)

"This fellow Hunt," President Nixon murmured in the Oval Office on June 23, 1972—on the "smoking gun" Watergate tape whose disclosure two years later would force Nixon's resignation—"he knows too damn much." A career spy and spy novelist, E. Howard Hunt appeared to many as the walking embodiment of all the exploits, secrets, and scandals of America's postwar intelligence community. Educated at Brown and the U.S. Naval Academy, Hunt served the OSS in wartime China and later joined the CIA. His Cold War clandestine career was less Ian Fleming than Hannah Arendt: He specialized in political and psychological warfare in the subversion of foreign leaders, such as the overthrow in 1954 of Guatemala's government. But Hunt's career was ruined by the failure of the Agency's next great effort at regime change: the Bay of Pigs, in which Hunt had played a planning role. In the Nixon White House, it was Hunt, partnering with G. Gordon Liddy, who recruited the Cuban Bay of Pigs veterans to commit the most consequential crimes of the 1970s: the break-ins at the office of Daniel Ellsberg's psychiatrist and the Democratic National Committee headquarters at the Watergate complex. Although history records that the Watergate cover-up collapsed and a president of the United States resigned because the White House never fully met Hunt's demands for "blackmail," or "hush money," Hunt always regarded the sums demanded as the traditional remuneration due to spies caught red-handed. Punished excessively by a publicity-seeking judge, Hunt served close to three years in prison, often in harsh conditions. Compounding his misfortunes was the plane crash that killed his wife, Dorothy, a covert operator who had couriered Watergate "hush money." WFB's view on the great scandal, and the sorrows of the Hunts, was personal: He had worked for Hunt in Mexico City in the early 1950s during a brief stint in the CIA and had become godfather to Hunt's children. During Watergate, Hunt confessed undisclosed aspects of the affair exclusively to Buckley. As late as 1977, lobbying for Hunt's release from prison, WFB pronounced his old friend, in a syndicated column, guilty of simple "foolishness"—but Buckley's judgment hardened over time. Outside of Ronald Reagan, no friend of Buckley's stood so squarely at the center of momentous events—and EHH, in Buckley's estimation, had sinned gravely. WFB's gift for friendship was universally recorded, but the arc of his friendship with Hunt was unique: a pitiable role reversal, set amid the moral vagaries of Watergate, that tested Buckley's reserves of faith, loyalty, and patience. The eulogy below shows how WFB struggled, where Christian morality did not compel otherwise, to err on the side of Christian mercy. [Note: WFB errs below in ascribing responsibility for the Ellsberg break-in to Attorney General John Mitchell; it was John Ehrlichman who gave the order, in writing, and was convicted at trial for it.]

"Howard Hunt, RIP"

Syndicated column, January 26, 2007.

My name has been linked to that of Howard Hunt, who died on Jan. 23, and I readily acknowledge that we were associates and close friends during the period (1951–52) when I worked for the Central Intelligence Agency in Mexico. Howard Hunt was my boss, and our friendship was such that soon after I quit the agency and returned to Connecticut, he and his wife advised me that they were joining the Catholic Church and asked if I would agree to serve as godfather to their two daughters, which assignment I gladly accepted, continuing in close touch with them.

Not so with their father. Howard Hunt, as has been widely recalled on his death, had a sensational career, including, in his 50s, 33 months in federal prison on charges of conspiracy, wiretapping, and burglary. Some time after leaving prison, he asked me to recommend presidential clemency, which would have had the effect of clearing his name and reauthorizing him to vote. I told him I was reluctant to do this because in fact he had been involved in conspiracy, wiretapping, and burglary, but I was careful to say that the reason he committed these crimes was that he thought himself engaging in public service by protecting the interests of President Richard Nixon.

He was terribly mistaken there, and in fact he was more responsible than any single other human being for bringing about Nixon's resignation. Because it was Hunt who organized the Watergate break-in, seeking to advance the partisan cause of Nixon in 1972. He had at the time already committed a crime by breaking into the offices of Daniel Ellsberg's psychiatrist, on a mission probably authorized by Nixon's attorney general, John Mitchell.

Hunt came to see me, with one of my goddaughters, shortly after his devoted and alluring wife was killed in an airplane crash. He recounted the story of Watergate, giving me information not known to the press or even to the prosecution. Notwithstanding his plight, he wore a jaunty sports coat and, pipe in hand, reported that, soon after his arrest, "I said to myself, 'Where's the fix? Why didn't they fix me up?'"

It was a genuinely appealing professional query. Howard Hunt had lived outside the law in the service first of his country, subsequently of President Nixon. The way things had worked for him, in Mexico, in Uruguay, in Japan, was the way he expected them to work now. You break the law in pursuit of your country's interest as prescribed by your superior or by your cognitive intelligence of political reality. You get caught; and, if feasible, your government looks after you. If it's bail that's needed, it materializes. If it's looking after your widow and children, that is done. If you are in Washington, D.C., having committed a crime on the authority of the attorney general or the president, why— Howard Hunt was saying—somebody . . . does something. And the charge against you for trespass, or burglary, or whatever, washes away.

But Hunt, the dramatist, didn't understand that political realities at the highest level transcend the working realities of spy-life. He ended up in prison, a widower with some of his children on drugs, and bankrupt. I got him a fine volunteer lawyer.

I remember with sad amusement an earlier experience of Hunt's with the law, this time involving his novels. Allen Dulles, then head of CIA, called him in one day and said, Howard, I know the rules are that this office has to clear all manuscripts by our agents. But you write so many, you're wearing us out. So go ahead and publish your books without our clearance, but use a pseudonym.

Hunt handed me his latest book, *Catch Me in Zanzibar*,* by Gordon Davis. I leafed through it and found printed on the last page, "You have just finished another novel by Howard Hunt." I thought this hilarious. So did Howard. The reaction of Allen Dulles is not recorded.

We visited once or twice after his remarriage, when he was trying to reestablish himself as an author. But estrangement crept in. A year ago he asked me, through an intermediary, to write the introduction to his memoirs [*American Spy: My Secret History in the CIA, Watergate and Beyond*]. I read them with great misgivings. There was material there that suggested transgressions of the highest order, including a hint that LBJ might have had a hand in the plot to assassinate President Kennedy. The manuscript was clearly ghostwritten.

I declined to write the introduction. But when the manuscript was resubmitted to me, with the loony grassy-knoll bits chiseled out, I said OK, but wrote an introduction restricted to describing our early friendship in Mexico. The book will be published (by John Wiley) in March.

And this former colleague here registers his old affection and admiration for a civil servant who ran into bad luck and lost his judgment, but who sought to serve his country and look after his children.

---

* The Library of Congress does not list a book with this title under Hunt's name or any of his aliases. Among the three novels "Gordon Davis" published during Dulles's tenure as CIA director, one—*I Came to Kill* (1953)—ended with: "THE END/of a novel by/Howard Hunt." However, the novel makes no reference to Zanzibar. It is possible that WFB got the title wrong or that he received a novel that never was published.

Martin Luther King, Jr.

(1929–1968)

WFB supported a national holiday for the Reverend Dr. Martin Luther King, Jr., but always insisted that we see "the other Dr. King." He believed MLK had achieved his legislative aims by 1965 and thereafter lost his moral clarity. As early as 1969, Buckley declared that for a memorial on the National Mall: "It is time that we mute the memory of one Martin Luther King, the advocate of civil disobedience who once likened America's foreign policy to Nazi Germany's; and stress instead the qualities that made him admirable—his courage, his moral strength, his great eloquence."

> The fact of it is that Dr. Martin Luther King was a hero and a martyr in one respect. In others—one thinks of his celebration of civil disobedience—he was the spokesman for a point of view on citizenship which in the opinion of some—e.g., me—is mortal to civil society.

When it was disclosed that the FBI had wiretapped the civil rights leader in flagrante delicto in various hotel rooms, Buckley denounced it: "I consider this the single most serious charge leveled against the FBI.... Assaults on his privacy, if they do not bear remotely on the security of the nation against crime or subversion, are inexcusable." Over time, Buckley saw the focus on the wiretapping and killing of King displacing thoughtful consideration of him. "I have been writing about Dr. King since 1955 and have not once mentioned the matter of the sex tapes," WFB wrote in 1987.

> What is scandalous, we are led to believe, is exclusively the tapes' existence and the uses to which they were put by the FBI. What we are not permitted to meditate is whether the subject matter of those tapes was scandalous.... Are we or are we not saying that that which is scandalous is that which offends the public ethic, and that even though we know about the prevalence of sin, we honor especially those who struggle successfully not only to preach the Commandments of God, but to follow them?

Buckley and *National Review* had, of course, been dreadfully wrong about civil rights in MLK's heyday, with Buckley arguing at the time that Southern whites, as "the advanced race," inherently possessed the power to take any measures necessary to preserve civil order during the period of blacks' transition to equality. The biographer Sam Tanenhaus, surveying Buckley's Southern roots, concluded that he had "actually inherited views on race that were fairly progressive for his time and place" and that his later recantations were "strenuous."

"Martin Luther King, RIP"

Syndicated column, April 9, 1968.

It is curious, and melancholy, that hours after the death of the Reverend Martin Luther King, and one-hundred thousand words after the doleful announcement of his murder, not a single commentator on radio or on television has mentioned what one would suppose is a critical datum, namely that Mr. King was an ordained minister in the Christian faith, and that those who believe that the ministry is other than merely symbolic servitude to God must hope, and pray, that he is today happier than he was yesterday, united with his Maker, with the angels and the saints, with the prophets whose words of inspiration he quoted with such telling effect in his hot pursuit of a secular millenarianism.

Those who take seriously Dr. King's calling are obliged above all to comment on this aspect of his martyrdom, and to rejoice in the divine warranty that eyes have not seen, nor have ears heard of, the glories that God has prepared for those who love Him.

No, it is the secular aspects of his death that obsess us; very well then, let us in his memory make a few observations:

1. Whatever his virtues, and whatever his faults, he did not deserve assassination. There are the special few—one thinks of Joan of Arc—whose career dictates, as a matter of theatrical necessity, a violent end, early in life. Dr. King was not of that cast. His virtues were considerable, most notably his extraordinary capacity to inspire. But although the dream he had seemed to many Americans, particularly the black militants, but not excluding many orthodox liberals,

less and less useful (freedom now, in the sense he understood it, *was* a dream, mischievously deceptive), it simply
wasn't ever required that, in order to reify that vision, he
should surrender his own life. In that sense his martyrdom
was simply not useful. Because it is plainly impossible that,
on account of his death, things are going to change. The
martyrdom he seemed sometimes almost to be seeking
may commend him to history and to God, but not likely to
Scarsdale, New York: which has never credited the charge
that the white community of America conspires to insure
the wretchedness of the brothers of Martin Luther King.

2. And concerning his weaknesses, it would take a luna-
tic (his murderer has not at this point been apprehended,
but he is sure to be one) to reason that Dr. King's faults justified a private assassination. The theory to which most of
us subscribe is that there is no vice so hideous as to justify
private murder. Even so, we tend emotionally to waive that
categorical imperative every now and then. If someone had
shot down Adolf Eichmann in a motel, the chances are that
our deploring of the assassin's means would have been ritu-
alistic. The only people who were genuinely annoyed by
Jack Ruby's assassination of Lee Harvey Oswald were those
who maintained a fastidious interest in the survival of Oswald, for the sake of the record.

Dr. King's faults, and they most surely existed, were far
from the category of the faults of those whose assassination
is more or less tolerated, as we all of us tolerated the assassination of George Lincoln Rockwell. Those faults were a terribly mistaken judgment—above all. A year ago he accused
the United States of committing crimes equal in horror to
those committed by the Nazis in Germany. One could only
gasp at the profanation. Ten days ago in his penultimate
speech, delivered at the Washington Cathedral, he accused

the United States of waging a war as indefensible as any war committed during the 20th century. Several years ago, on the way back from Stockholm, where he received the Nobel Peace Prize, he conspicuously declined to criticize the Gbenye movement in the North Congo, which was even then engaged in slaughtering, as brutally as Dr. King was slaughtered, his brothers in Christ. But for such transgressions in logic and in judgment, one does not receive the death sentence.

3. The sickening observation of the commentators is therefore particularly inapposite. The commentators (most of them) said: How can we now defend nonviolence? Surely the answer is: more perfervidly than ever before. It was, need we remark, violence that killed Dr. King. Should we therefore abandon nonviolence?

Those who mourn Dr. King because they were his closest followers should meditate the implications of the deed of the wildman who killed him. That deed should bring to mind not (for God's sake!) the irrelevance of nonviolence, but the sternest necessity of reaffirming nonviolence. An aspect of nonviolence is subjugation to the law.

The last public speech of Martin Luther King described his intentions of violating the law in Memphis, where an injunction had been handed down against the resumption of a march which only a week ago had resulted in the death of one human being, and the wounding of fifty others.

Dr. King's flouting of the law does not justify the flouting by others of the law, but it is a terrifying thought that, most likely, the cretin who leveled his rifle on the head of Martin Luther King, may have absorbed the talk, so freely available, about the supremacy of the individual conscience, such talk as Martin Luther King, God rest his soul, had so widely, and so indiscriminately, made.

Golda Meir

(1898–1978)

"Israel is more than merely a state, is it not?" WFB asked Golda Meir during an interview in her Tel Aviv office in March 1972. "It is and it isn't," the prime minister replied warily. Buckley's visit predated the Munich Olympics and the Yom Kippur War, but even before those wrenching events, he saw Meir presiding over two Israels: one a state bound by convention yet fiercely survivalist, the other a universal ideal, the locus of man's hopes. "What then is Israel?" WFB asked afterward. "What is it that defines a Jew? To which question the accepted answer has come to be: to believe oneself to be one. By the same token, Israel is whatever the individual Israeli believes it to be."

"Golda Meir, RIP"

National Review, January 5, 1979.

Behind her desk in her office—surely the most tatterde-malion of any occupied by a chief of government anywhere in the world—were two pictures, one of Richard Nixon (the year was 1972), one of John Lindsay. On being asked about the criteria for qualifying to have one's picture on her wall, she chuckled and said that the President of the United States (whoever he is) is regularly there. As for John Lindsay, then mayor of New York, she said she loved him, and indeed that she had got him elected in 1969 during his crisis with the Republican Party. "Yes," she said, "I did it," and chuckled. "I get along very well with American politi-cians. I make it my business." Asked about McGovern, she warned of the implications of his anti–Defense Depart-ment policies. Why didn't she speak out to world Jewry on the subject? Well, she agreed she was chief of government of a Jewish state, but she wasn't going to start giving Jews or-ders whom to vote for in American elections. Israel needed U.S. good will and U.S. support, but Israel would other-wise look after itself. There was no alternative. "I was in the Waldorf Astoria when at the Security Council they were talking about a cease-fire resolution, and the talk talk talk went on for three days, and before they got to the resolu-tion, India had overrun East Pakistan. And you know what the delegates were doing? While Pakistan was going down the drain? They were laughing! It could have been Israel." She leaned back and lit another cigarette and talked about the reluctance of Israel to give up the captured territories in the absence of believable guarantees, nowadays defined as guarantees with a higher Moody rating than those we gave to Taiwan. "You know, I just love American Presidents. They are so nice to me. But—" her laughter, though coarse, was infectious—"you know, I have *yet* to find a U.S. President who has offered me command of the Sixth Fleet." Golda looked after her people with ruthless disregard for lesser matters. And all other matters were lesser matters. If she had been President of the United States, we'd have had peace in Indochina, in the Mideast, in the Far East; and Moscow, a quaint duchy in the heartland of Asia, would be exporting wheat and importing Jews. God be with her. She will look after Him. —WFB

John Mitchell

— ⟡ —

(1913–1988)

Present at the creation: In 1968, Henry Kissinger, a Harvard professor and Rockefeller adviser, contacted WFB—a friend since the 1950s, when Buckley had lectured Kissinger's international relations seminar (attended, Buckley observed, "only by students who intended to become prime minister or emperor")—to ask if he would relay a private message to President-elect Nixon. Buckley dutifully placed a call to John N. Mitchell, Nixon's law partner and campaign manager and the closest thing Nixon had to a friend; the result was the Nixon–Kissinger foreign policy. Long Island–raised, Jesuit-educated, Mitchell was Wall Street's premier municipal bond lawyer. Using JNM's innovation, the "moral obligation bond," cities and states across the country financed countless public works. When Mitchell's law firm merged with Nixon's, the former vice president, plotting his comeback, eyed his new partner's network of contacts and steely-eyed taciturnity. "I believed," Nixon later wrote, "that I owed my election as president in 1968 largely to his strength as a counselor and his skill as a manager."

Concerned about his second wife, Martha, an alcoholic with psychiatric problems, Mitchell only reluctantly capitulated to Nixon's pleas to serve as attorney general in the tumultuous era that produced Kent State and the Weather Underground. Amid all that, JNM advised on Vietnam and China, picked four Supreme Court nominees, desegregated the Southern schools, and defused the crisis when Nixon's "plumbers" discovered that the Joint Chiefs of Staff had spied on the president. Running Nixon's reelection campaign, Mitchell became ensnared in Watergate, making him the highest-ranking U.S. official ever to serve time. Buckley erred in ascribing responsibility for the Watergate break-in to Mitchell; the former attorney general's denials on that score were truthful. But WFB harbored a soft spot for JNM—it was a grant from Buckley, in 1991, that launched my work on a biography of Mitchell—and Buckley's eulogy draws both on his novelistic skills, with a comic rendering of Mitchell's Hitchcockian appearance, and on WFB's own memories, uniformly unhappy, of the tormented Martha.

"John Mitchell, RIP"

National Review, December 9, 1988.

A bond dealer! It was a part of the grander design that John Mitchell should have had that profession, and that face. He looked like the Anonymous Man, clerking his time away until the Social Security payments began. And all the while, in private life and in public, he was a picaresque figure.

Anyone married to Martha Mitchell had to be, in hidden life, one true gay blade. At his request, received by radio from my office while I was on a sailing vacation, I stopped at a little village in Maine and telephoned his home number.

Mrs. Mitchell answered the phone: "Naaargh, operator, whoever is calling CANNOT speak to John Mitchell and I don't care if it's the man who is running for President. John Mitchell needs to relax. And that's MY business."

There were those who doubted his professional talents as a campaign manager, given that Richard Nixon, after Chicago, 1968, was ahead of Hubert Humphrey by 15 points; ten weeks later, on election day, he won by less than a single point. But John Mitchell was always imperturbable, always certain (in the company of others, anyway) that things would work out. Six years after this triumph—the return of a Republican President after the long winter 1960–1968—John Mitchell had stepped down as attorney general, had been divorced by Martha, and was in jail.

The daemon prevailed, and we know that John Mitchell authorized the Watergate burglary and then lied about it. We take these matters very seriously in the United States, and we should. But we should also be aware that there are other cultures commonly thought of as civilized in which what Mitchell did would be laughed at as nothing more than the games pols play. I remember especially the French intellectual who during the months just before Mr. Nixon's resignation commented that if it was absolutely proved that Mr. Nixon did *not* authorize Watergate, he should then be impeached as incompetent.

Beyond denying, while he could, what he had done, Mitchell clammed up. One needs to go back to George Marshall to find anyone whose memoirs—in Mitchell's case so greatly relevant to a political understanding of exactly what had happened—were so sought after. But he lived quietly in Washington, with a companion. And, it is said, spoke discreetly from time to time with his old comrade-in-arms, who had been spared jail, but not the humiliation of having to resign, for the first time in American history, the Presidency.

John Mitchell's stoicism can be admired quite apart from the weakness that seized him on that fatal day, when his anxiety to know everything the Democrats were up to led him to authorize a little caper that became the greatest political crime in U.S. history. As Jesse Jackson would say, From Watergate to Pearly-gate. We wish him safe passage. —WFB

Jacqueline Onassis

—◆—

(1929–1994)

"I think more of her now than ever," WFB wrote of Jacqueline Onassis in July 1969, after publication of a tell-all book by Jackie's secretary. "The most sensational revelations about Mrs. Kennedy," Buckley noted happily, "are utterly unsensational." Buckley had earlier befriended the widowed first lady in the company of John Kenneth Galbraith, who had taken Jackie to Gstaad for a weeklong skiing vacation in 1967. "Galbraith had undertaken her protection, and looked out, too, for her social life. Did I want to join them for dinner at the chalet of David Niven and his wife Hjordis?... [Niven] was a radiant host, attentive to every need.... What Jackie most needed, during that extended period of shock, was to laugh. Making people laugh was a specialty of his." WFB's eulogy for Jackie offers a glimpse into a society world long gone in which manners still prevailed and the two could happily encounter each other in the usual settings—one memorable fire drill aside—with mutual admiration, good cheer, and care not to impose.

"Jacqueline Onassis, RIP"

National Review, June 13, 1994.

Whenever I think back on it, as I am now forced to do, it is with utter dread & horror. It was late in the afternoon of a very full day in the Sixties. I stumbled into the receiving line, made up of four lovely ladies, self-evidently the sponsors of the charity affair. The first in line was my wife, the other three all very familiar faces—no doubt I had been in their company dozens of times. But in that harassed moment I could not instantly remember their first names, so I did what one generally does in these situations. After kissing my own wife, I went on to buss Lady B (whom indeed I did know), then Lady C (whom indeed I did know), then Jackie Kennedy—whom I had never laid eyes on in my life. It was only after I had treated her like one of my old lady-buddies that recognition set in. I felt exactly as I'd have felt if I had accidentally kissed the Queen of England. Not because Jackie was Untouchable; but because the national mania to touch her made her correspondingly vulnerable. For a while, a long while, I felt like that awful paparazzo she finally took to court [Ron Galella] because he was following her about with his camera day after day, week after week, month after month.

In the years ahead, we became moderate friends, and once during a fire drill at Doubleday I shared a concrete stair with her for the duration. Our contacts were infrequent, and I rather liked that about her. She had a set of friends, and as the years went by, she gave more time to consolidating friendships that especially appealed to her than to quick-processing fresh friends. If it had happened that, a month ago we had been seated together, whether in a staircase during a fire drill or at a fancy dinner party, the conversation would have been fresh and lively and spontaneous, utterly lacking in strain; in part, I must suppose, because she knew that notwithstanding the first awful misadventure, I was not engaged in cultivating Jacqueline Kennedy Onassis. I did once ask her to engage in an enterprise that would have required her to spend ten minutes at the Sistine Chapel, reflecting on the continuing relevance of one of the parables in the New Testament. Her negative was charmingly delivered over the telephone. "Bill, the only time I ever appeared on television was when I took the camera around the White House after the renovations. I was so awful I decided never to do it again."

It seems, on reflection, that her life, for all its vicissitudes, was about as perfectly conducted as anyone with her beauty, skills, and glamour could hope to manage. She did what she wanted to do. If her second marriage was emotionally impulsive, it was strategically prudent. Books could be written (probably have been written) on the skills she showed in bringing up her two exemplary children in that magnetic field she moved in. She worked not as a dilettante but as a truly engaged editor, an average of three days every week. She exhibited only as much of herself as she thought she owed as reciprocity to a country that loved her and was fascinated by her.

And she was true to her Christian faith, which in the final ceremony irradiated Jackie's class, a creature of God. —WFB

Vernon Walters

∽

(1917–2002)

It was fitting that Lieutenant General Vernon M. Walters, a soldier, spy, linguist, translator, and diplomat, should have titled his 1978 memoir *Silent Missions*. In more than fifty years of public service, he remained to the end the model of the discreet public servant. An army veteran of allied campaigns in North Africa and Italy in World War II, Walters mastered at least seven foreign languages. He was the official note taker present when President Truman fired General Douglas MacArthur. As a staff aide to President Eisenhower, he made an impression on Vice President Nixon, particularly when he served as Nixon's interpreter during the latter's famous trip to Caracas in 1958 (when anti-American mobs violently attacked Nixon's motorcade). As the military attaché in Paris during Nixon's first term as president, Walters helped smuggle Henry Kissinger to and from secret talks with the North Vietnamese negotiator Le Duc Tho. In 1972, Nixon appointed Walters deputy director of the Central Intelligence Agency, a position in which the taciturn general played a critical early role in frustrating, and documenting, efforts by White House aides to enmesh the Agency in the Watergate cover-up. Later, President Reagan tapped Walters to serve as U.S. ambassador to the United Nations, and President George H. W. Bush made him ambassador to the Federal Republic of Germany. Never married, he died alone at a hospital in Florida at the age of eighty-five. Between 1978 and 1993, WFB welcomed Walters to the set of *Firing Line* five times, reveling always in the older man's singular gift for language—both the spoken word and those best left unsaid.

"Vernon Walters, R.I.P."

National Review, March 11, 2002.

The Quiet Man departed this world at Good Samaritan Medical Center, the cause of death, as he'd have wished, unstated. On hearing of his unobtrusive death in Palm Beach, friends and admirers took it for granted that the Good Samaritan hospital took the very best care of the good Samaritan dying in its hands. If Vernon Walters was conscious, he'd have received the last rites of the Catholic Church, whose God he thought himself as having committed his life work to, although what he did was work for the United States, an ungodly nation much of the time Walters was active, but reasonably adjudged the best-intentioned country of the 20th century.

Walters was at once the invisible man, and the man, asked to speak out, utterly plainspoken, wittily dogmatic, searchingly thoughtful. He was a consummate craftsman: You had to be out of sight when you were interpreting for Eisenhower and de Gaulle, Kissinger and Pompidou, note-taking for Truman when he fired Douglas MacArthur,

sneaking Kissinger into Paris to meet secretly with the
Vietnamese, serving as deputy chief, then acting director,
of the CIA. But when his views were asked, on questions
he thought himself entitled to speak out about, the words,
thoughts, reflections, history, and witticisms poured forth,
ingenuous questions corrected, sarcasm and cynicism handled, the questioner left barely alive to tell the tale.

It happens that I saw him often, because he spent many
days on passenger liners participating in seminars we both
engaged in. He was getting creaky, at 85, and needed his
nephew to get him about, but he omitted nothing that was
going on, in part a preternatural disposition to do his duty,
in part an appetite to see and hear everything. The intelligence officer off-duty is sometimes governed by the habits of an intelligence officer on-duty. In his company one
found oneself supposing, on hearing Walters handle German and Spanish, French and Italian, Dutch, Portuguese,
and Russian, that his mind traveled from any one language
to any other seriatim, because his mind worked that way,
taking it all in.

Although his business in later years was diplomacy, his
craft was intelligence, and the two blended in his hands.
His mien was grouchy, the corners of his lips turned down,
his arms crossed, as he might have looked receiving a ti-
rade from Khrushchev with duties to pass the ordure on
to Jack Kennedy. I asked him, on a television program at
a time when the CIA was under especially heavy pressure,
about his calling. He replied in one breath, "We have a
great ambivalence toward intelligence. The average American thinks it's something that isn't very clean, it isn't very
American, and the Founding Fathers wouldn't like it. Well,
I have news for them. George Washington was one of the

most prolific readers of other people's mail. Benjamin Franklin was assistant postmaster of British North America before the Revolution when we were all loyal subjects of George III. He was busy opening all the British mail. They caught him. They sent him to London to stand trial before the Privy Council. They found him guilty. Before they could sentence him, he skipped off to France to conduct the covert operation that was to bring France into the war on the side of the Revolution. Now this was a remarkable achievement, seeing that Anthony Eden's great-great-great-grandfather had fully penetrated Benjamin Franklin's office. Franklin's valet was a British agent, his secretary was a British agent, and we have some doubts about one of the three commissioners."

That was a mouthful, and he spoke in mouthfuls. But he was, in spite of it, a man of great diffidence. My most memorable encounter with him was at the steps of the White House. He was passing through the usual checkpoint at the west gate and had his sister with him.

The Secret Service would not let them in: They had no data on his sister, and for all the Secret Service knew, this septuagenarian lady was really Mata Hari. I was behind in line, and behind me was Ted Williams, conversing with the chancellor of the University of Chicago. Ours was a line of people invited to the White House that day in January 1991 to receive the Presidential Medal of Freedom; and there the former head of the CIA was holding up the line. He just stood there, waiting for something to happen, so that he could have a family member at hand when the president of the United States hung a medal about his neck. —WFB

FRIENDS

Whittaker Chambers

(1901–1961)

"The contest between Whittaker Chambers and Alger Hiss was a gripping judicial Armageddon," WFB wrote in 1978. "But to deposit Chambers, as has been done in most references to him, as the man who got Hiss is on the order of remembering Ezra Pound as the man who broadcast for Mussolini."

The main event . . . is the political and literary art of Whittaker Chambers. . . . His genius lay in an analytical and descriptive intensity that touched even the most awful concerns with a kind of transporting lyricism.

Gripped by the Hiss–Chambers case, enraptured by *Witness* (1952), WFB saw Chambers in heroic terms. But he also counted the rumpled ex-communist and *Time* editor a colleague and pal. Twenty years after recruiting the older man to *National Review,* Buckley would write of Chambers's "closest friends (I was one of them)." Sometimes WFB found his friend's writing obscure, his reasons for leaving the magazine, after two years, even more so, but he remained awed by Chambers's epiphany and its consequence. "The Hiss Case is a permanent war," Chambers wrote in his first letter to WFB, in 1954. When WFB published their correspondence—in *Odyssey of a Friend* (1969)—no letter provided greater insight into Chambers's innate contradictions than the 1957 missive in which he remarked with "sadness" on how much he had come to "enjoy" writing for *NR:* "I have been grateful to you in a way that I could not express without courting extravagance." Buckley's original 1962 eulogy, "The End of Whittaker Chambers," quoting at length from the letters, consumed 10,000 words in *Esquire* (and was republished in *Rumbles Left and Right* [1963]). Here we present WFB's remarks, adapted from the longer piece, at a White House event commemorating Chambers's centenary.

"Witness and Friend"

National Review, August 6, 2001.
[originally delivered July 9, 2001, at the Eisenhower Executive Office
Building, Washington, D.C.; adapted from "The End of Whittaker
Chambers," *Esquire,* September 1962]

We were to meet at the National Gallery here in Washington, and I had been waiting for him at the specified corner. I spotted him far down the corridor. It could only have been he, or Alfred Hitchcock. The Sunday before, he had asked me to come down that day, the 8th of June. We had lunch. He had asked me to keep the evening free. "You've guessed what's up, haven't you?" he asked, his face wreathed in smiles.

"I haven't the least idea."

"John!" he said proudly. His son would be married that afternoon, and I was to go to the wedding and the reception.

As he stepped into the elevator that evening, after the ceremony, I saw him framed by the door, his hand and Esther's clutched together, posing while his son-in-law popped a camera in his face—a grim reminder of all those flashbulbs ten years before. I never saw him again. He died a month later, on July 9, 1961, forty years ago, exactly. Free at last.

I first met Chambers in 1954. An almost total silence had closed in on him. Two years earlier he had published *Witness*. When the preface of *Witness* appeared as a feature in *The Saturday Evening Post,* that issue of the magazine sold a startling half million extra copies on the newsstand. The book came out with a great flurry. The bitterness of the Hiss trial had not subsided. For some of the reviewers, Hiss's innocence had once been a fixed rational conviction, then blind faith; and now, after the publication of that overwhelming book, rank superstition.

But the nature of the author was not grasped by the reviewers. *I am a heavy man,* Chambers once wrote me, apologizing for staying two days at my home. There is a sense in which that was true. But he never appreciated, as others could do, the true gaiety of his nature, the appeal of his mysterious humor, the instant communicability of an overwhelming personal tenderness; his friends—I think especially of Ralph de Toledano—took endless and articulate pleasure from his company.

Witness was off to a great start. But, surprisingly, it did not continue to sell in keeping with its spectacular send-off.

The length of the book was forbidding; and the trial, in any case, was three years old, and the cold sweat had dried. Alger Hiss was in prison, and now the political furor centered about Senator McCarthy. Those who did not know the book, and who were not emotionally committed either to Chambers's guilt or to his innocence, seemed to shrink even from a vicarious involvement in the controversy, to a considerable extent because of the dark emanations that came from Chambers; depressing when reproduced, as was widely done, in bits and snatches torn from the narrative. "Until reading *Witness* it had been my impression," Hugh Kenner, the author and critic, had written me, "that his mind moved, or wallowed, in a setting of continuous apocalypse from which he derived gloomy satisfactions, of an immobilizing sort. The large scale of *Witness* makes things much clearer. It is surprisingly free from rhetoric, and it makes clear the genuine magnitude of the action which was his life; a Sophoclean tragedy in slow motion, years not hours."

In 1954 I asked if I might visit him. He had written to a long-standing friend, Henry Regnery, the publisher of my book on Senator McCarthy, to praise the book while making clear his critical differences with its subject. Chambers had been struck down by a heart attack and it was vaguely known that he spent his days in and out of a sickbed, from which the likelihood was that he would never again emerge physically whole. I had every reason to believe that I would be visiting Jeremiah lying alongside a beckoning tomb.

I was taken to his bedroom. The doctor had forbidden him even to raise his head. And yet he seemed the liveliest man I had ever met. I could not imagine such good humor from a very sick man, let alone anyone possessed by the conviction that night was closing in all over the world, privately tortured by his continuing fear that the forces aligned against him would contrive to reorder history, impose upon the world the ghastly lie that he had testified falsely against Alger Hiss, and so erase his witness, his expiation for more than ten years' complicity with Communism.

We did not, of course, speak of Hiss, nor did we for several months; though later he spoke of him, and of the case, with candor. But we talked about everything else, and I left Westminster later than I should have, hustled anxiously to the door by a wife who knew she was helpless absolutely to enforce the doctor's rules.

As he began to recover he was, for a period, greatly renewed by a physical and spiritual energy that were dialectically at odds with his organic ill health and his intellectual commitment to the futility of all meliorative action in the Cold War. I talked with him about the magazine I proposed to publish and asked whether he would join the staff. To my astonishment the answer was yes—he would consider doing just that. We corresponded through the summer. He was to make up his mind definitely during the fall, after we visited again. I made the mistake in one of my letters of expressing exorbitant hopes for the role *National Review* might play in political affairs. He dashed them down in a paragraph unmatched in the literature of supine gloom, sentences that President Reagan, who was in awe of their eloquence, and defiant of their fatalism, publicly recalled more than once. *It is idle,* he rebuked me, *to talk about preventing the wreck of Western civilization. It is already a wreck from within. That is why we can hope to do little more now than snatch a fingernail of a saint from the rack or a handful of ashes from the faggots, and bury them secretly in a flowerpot against the day, ages hence, when a few men begin again to dare to believe that there was once something else, that something else is thinkable, and need some evidence of what it was, and the fortifying knowledge that there were those who, at the great nightfall, took loving thought to preserve the tokens of hope and truth.*

The tokens of hope and truth were not to be preserved, he seemed to be saying, in a journal of opinion, not to be preserved by writers or thinkers. Only by activists, and I was to know that he considered a publication—the right kind of publication—not a word, but a deed. In the final analysis it was action, not belletrism, that moved him most deeply.

And so in time I came to understand why in 1932 he resigned as editor of the Communist *New Masses,* where he had earned an international reputation as a writer, to go scurrying about the streets of Washington, Baltimore, and New York, carrying pocketfuls of negatives and secret phone numbers and invisible ink. *One of the great failures of* Witness, he wrote me, *is that there was no time or place to describe the influences, other than immediate historical influences, that brought me to Communism. I came to Communism . . . above all under the influence of the Narodniki. They have been deliberately forgotten, but, in those days, Lenin urged us to revere the Narodniki—"those who went with bomb or revolver against this or that individual monster." Unlike most Western Communists, who became Communists under the influence of the Social Democrats, I remained under the spiritual influence of the Narodniki long after I became a Marxist. In fact, I never threw it off. I never have. And, of course, it was that revolutionary quality* [in me] *that bemused Alger—mea culpa, mea maxima culpa.*

Activism. From the Narodniki to the Republican Party, in one defection.

But now he would stay on at his farm, and worry from his sickbed.

He had a great deal to worry about. His broken health and near penury enhanced an insubordinate restlessness. *I do not even have the capital to farm halfheartedly,* he wrote me, *and I cannot, as in the past, make good the capital by my own labor power. This inability to work is perhaps the greatest burr in my mind. It torments me since, among other disabilities, I have no talent for being a country gentleman.*

He reached the low point of his spirits as he sweated in philosophical bedrock, gathering his thoughts: *I have been splashing about in my private pool of ice water.* In another letter, *I have ceased to understand why I must go on living.* In still another, *The year was, for me, a long walk through the valley. No one but me will ever know how close I came to staying in it.*

Did he isolate the trouble? Yes. *It had to do with my inability to fix the meaning of the current period of existence in some communicable way. I knew the fault lay in me. So that, all the while I was trying to write, I was simply trying to grow.*

But the weeks went by. Eisenhower ran and was reelected. Nixon was safely vice president. Six months later Chambers wrote to say he was ready to sign up with *National Review.* Having made the decision, he was elated. After five years of isolation and introspection, he was like a painter who had recovered his eyesight. He felt the need to practice his art. How many things he wanted to write about, and immediately! Mushrooms, for one thing. Albert Camus. What a lot of things needed to be said instantly about *The Myth of Sisyphus*! Milovan Djilas's *New Class* was just out, and most of the critics, he said, had missed the whole point.

But what he wrote about first was the farmers. He anticipated a gradual end to their independence. *Perhaps* [in the future, the socialized farmer] *will not be able . . . to find or frame an answer* [to why he lost his freedom]. *Perhaps he will not need to. For perhaps the memory of those men and women* [who fought socialism] *will surprise him, as with an unfamiliar but arresting sound—the sound of spring-heads, long dried up and silent in a fierce drought, suddenly burst out and rushing freely to the sea. It may remind him of a continuity that outlives all lives, fears, perplexities, contriving, hopes, defeats; so that he is moved to reach down and touch again for strength, as if he were its first discoverer, the changeless thing—the undeluding, undenying earth.*

Chambers decided in the summer of 1958 to come up to New York every fortnight and spend two days in the office with his colleagues, writing editorials and features for the magazine. He would arrive on the train from Baltimore at noon and come directly to the editorial lunch, always out of breath, perspiring in his city clothes. He liked his little cubicle at *National Review* which, five minutes after he entered it, smelled like a pipe-tobacco factory. He puffed away devotedly, grinding out memorable editorials and paragraphs.

Yet anyone meeting Chambers casually, without preconception, would judge him an amusing and easily amused man. The bottomless gravity seldom suggested itself. He was not merely a man of wit, but also a man of humor, and even of fun. Often, in his letters, even through his orotund gloom, the pixie would surface. (*Would that we could live in the world of the fauves,* he wrote me at Christmas, *where the planes are disjointed only on canvas, instead of a world where the wild beasts are real and the disjointures threaten to bury us.*)

On Tuesday nights we worked late, and four or five of us would go to dinner. By then he was physically exhausted.

But he wanted to come with us, and we would eat at whatever restaurant, and he would talk hungrily (and eat hungrily), talk about everything that interested him, which was literally everything in this world, and not in this world. He talked often around a subject, swooping in to make a quick point, withdrawing, relaxing, laughing, listening—he listened superbly, though even as a listener he was a potent force.

The next morning, press day, he was at his desk at eight, and, for lunch, a sandwich. At five he was on the train back to Baltimore, where his wife would meet him. On reaching his farm he would drop on his bed from fatigue. Three months after coming to New York, he collapsed from another heart attack. But in the summer of 1959 he felt well enough to indulge a dream, more particularly his gentle wife's dream, to visit Europe. We drove them to the airport after a happy day. I noticed worriedly how heavily he perspired and how nervously his heavy thumbs shuffled through the bureaucratic paraphernalia of modern travel, as he dug up, in turn, passports, baggage tags, vaccination certificates, and airplane tickets. His plans were vague, but at the heart of them was a visit to his old friend, Arthur Koestler.

They were at Koestler's eyrie in Austria for a week.

Alpach, where AK lives, is some four hundred meters higher into the hills than Innsbruck, he wrote me. *So there we sat, and talked, not merely about the daily experiences of our lives. Each of the two men with us had tried to kill himself and failed; Greta Buber-Neumann was certainly the most hardy and astonishing of the three. Then we realized that, of our particular breed, the old activists, we are almost the only survivors. . . .*

They went on to Rome (*In Rome, I had to ask Esther for the nitroglycerine. Since then, I've been living on the stuff. . . .*).

And then Venice (*I came back to Venice chiefly to rest. If it were not for my children, I should try to spend the rest of my life here*). Berlin (*I feel as though I had some kind of moral compulsion to go at this time. . . .*). Paris ("You will look up Malraux?" I wrote him—I remembered the gratitude Chambers felt on receiving a handwritten note from Malraux with his judgment of *Witness:* "You have not come back from hell with empty hands.")

But he took sick again and, abruptly, they flew back; again he was in bed. He wanted now to resign from *National Review*. It was partly that his poor health and his unconquerable perfectionism kept him from producing a flow of copy large enough to satisfy his conscience. Partly it was his weltanschauung, which was constantly in motion. He resisted *National Review*'s schematic conservatism, even its schematic anti-Communism. *You . . . stand within, or at any rate are elaborating, a political orthodoxy,* his letter explained. *I stand within no political orthodoxy. . . . I am at heart a counter-revolutionist. You mean to be conservative, and I know no one who seems to me to have a better right to the term. I am not a conservative. I am a man of the Right. I shall vote the straight Republican ticket for as long as I live.*

And, always looking within the Marxist world for amplification, he found it. *You see, I am an Orgbureau man. But if the Republican Party cannot get some grip of the actual world we live in and from it generalize and actively promote a program that means something to the masses of people—why somebody else will. Then there will be nothing to argue. The voters will simply vote Republicans into singularity. The Republican Party will become like one of those dark little shops which apparently never sell anything. If, for any reason, you go in, you find at the back an old man, fingering for his own pleasure some oddments of cloth.*

Nobody wants to buy them, which is fine because the old man is not really interested in selling. He just likes to hold and to feel. . . .

He had made up his mind to do something else. He enrolled at Western Maryland College as an undergraduate.

He had quit *National Review,* he had failed to complete the book that Random House had been expecting for six years. He did not want to sit at home, half crippled and denied the life he would, I think, have liked most to lead, the life of a dawn-to-dusk farmer. Whittaker Chambers was all Puritan about work. Idleness was incomprehensible to him. But there was another reason for going back to school. In Europe, Koestler had said to him sharply: "You cannot understand what is going on in the world unless you understand science deeply." Very well, then, he would learn science.

He threw himself into his work. Science courses galore. For relaxation, Greek, Latin, and advanced French composition. Every morning he drove to school and sat among the farmers' sons of western Maryland, taking notes, dissecting frogs, reciting Greek paradigms, working tangled problems in physics. Home, and immediately to the basement to do his homework. Everything else was put aside.

He signed up for the summer session but in the interstice between terms he drove north to see his daughter, Ellen. En route he spent a day with us on a hot afternoon. How do you get on, my wife asked, with your fellow undergraduates? "Fine," he said, puffing on his pipe. In fact, we learned, he had an admirer. A young lady—aged about nineteen, he guessed—shared with him the allocated carcasses of small animals, which the two of them, in tandem, proceeded to disembowel. He had written to me about her. *For months while we worked together she addressed me not a word, and I was afraid my great age had frightened her. But last week she broke silence. She said breathlessly: "Mr. Chambers?" "Yes," I answered her anxiously. "Tell me, what do you think of 'Itsy Bitsy Teenie Weenie Yellow Polkadot Bikini'?"* He recalled the question now with laughter. He hadn't, at the critical moment, any idea that the young lady was talking about a popular song, but he had improvised successfully until he could deduce what she was talking about, and then confided to his covivisectionist that it just happened that this was one of his very favorite songs. Her excitement was indescribable. From that moment on they chirped together as soulmates, pooling their knowledge of spleens and livers, kidneys and upper intestines.

I imagine that he was a very quiet student, giving his teachers no cause whatever for the uneasiness they might have expected to feel in the presence of so august a mind. During examination weeks he was in a constant state of high boil. He slaved for his grades and achieved them, even in the alien field of science; all A's, or A minuses; once, as I remember, a humiliating B plus. After the spring term his fatigue was total, overwhelming. *Weariness, Bill,* he wrote in the last letter I had from him, a few days before John's wedding, *you cannot yet know literally what it means. I wish no time would come when you do know, but the balance of experience is against it. One day, long hence, you will know true weariness and will say: "That was it." My own life of late has been full of such realizations.*

He learned science, and killed himself. Those were the two things, toward the end, for which he strived.

'Why on earth doesn't your father answer the phone?" I asked his daughter Ellen in Connecticut on Saturday afternoon, the 8th of July. "Because," she said with a laugh, shyly, "Poppa and the phone company are having a little tiff, and the phone is disconnected. They wanted him to trim one of his favorite trees to take the strain off the telephone line, and he put them off. So . . . they turned off the phone." I wired him: WHEN YOU COME TO TERMS WITH THE PHONE COMPANY GIVE ME A RING. But he didn't call. The following Tuesday when I walked into my office the phone was ringing. I took the call standing in front of my desk. It was John Chambers. He gave me the news. A heart attack. The final heart attack. Cremation in total privacy. His mother was in the hospital. The news would go to the press later that afternoon. I mumbled the usual things, hung up the telephone, sat down, and wept.

He had written me once, *American men, who weep in droves in movie houses, over the woes of lovestruck shop girls, hold that weeping in men is unmanly. I have found most men in whom there was depth of experience, or capacity for compassion, singularly apt to tears. How can it be otherwise? One looks and sees: and it would be a kind of impotence to be incapable of, or to grudge, the comment of tears, even while you struggle against it. I am immune to soap opera. But I cannot listen for any length of time to the speaking voice of Kirsten Flagstad, for example, without being done in by that magnificence of tone that seems to speak from the center of sorrow, even from the center of the earth.*

For me, and others who knew him, his voice had been like Kirsten Flagstad's, magnificent in tone, speaking to our time from the center of sorrow, from the center of the earth.

Richard Clurman

(1924–1996)

"My friend Buckley," Richard M. Clurman wrote in 1980, "is a real lover of his friends, not just his sailing friends, but his writing, painting, piano-playing, economizing, computerizing, lawyering, banking—all his real friends. Not that he's profligate with friendship nor does he debase the coinage. He's just intense about it." A longtime editor at *Time* magazine, Clurman also served on the boards of various arts institutions and as head, in the final year of the Lindsay administration, of New York City's parks department. In that capacity Clurman earned WFB's admiration for the declaration, in his first public appearance on the job, that he intended to withdraw municipal maintenance from any park where local residents appeared to acquiesce in its neglect. As he wrote in *Atlantic High* (1982), Buckley considered the bespectacled and schlemiel-like Clurman "among the most sentimental of men," an engaging mind that was, by turns, "trenchant, pointed, fluent, philosophical." The two sailed often, if not annually, despite Clurman's singular inaptitude for the required tasks, and these were special times for them. "Even more

at sea than on land," Clurman noted in his seafaring journal, "Bill re-
fuses to allow around him, not only by noncontribution, but by his
very attitude, unpleasantness among his friends." The grief WFB felt at
Clurman's passing, at seventy-two, is palpable in this eulogy.

"Richard M. Clurman, R.I.P."

National Review, May 20, 1996.

Three years ago, one evening in July, he asked whether I'd
cross the ocean again in 1995, what would have been the
fifth such venture, done at five-year intervals beginning in
1975. "I'm prepared to go," he told me. I suppose I smiled;
it was dark on the veranda when he spoke. I told him I
doubted my crew could be mobilized for one more such
trip, and just the right crew was indispensable. He had
done with me two Atlantic crossings, one Pacific crossing.
He was an instant celebrity for his ineptitudes at sea, done
in high spirit with a wonderful, persistent incomprehension
of what was the job at hand. He was the object of hilarious
ridicule in my son's published journal—and he loved it all,
even as Christopher loved him; even when, while discours-
ing concentratedly on matters of state, he would drop his
cigarette ash into Christopher's wine glass, or very nearly
set fire in the galley when trying to light the stove. He
thrived on the cheerful raillery of his companions, but on
one occasion thought to say to me, in a voice unaccustom-
edly low: "I'm good at other things."

He hardly needed to remind me. Yes, and from everything he was good at he drew lessons, little maxims of
professional and extraprofessional life of great cumulative

impact, instantly imparted to all his friends, at the least suggestion from them, or from their situation, that they needed help, or instruction. It is awesome to extrapolate from one's own experience of his goodness the sum of what he did for others.

When [*Newsweek* editor] Osborn Elliott, on Shirley's [Mrs. Clurman] behalf, asked me to say something today I went right to my desk, but I found it impossible to imagine his absence from the scene. Was it true that there would be no message from him tomorrow on our E-mail circuit? That we would not be dining together during the week, or sharing a tenth Christmas together? In the strangest sense, the answer is, No, it isn't impossible that we will continue as companions, because his companionship left indelible traces: how to work, how to read, how to love.

It came to me last Thursday when just after midnight my son reached me at the hotel, that I have always sub-consciously looked out for the total Christian, and when I found him, he turned out to be a nonpracticing Jew. It will require the balance of my own lifetime to requite what he gave to me. —WFB

Evan Galbraith

―✦―

(1928–2008)

Evan G. ("Van") Galbraith was almost a lifelong friend of WFB's and probably his closest. They met at Yale on Election Day 1948. A graduate also of Harvard Law School and a Wall Street banker, Galbraith would go on to serve as chairman of the *NR* board of trustees, as President Reagan's ambassador to France, and as president of Moët & Chandon. Like Buckley, Galbraith also served a brief stint as a CIA officer. He was a frequent skiing and sailing companion of WFB's, and his journal entries, bursting with salty wit, enlivened Buckley's books about their adventures at sea. Christopher Buckley, who accompanied WFB and Van on their three transoceanic voyages, recalled that Galbraith, "handsome, blond, brawny, broken-nosed," possessed "the rare gift of being able to make almost any unpleasant situation funny." Case in point: After wrapping up his watch duty, Galbraith would startle awake the next passenger slated for that duty, in the dead of night, with absurd cheerfulness: "Good news—you don't have to sleep anymore!" Given the length and depth of their bond—Galbraith was one of two friends who celebrated WFB's eighty-second, and final, birthday with him, at a moment when Galbraith had just completed his thirtieth radiation treatment for cancer and himself had only months to live—it is fitting that Galbraith should have been the subject of the last eulogy Buckley ever wrote, published about two weeks before his own death. Its brevity, however—fewer than 350 words—probably reflects WFB's rapidly declining health, for in more vigorous times he had been in the habit of remembering even more distant friendships at greater length and almost surely would have done that for this accomplished man he so loved and admired.

"Evan Galbraith, R.I.P."

National Review, February 11, 2008.

Van Galbraith's credentials were pretty impressive. We were classmates at Yale and then he went to Harvard Law School. After that came service as a naval officer, in the folds of the CIA. Then a top law firm in New York City, and on to London, where he represented his firm and did private business. But his interest in public affairs was irresistible, and when Ronald Reagan was sworn in as president, Galbraith was sworn in as ambassador to France, abandoning even his post as chairman of the board of trustees of *National Review.* After Paris, back to the law and to business, but soon he was in Europe again, this time in Brussels as defense adviser to the U.S. mission at NATO. He pulled away from that in November, and died January 21 in New York of problems that traced to a cancer discovered, but not arrested, years ago.

A deskbound life? Hardly. He made four transoceanic

passages with me on sailboats, performing duties at sea without ever learning, quite, how to sail. We skied together every winter and his proficiency there was that of an expert. He wrote and published two books and loved to give advice, oracular in tone, shrewd in conception—underestimated only by those of invincible ignorance who set his advice aside. They included an illustrious if wrongheaded company of presidents and kings and commissars.

In one enterprise he was unfailing. Everyone he knew came up upon his brightness of spirit. The acuity of his wit was always inflected through his personal generosity. When you add the hours at sea and the snows traversed together to the classroom work taken jointly, I must have spent more time with Evan Galbraith than with any other human being outside my family. The loss to his own family is awful to contemplate, while the pleasures he gave, in his seven decades, to all he brushed up against are as incalculable as the depths of his laughter and the joy he gave to the world.

John Kenneth Galbraith

—◆~—

(1908–2006)

The first words John Kenneth Galbraith spoke to WFB were "I regret that." The setting, in November 1966, was an elevator in New York's Plaza Hotel, where the two men and their wives were arriving for Truman Capote's masked ball; Buckley had asked JKG to explain why he had warned a colleague not to publish in *National Review*. Thus commenced one of the deepest, most affectionate friendships of Buckley's adult life, played out on the ski slopes of Gstaad and countless TV news sets and debate stages. At six-foot-eight, Galbraith cut an imposing figure, but the Harvard economist, who served as President Kennedy's ambassador to India, never intimidated WFB: The conservative godfather delighted in mocking his friend's liberal theories. Galbraith's works were widely read—several of his coinages entered the national lexicon, from "the conventional wisdom" to "the affluent society," the title of his 1958 book—and Buckley considered his friend, however misguided, as influential as Adam Smith and John Maynard Keynes. Their differences remained acute: Not long after their elevator encounter, Buckley accused JKG, in a column, of "seem[ing] to want most of all a military defeat and the psychological humiliation of this country." Still, Galbraith's eleven appearances on *Firing Line* set the standard for elevated, witty debate. In a 1969 show, Galbraith suggested that Buckley knew all too well the feelings associated with recantation. "I may be guilty of heresies," WFB said, "but I don't remember deserting any of my heresies." "Oh, yes, yes, Bill," JKG shot back. "I remember that very good book of yours, *The Unmaking of a Mayor,* where you deserted your whole conservative doctrine." And on the special occasion in July 1972 when *Firing Line* welcomed JKG and two of his sons, distinguished academics both, WFB began: "I regret to report that there is no generation gap between father and sons." On a Mideast trip in February 2013, I asked Secretary of State John Kerry if he had ever met WFB; Kerry replied that he had once appeared on *Firing Line* and added, "I *loved* Bill Buckley." Asked why, he cited WFB's abiding friendship with J. K. Galbraith: "That's what's missing from politics today."

"John Kenneth Galbraith, R.I.P."

National Review, May 22, 2006.

I file this story, remarking the death of John Kenneth Galbraith, only with the forbearance of the editors of *National Review.* I draw deep into the forbearing capital I have accumulated in this journal by writing so personal an account of his life. It pleases me that he knew the value I placed on his friendship, which here impels something of a corruption of my duties.

The public Galbraith I knew and contended with for many years is captured in the first paragraph of my review of his 1992 book, *The Culture of Contentment.* I wrote then:

"It is fortunate for Professor Galbraith that he was born with singular gifts as a writer. It is a pity he hasn't used these skills in other ways than to try year after year to bail out his sinking ships. Granted, one can take satisfaction from his antihistorical exertions, and wholesome pleasure from his yeomanry as a sump-pumper. Indeed, his rhythm and grace recall the skills we remember having been developed by Ben-Hur, the model galley slave, whose only request of the quartermaster was that he be allowed every month to move to the other side of the boat, to ensure a parallel development in the musculature of his arms and legs. I for one hope that the next time a nation experimenting with socialism or Communism fails, which will happen the next time a nation experiments with socialism or Communism, Ken Galbraith will feel the need to explain what happened. It's great fun to read. It helps, of course, to suppress wistful thought about those who endured, or died trying, the passage toward collective living to which Professor Galbraith has beckoned us for over forty years, beguiling the subliterate world, here defined as those whose knowledge of what makes the world work is undeveloped, never mind that many of them have Ph.Ds."

So it is said, for the record; and yet we grieve, those of us who knew him. We looked to his writings not for his social indenture to a progressive state, but for the work of a penetrating mind who turned his talent to the service of his ideals. This involved waging war against men and women who had, under capitalism, made strides in the practice of industry and in promoting the common good. Galbraith denied them the tribute to which they were entitled. It was bad enough, for him, that some Americans contributed to the commonweal the fruit of their industry. When they went further and offered their intellectual insights, Galbraith was unforgiving. Prof. Arthur Laffer, the idiomatic godfather of supply-side economics, Galbraith dismissed as if his work were of zero interest. His appraisal of such intellectual dissenters from his ideas of the common good derived from the psaltery of his moral catechism, cataloguing the persistence of poverty, the awful taste of the successful classes, and the wastefulness of the corporate and military establishments.

He dismisses conflicting notions with a wonderful contempt. "It is not clear that anyone of sober mentality took Professor Laffer's curve and conclusions seriously," Galbraith writes. Watch now the mortal dig: "He must have credit, nonetheless, for showing that justifying contrivance, however transparent, could be of high practical service." Where Mr. Galbraith is not easily excusable is in his search for disingenuousness in such as Charles Murray, a meticulous scholar of liberal background, whose *Losing Ground* is among the social landmarks of the postwar era. "In the mid 1980s," Galbraith writes, "the requisite doctrine needed by the culture of contentment to justify their policies became available. Dr. Charles A. Murray provided the nearly perfect prescription. . . . Its essence was that the poor are impoverished and are kept in poverty by the public measures, particularly the welfare payments, that are meant to rescue them from their plight." Whatever Murray's modifications, "the basic purpose of his argument would be served. The poor would be off the conscience of the comfortable, and, a point of greater importance, off the federal budget and tax system."

One needs to brush this aside and dwell on the private life of John Kenneth Galbraith. I know something of that

life, and of the lengths to which he went in utter privacy to
help those in need. He was a truly generous friend. The
mighty engine of his intelligence could be marshaled to
serve the needs of individual students, students manqué,
people who had a problem. Where he would not yield was
in intellectual and social perspective. I had a letter from
him a week before he died, pressing a point he had made
orally when we last visited a few weeks ago. He added:
"Nothing, of course, gives me more pleasure than lectur-
ing on the nature of true conservatism."

   Two or three weeks ago he sent me a copy of a poll in
which he and his accomplishments were rated by the academic economics profession. He was voted the third most
influential economist of the 20th century, after Keynes and
Schumpeter. I think that ranking tells us more about the
economics profession than we have any grounds to cele-
brate, but that isn't the point I made in acknowledging his
letter. I had received, only a day or two before, a book about
the new prime minister of Canada, Mr. Stephen Harper,
in which *National Review* and its founder are cited as the
primary influences in his own development as a conservative leader. But I did not mention this to Galbraith either.
He was ailing, and this old adversary kept from him loose
combative data which would have vexed him.

   I was one of the speakers at his huge 85th-birthday
party at the Boston Public Library. My four-minute talk
was interrupted halfway through by the master of ceremonies. "Is there a doctor in the house?" The acoustics at the
library were bad, and the next day I sent Galbraith the text
of my talk. A week later I had his acknowledgment. It read:
"Dear Bill: That was a very pleasant talk you gave about me.
If I had known it would be so, I would not have instructed

my friend to pretend, in the middle of your speech, to need the attention of a doctor."

Forget the whole thing, the getting and spending, and the Nobel Prize nominations, and the economists' tributes. What cannot be forgotten by those exposed to it is the amiable, generous, witty interventions of this man, with his singular wife and three remarkable sons, and that is why there are among his friends those who weep that he is now gone. —WFB

Tom Hume

(1928–2003)

Tom Hume was an architect, sailor—part of the crew aboard the 1966 winner of the Mallory Cup—and father of six in a family with long roots in Connecticut. He and Buckley graduated from Yale together and remained sailing buddies until a stroke incapacitated Hume, in 1981, at the age of fifty-three. He would live, trapped within himself but still able to communicate in a limited fashion to those who knew him best, for another twenty-two years. In this eulogy, delivered at Hume's funeral service, WFB remembers his friend, whom Pat Buckley, more than a half century earlier, had declared "the most handsome man I have ever laid eyes on."

Remarks at the funeral service for Thomas Hume, St. Clement's Church, Stamford, Connecticut, November 6, 2003; published in *National Review,* December 8, 2003.

We were all of us, in the Yale Class of 1950, asked to give a few sentences of biographical information for the 50th anniversary yearbook. Tom Hume wrote: "My life changed on November 16, 1981, when I suffered a stroke at age 53. After a difficult recovery, stretching over two years, I have limited ability to read, write, or converse." But he did manage, with appropriate contrivances, to drive a car, and to captain a Dyer 29 frequenting Long Island Sound, which, as he put it, "I know well and find endlessly fascinating." And he cruised in the waterways of Europe, and spent happy days with his ten grandchildren. He cultivated, also, his artistic skills and painted in watercolor.

When in 1949 I introduced Tom, at Yale, to my fiancée, Pat Taylor, she turned to me after he had left the room and said, "That is the most handsome man I have ever laid eyes on." I suppressed my jealousy, and concurred. He was, also, a brilliant student. As an architect, years later, he did wonderfully imaginative work for me, including a subterranean swimming pool which I cheerfully hailed in one of my books as the most beautiful this side of the mosaic pool in Pompeii, which caused my critics to croak forth that I was advertising my own artistic talents, requiring me to rebuke them publicly by saying that I had nothing to do with the pool, except to pay for it: The artistry of it was Tom Hume's, and Robert Goodnough's.

One evening in October 1981, we set out on my sloop at 6 P.M., headed for Newport. We arrived just after 10 the next morning, a heady propulsion. Stamford to Newport, 135 miles in 16 hours. All of nature, wind and tides, colluded to get us there at maximum speed, with a southerly wind, in bright autumn weather. Tom, the expert sailor, had sailed and raced with me from time to time, including one trip to Bermuda. He was always calm, decisive, inquisitive, companionable. But six weeks later he was lying on his back in a hospital bed.

I wrote about that visit in one of my books back then. "The omnicompetent Tulita, having brought up six children," I reported, "had now been working for Channel 13 in New York, but substantially she has become a therapist, wholly confident of Tom's recovery. Tom can't talk, though one has the feeling that he can understand. His eyes are luminous with intelligence, and every now and again he attempts a phrase, but it usually reduces, smiling through his effort, merely to 'shit,' a word, in his frustration, he seems to utter with abandon and security. His right arm is lifeless, and he has been practicing pencil strokes with his left hand. I dumped on him last week a supply of oils, brushes, and crayons. He has not broken them out—probably he is having trouble concentrating. His ambition, Tulita tells me, is to leave the hospital and go directly to the therapeutic center; and from there right back to his desk at the office, say in six months. Let us pray. I told him I had done just that at church, and he didn't say shit, perhaps because he is himself a believer. His uncle founded Canterbury School, his cousin is head of St. David's in New York."

Those hopes were denied. What never altered was the devoted care Tulita gave him. In my lifetime, I have known two women about whom I could say that their pledges to stand by, in sickness and in health, were wholly tested, Tulita Hume and Nancy Reagan.

My wife and I saw the Humes from time to time, and although by now there was no substantial relief in store for Tom, he was always cheerful. He loved to laugh, and he had help from the Lord, whose temple he frequented almost daily, one final time this morning, when we mourn his death, while reaffirming the joy we took from his friendship, commending him to eternal rest, and resolved always to remember him as a most handsome man, in our eyes, and, surely, in the eyes of the Lord. —WFB

Nan Kempner

﹎﹏

(1930–2005)

Nan Kempner was one of Manhattan's most prominent socialites: a leading hostess and philanthropist, patron of the arts, and unabashed diva of the fashion world. Considered by many to have been the model for the "social X-rays" Tom Wolfe anatomized in *Bonfire of the Vanities* (1987)—the too-rich, too-thin women whose Park Avenue parties marked the epicenter of high society—Kempner proudly acknowledged having been one of the first Americans to undergo plastic surgery. Blessed with a slim figure she maintained through rigorous daily exercise, Kempner was a fixture at the premier fashion shows in New York and the capitals of Europe. Yves Saint Laurent proclaimed her *"la plus chic du monde"*; *Vanity Fair* crowned her "the world's most famous clotheshorse." Asked once to define her "look," she replied with characteristic guilelessness: "Artificially relaxed." WFB had known her "rather aloof" husband, the investment banker Thomas Kempner, since 1946, when they had entered Yale as freshmen; Pat Buckley—no slouch in the elite precincts of entertaining, philanthropy, and haute couture—considered Nan, a frequent visitor to the Buckleys' Gstaad chalet, her best friend. "She has," WFB writes here, "no successor."

"Notes & Asides"

National Review, October 24, 2005.
[reprinting WFB's remarks at a memorial service held at Christie's auction house in Manhattan, September 23, 2005]

I thought, apropos of my duties here, to ask myself when did I first meet her, and of course the answer was: I cannot remember. It seemed, on reflection, to be an idle question: When did one not know Nan Kempner? By contrast, her rather aloof husband I could very well remember first encountering. It was at the gymnasium in New Haven, filing through the obstacle course designed to record individual physical weaknesses, so that Yale University could, in pursuit of *corpore sano,* address such problems while simultaneously moving whole landfills designed to remedy our intellectual ignorance. We were freshmen; it was September 1946, fifty-nine years ago.

Tom, I would eventually learn, extruded most of the planted axioms of Yale economics, emerging not only as a conservative, but also as a conservative with something of a sense of mission. I say this because every Christmas I receive, along with 100 other recipients, one or more didactic books from him with a covering letter describing their singularity. You would think that after almost sixty years of companionship, he'd have elected to send around at least one book written by me. On the other hand, I doubt very much that Nan was on this particular gift list, because if she ever expressed a political thought, it was done outside my hearing.

This wasn't owing to any indifference to modern thought or to attempts to undermine it. It was, rather, just one more stroke in pursuit of that otherworldliness which she celebrated and adorned. She'd have made an absolutely superb White Russian. Her eyes were on her family and friends, on their needs and pleasures, and her own. Her delight was in those things that ideology can't really suppress. Who is going to require us to eat badly prepared cuisine? Good food is an embellishment of life, and I first knew from her that what one thought one's own food, she considered common property if she was seated anywhere near you. She wanted to taste it, and her face graphically registered her reactions to it.

She managed all of this year after year, decade after decade, while simultaneously maintaining her famous figure. No dress was ever designed or produced too slender for Nan Kempner to display, causing delight for so many, who marveled at her ability to enhance with her couture any scene at all, and the sense we always had that she *knew* she was bringing pleasure to an entire world, disposed not merely to approve her taste but to marvel at it and at her near-sensual devotion to the art of clothing.

Three years ago she fell ill at our chalet in Switzerland, to which she had invited herself on her entirely well-reasoned assumption that she would be welcome. "I'm coming to you for a week," she would say, and my wife Pat, whom Nan acknowledged, in the essay about her in *Vanity Fair* in April, as her "best" friend, would worry about the possibility that one of the seven evenings ahead would be insufficiently peopled with men and women who would entertain Nan Kempner, or, inconceivable, that someone would fail to be entertained by her.

That winter she stayed many weeks at the Saanen Hospital, which had now become the social center of Gstaad. But eventually she decided to call an end to that season's illness and get back to her obligations to friends and admirers in other capitals of the world. There were a few days there, that winter in Switzerland, when we feared for her survival. Her illness seemed to affect even the snows outside, which gave way to a wet emaciation, discouraging the exercise of the sport she had come to Switzerland to pursue. She was entirely philosophical about this bad turn in the weather, as she had been about the bad turn in her own health. Nan simply did not criticize. She deplored, but did not criticize.

She gave us another three years, living with restrictions which are the legacies of the cigarettes she so much enjoyed, but she did not repine. When finally she left us, the pain was mostly ours, as also the gratitude for her company so kind and generous, so animated and so cheered by life's extravagant endowments. She is greatly missed. She has no successor, but the memory of her is in the minds of the legions she entertained and loved. —WFB

Hugh Kenner

(1923–2003)

A native of Canada who studied under Marshall McLuhan, Hugh Kenner was one of the most revered literary scholars and critics of the twentieth century. *The New York Times*'s Christopher Lehmann-Haupt hailed him as "America's foremost commentator on literary modernism, especially the work of Ezra Pound and James Joyce." WFB's eulogy for Kenner ranks among Buckley's longest, exceeding 2,200 words; it is also rare for its explicit reference to periods of quarreling between them, something Buckley generally avoided mentioning in remembrances of departed friends. This alone speaks to their "very close" bond: WFB served as best man at Kenner's second wedding and as godfather to one of Kenner's seven children. The two men, sometimes with their families in tow, vacationed and sailed together, and Buckley records solemnly: "It was he who introduced me to computers." While keenly appreciative of the "special mind" Kenner possessed, WFB confesses here to occasionally finding his friend's work "dense" and to not always being able to "comprehend it fully"; only on

Firing Line—specifically, the June 28, 1974, episode, Kenner's lone appearance—would American television audiences hear a white-haired academic proffer observations such as: *"Paradise Lost* is very largely an apolitical tract, in which Satan coming back to disrupt the harmony of the new creation is marvelously plausible and attractive because he is modeled on Charles II, who had just done the same thing. . . ."

"Hugh Kenner, R.I.P."

National Review, December 22, 2003.

He died late on November 24, and I had the news of his death early the next day. Mary Anne Kenner was weeping as she spoke, and I wasn't able to hear everything she told me, though I learned that his daughter Lisa, my goddaughter, had been with them, and that father, mother, and daughter had attended Mass the day before.

I called my friend Christopher Lehmann-Haupt on the *New York Times,* but got only his answering service. But he returned my call some time after noon, and called again a few moments later to say that the "desk" at the *Times* demanded an obituary by 6 P.M. Could he prepare an obit on Hugh Kenner in three hours? Impossible! Happily, Lehmann-Haupt had himself reviewed the most famous of the 25 books that Kenner wrote, and was well informed on the enormous impact *The Pound Era* had and continues to have on the literary community. It conferred on Kenner a near-undisputed eminence. The deadline was met, and the next day's paper carried the headline right across the page: "Hugh Kenner, Commentator on Literary Modernism, Pound and Joyce, Is Dead at 80." On Saturday, the *Times* carried a candidly appreciative essay by Benjamin Ivry. The headline here was, "A Critic Whose Scholarship / Gleamed With His Writing." The lead sentence: "Hugh Kenner, who died at 80 at his home in Athens, Ga., this week, was among the finest writers of critical prose in America. He was one of the few commentators whose books and articles cause delight and stand as literary achievements in their own right, including *Gnomon: Essays in Contemporary Literature* (1958); *Dublin's Joyce* (1955); *The Stoic Comedians: Flaubert, Joyce and Beckett* (1964); *The Counterfeiters: An Historical Comedy* (1968), the latter two illustrated by the writer and artist Guy Davenport; *The Pound Era* (1971)."

We were very good friends and, for many years, very close friends (I served as best man at his wedding in 1965 to Mary Anne Bittner, a year after the death of his first wife, Mary Josephine Waite). We had met in the late Fifties by chance—we both had books scheduled for publication by the same publishing firm, McDowell Obolensky. A friendship ripened. He and Mary Jo visited with me in Connecticut, I with them in Santa Barbara; later with him and Mary Anne in Baltimore, still later in Athens. We sailed a half-dozen times on my boat, and when it ran fatally onto the rocks during a hurricane, his grief moved him to an uncharacteristic mode. His threnody spoke of a boat that had "done much for her friends, in the summers before her side was stove in. She had taken them all around the Sound and along the New England coast, and even to Bermuda (thrice), and shown them Wood's Hole, and the Great Fish that eats taffrail logs, and the Kraken, and the strange men of Onset with their long faces, and perfect Edgartown; and lapped them at night gently to rest; and given them the wind and sun and made for them a place of adventure and refreshment and peace; and taught them this, that beyond illusion it is possible to be for hours and days on end perfectly and inexpressibly happy."

Happiness of any kind was sharply interrupted soon after the boat's end when Mary Jo, the mother of five children, contracted cancer, dying in a few months. Hugh recovered with the help of Mary Anne, with whom he would have two more children. He industriously pursued his academic career at the University of California at Santa Barbara, then at Johns Hopkins, and finally at the University of Georgia. "How come you agreed to move to Athens?" I asked him. We spoke to each other with great candor. He answered, in the clinical mode in which he often spoke, that the University of Georgia was seeking academic eminence. "If they want to do that in the field of chemistry or engineering they have to invest 25 million dollars in a new lab. If they want it in the humanities, they can just hire me."

He was happy in Athens, where, he told me, he taught the most talented students he had ever encountered, as also the dumbest. And he was busy worldwide. "It seems that we shall be making our first visit to Spain early in June. They are having a Pound Conference in Barcelona. It fits nicely just before the Joyce Conference in Monaco, which we were scheduled to attend anyway but must leave prematurely to be in Evanston for Lisa's graduation June 16. Any recommendations re Barcelona?" On his 70th birthday at his home, his son Rob and I were summoned as guests to an intimate dinner, marred only by his resolution to quit tobacco.

His sense of his own standing was probably resented by some of his colleagues. Envy is easy to do, but it wasn't easy to dispute his claims to preeminence. When talking about himself—until recent years, always with lit cigarette in hand—he was a singular phenomenon. There was the disordered crown of bushy hair stretching from ear to ear atop a 6-foot-4 frame. Most noticeable was the odd accent. He spoke as though to a computer wired to learn the range of phonemes in the language. To communicate these exactly, the speaker was pronouncing his words with exaggerated clarity. The reason for this oddity was that as a very young child, the son of a schoolmaster in Canada, he was abandoned medically as deaf. His hearing, however, returned, though never wholly. The years of muteness required him to learn to speak afresh, causing that odd exactitude of enunciation. The words came with an astonishing lucidity. He wrote as he spoke, his command of language mesmerizing and awesome. He did not question his powers, or belittle his accomplishments. He managed a look of childlike innocence whenever the subject of his attainments was tangentially raised, much as a prince would react to mention of his bloodline. Anyone questioning it was thought of by everyone, himself included, as simply uninformed.

Not everyone (myself included) has the background to evaluate his scholarship, or even, in the densest of his work, to comprehend it fully, let alone revel in it. His knowledge in his own field was comprehensive, and his use of it, fluent, commanding, and enterprising. We dined once in Switzerland with Charlie Chaplin, and went on to a nightclub. Chaplin was spotted at the door, and the musicians swung immediately into "Terry's Theme" from [the 1952 Chaplin film] *Limelight*. Chaplin acknowledged the greeting by doing a gig from vaudeville. He turned his back to the assembly and squatted down so that all the viewers

could see was his black homburg over the black overcoat.
His head swaying to the beat of the music, he is examining
the window of the art shop, and now he spots the painting
of the naked lady. His interest springs to life and with deft
use of a hidden cane, he appears to elongate to eight feet
tall, the better to appease his appetite. The band played on
as Chaplin sat down at the bar and lectured to Hugh Kenner about comedy. But the next day, pleading preoccupa-
tions, he denied Kenner's petition to spend time with him
at his home in Corsier to elaborate on the subject; Hugh
completed his book (*The Stoic Comedians*) without the benefit of more time with the master.

The range of his interests was extensive. Before deciding
finally to get his doctorate in English (at Yale) he considered mathematics as an alternative discipline. It was he who
introduced me to computers. My own interest was all but
exclusively in the use of the computer as a word processor.
But imposing on his familiarity with the general discipline
and preying on his exposure to sailing, I took to him some
years ago a problem. For the purpose of celestial navigation,
I wanted to be able to take a star sight, or a planet sight,
without knowing what the object was when I shot it and
then, knowing the time of the observation, to identify the
star and establish the exact position of my boat. Such a program would prove very useful for the sailor. Suddenly, at sea,
you spot a little, nubile spark overhead. But perhaps clouds
are moving in. Or perhaps there is overcast, and the star
peeps out at you only for an instant or two. You grab your
sextant and shoot it; then you go below. There you struggle,
not knowing which was the star that bared itself to you. You
fuss with the Star Finder, you diddle with the HO 249 tables,
play out your assumed position. And after ten minutes of

work, maybe fifteen, you say, Er, that ecdysiast star must have been Achenar. Maybe it was—but then maybe it wasn't.

"What did you ask Professor Kenner to do, and by the way, why him?" the editor of *Yachting* asked me.

"To answer the second question first," I replied, "I tapped him because he is a personal friend and was willing to take the 200 hours it required to dope out and write the program. I needed someone who is a whiz with computers; but I also wanted a sworn enemy of clumsy instructional prose. As a supremely gifted writer, Hugh Kenner would devise instructions for WhatStar (catch . . . already . . . the simple beauty of the program's name?) that anyone could read and understand." So to speak.

I concluded the piece for *Yachting* by asking myself with grand condescension a loaded question, and then giving my own confident answer to it: "I am told by the blasé community that the sextant is going out of fashion, that what with Loran in so many parts of the world, and GPS only a season or two away, the sextant is anachronized." My comment: "Yawp. And cigarette lighters will anachronize the match. . . . So, when you next use your sextant, avoid such pains in star identification as are associated with it which are avoidable. And think lovingly of Hugh Kenner when you use WhatStar." Twenty years after Hugh Kenner devised WhatStar, the Naval Academy stopped teaching celestial navigation to its students.

He wrote often, always by e-mail when that became possible, and always brightly. He was generous to friends with whom I involved him, while never compromising the remove he felt as a teacher with definitive things to say. There was sometimes a trace of impatience when he suspected sluggishness at the other end. He once addressed me so abruptly—I had not carried out a particular instruction, and so confused Antares with Saturn—that I felt the need to rebuke him. I did this by failing to acknowledge two or three of his missives; all of that was quickly repaired.

His dismissive skills were not retired. I introduced him to a regular correspondent, an elderly man who managed to feign an office job while spending his entire time reading books and writing letters. Charles Wallen had remarked, reprovingly, my use of a word he thought arcane. I defended the word and forwarded his complaint to Kenner, our mutual friend. Kenner wrote him,

Dear Charles:

Bill's point is precisely that there is no substitute for "solipsism." If what pains you about it is simply the fact that you seldom hear it, then the fault is not in the man who grinds it against your ears, but in the millions of part-time and largely inadvertent solipsists who are so convinced the universe emanates from them that they feel no need of a word to designate such a condition. Fish, on the same principle, know nothing of water and for aqueous terminology you should not apply to a fish.

If on the other hand your ears are assaulted by its impacted sibilants (as the ears of Tennyson were aggrieved by the word "scissors") then I can only fetch you the cold comfort that for a graceless condition the wisdom inherent in the language has afforded us a graceless word. And if, finally, your grievance is that Bill uses it too often, then I can only tax you with inconsistency, since you report that after one to two years of not hearing it from his lips you were wounded anew by a single occurrence—perhaps, I will grant, on the principle of a man who has been sensitized

*to penicillin. Such a man's comfort should be that others need the
remedy that inflames him, and that principle I commend to you.*

Hugh Kenner

Some years ago I felt a lessening in his concerns for me
and for my world, his interventions in it having reduced
sharply. Our exchanges dwindled, and there came a total
end to his long, disquisitional letters about this and that.
I felt the possibility of Alzheimer's lurking in that special
mind. But he never forgot to remind me of the anniversary
of his wedding, in which I had served as best man. And he
nursed something of a fixation on *National Review Online*'s
posting of the word-of-the-day. If that day's word was missing, he would complain to me. The letter might be only a
sentence long. Always he closed his letters, as he had done
for forty years, "Ever affectionately." I would always reply in
equivalent language, while knowing that this remarkable
intellect, and friend, was slipping away, as he did on my
78th birthday, in the arms of his beloved wife. —WFB

Allard Lowenstein

◆ ～ ◆

(1929–1980)

Ninety days before he was shot to death in his Manhattan office by a deranged acquaintance, Allard Lowenstein, the former New York congressman, made his ninth appearance on *Firing Line*. "What is 'the Left'?" he asked. "I think that there's a laziness on the part of some people—left or right, whatever those labels mean—in selective denunciations." Bespectacled and nebbishy, Lowenstein worked fearlessly to advance liberal and humanitarian causes. He documented South African apartheid, prodded Eugene McCarthy to challenge LBJ in the 1968 Democratic primary, and, as head of Americans for Democratic Action, made the Nixon White House "enemies list" by urging impeachment in 1971—a year before Watergate—over Vietnam. His gift for "transideological" bonding matched WFB's own. "Who but Al Lowenstein," Ted Kennedy asked at the funeral service where WFB delivered the eulogy below, "could claim among his best friends both Bill Buckley and Robert Kennedy?"

"Allard Lowenstein, RIP"

Remarks at memorial service for Allard Lowenstein, Central Synagogue,
Manhattan, March 18, 1980; published in *National Review,* April 4, 1980.

Possibly, as a dissenter, my own experience with him was
unique, in that we conservatives did not generally endorse
his political prescriptions. So that we were, presumptively,
opponents of Al Lowenstein, in those straitened chambers in which we spend, and misspend, so much of our
lives. It was his genius that so many of those he touched—
generally, arriving a half hour late—discovered intuitively
the underlying communion. He was, in our time, the original activist, such was his impatience with the sluggishness
of justice; so that his rhythms were more often than not dis-
harmonious with those that govern the practical, banausic
councils of this world. His habits were appropriately disar-
rayed. He was late to breakfast, to his appointments; late
in announcing his sequential availability for public service.
He was punctual only in registering (though often under-
age) for service in any army that conceived itself bound to
righteousness.

How did he live such a life, so hectic with public concern, while preoccupying himself so fully with individual
human beings: whose torments, never mind their singularity, he adopted as his own, with the passion that some give
only to the universal? Eleanor Roosevelt, James Burnham
once mused, looked on all the world as her personal slum
project. Although he was at home with collectivist formulations, one had the impression of Allard Lowenstein that he
might be late in aborting a Third World War—because of

his absorption with the problems of one sophomore. Oh, they followed him everywhere; because we experienced in him the essence of an entirely personal dedication. Of all the partisans I have known, from the furthest steppes of the spectrum, his was the most undistracted concern, not for humanity—though he was conversant with big-think idiom—but with human beings.

Those of us who dealt with him (often in those narrow passages constrained by time-clocks and fire-laws and deadlines) think back ruefully on the happy blend of purpose and carelessness with which he arranged his own career and his own schedule. A poet might be tempted to say, "If only the Lord had granted us that Allard should also have arrived late at his own assassination!"

But all his life he was felled by mysteries, dominant among them those most readily understood by more worldly men—namely, that his rhythms were not of this world. His days, foreshortened, lived out the secular dissonances. "Behold, Thou hast made my days as it were a span long: and mine age is even as nothing in respect of Thee; and verily every man living is altogether vanity." The psalmist spoke of Al, on Friday last—"I became dumb, and opened not my mouth; for it was Thy doing." To those not yet dumb, the psalmist also spoke, saying, "The Lord is close to the brokenhearted; and those who are crushed in spirit. He saves." Who was the wit who said that Nature abhors a vacuum? Let Nature then fill this vacuum. That is the challenge which, bereft, the friends of Allard Lowenstein hurl up to Nature, and to Nature's God, prayerfully, demandingly, because today. Lord, our loneliness is great.

David Niven

(1910–1983)

For six weeks each year, Pat and Bill Buckley decamped to their chalet in Gstaad, Switzerland, where WFB would knock out one of his spy thrillers between skiing runs and dinners with friends. The Buckleys' Swiss social circle overlapped with their New York set, but Gstaad and the friends who vacationed there annually, as the Buckleys did, held special significance for them. One such friend, on the slopes and for hours on end in the converted playroom where WFB set up a painting studio, was the Scottish-born actor and novelist David Niven. A veteran of the British Army in World War II, Niven was slight of build and dashing of mustache, good company and a lively wit. He appeared in more than 100 plays and films, including *Around the World in Eighty Days* (1956), *Separate Tables* (1958)—for which Niven won the Academy Award for best actor—*Please Don't Eat the Daisies* (1960), *The Guns of Navarone* (1961), *Casino Royale* (1967), and several installments of the Pink Panther franchise. Niven also published two best-selling memoirs of Hollywood's Golden Age, *The Moon's a Balloon* (1971) and

Bring on the Empty Horses (1975), the latter of which, in a *New York Times* review, WFB hailed as "a masterful self-portrait." Across two decades of friendship, Buckley delighted in Niven's storytelling. In a 1991 article on gift giving published in *Playboy,* WFB recounted the tale Niven told of a 1940s Christmas spent, as a recent widower, sharing an apartment with fellow Hollywood star Errol Flynn, a recent divorcé. As the holiday approached, the two decided not to open the pile of wrapped gifts they had received but to replace each label and card addressed to them with one *from* them to another recipient. "A tidy operation," WFB wrote, "except that [MGM studio chief] L. B. Mayer received from Flynn a silver cigarette case on which was engraved, TO DAVID NIVEN, FROM HIS DEAR FRIEND, L. B. MAYER." For his eulogy, published as a column and again in *National Review,* WFB drew heavily on an earlier essay, about ten of his best friends; the portion of that essay relating to Niven is reprinted here in its entirety.

———◆———

Excerpted from "10 Friends," *Forbes FYI,* September 2000.

The first time. . . . On the telephone was John Kenneth Galbraith. He had under his wing Jacqueline Kennedy, who was trying to get a week's vacation, skiing. It had been more than three years since the assassination but she was followed everywhere and now Professor Galbraith had undertaken her protection, and looked out, too, for her social life. Did I want to join them for dinner at the chalet of David Niven and his wife Hjordis?

That's when I met him. He was a radiant host, attentive to every need and whim; indeed after a while my wife (who became, arguably, his closest friend) suspected that his magic was to induce a whim, so that he could gratify it.

What Jackie most needed, during that extended period of shock, was to laugh. Making people laugh was a specialty of his. I remember the evening with him years later in Monaco. We'd have drinks in the palace with Prince Rainier and then dinner at a restaurant as guests of David Niven.

There was one problem. We had hit Rainier in one of his grumpy moods. That kind of situation was, for old friend and neighbor David Niven, a challenge.

Waiting for the first course to arrive, David launched into an autobiographical account of his seduction at age fifteen by an accomplished lady of the night. He imitated sundry accents. The words spoken were lightly ribald, amusing, evocative. Before the second course was served, the prince was a rollicking companion. In Niven's company, nobody had a *chance* to live very long as a wallflower.

He continued, in the eighteen years of our friendship, to make movies, of uneven quality, but his life was heavily involved in domestic traffic. He would drive his two little girls to school and bring them back to their chalet after skiing in the late morning. Every two or three days he would come to our place, with its huge playroom, one half of it my writing quarters, the other half an improvised studio built around a ping-pong table.

He was greatly skilled, and seldom spoke during the hour or two he devoted to the canvas at hand. His six paintbrushes were carefully positioned in his left hand. He washed and cleaned them meticulously and proudly recalled that he had bought them in his earliest days in Hollywood, even before his first wife was killed in that crazy accident playing hide-and-seek. In the last winter he came over to paint more frequently, because what he mostly didn't want, at that point, was to have to talk: His disease

(Lou Gehrig's) was creeping up on him and it was a strain to talk through its strangulations. He would just come, set up his paints and leave after about an hour because, he explained to me, the turpentine fumes soon overcame him.

I remember one afternoon, coming back from skiing to go to work. He was there with his paintbrushes and hailed me. He wanted to tell me something.

His face choked up with laughter. It was hard to make out what he was saying, but I managed. He had been in his car when stopped by the red light in Gstaad. An old friend who knew nothing about the illness was coincidentally stopped opposite him, headed in the other direction.

He leaned out the window. "What have you got?" he asked David.

"I tried to get out to him," he had a problem with the words, "that I had amytrophic lateral sclerosis. He could hear me well enough but couldn't make out what I said. He yelled back just as the light changed. 'Oh? Well I've got a Lamborghini 500S!'" It hurt David to laugh, and that was the truly unbearable burden.

Warren Steibel

(1925–2002)

The most overlooked figure in the story of William F. Buckley—his way with words, his good looks, his multimedia celebrity, the long reach of his influence—was Warren Steibel: producer of virtually every episode of *Firing Line*. From my 2000 interview:

ROSEN: Which was more important in advancing conservatism, and bringing it to where it is today: the forming of *National Review* or *Firing Line*?

WFB: Well, there's an eleven-year difference. *National Review* began in 1955, *Firing Line* in 1966. I think that *Firing Line* had enormous influence in suggesting to people—who were alert to the question—that liberals weren't simply dispositively correct on all issues, because they all appeared on *Firing Line* and were contested. Now it had, of course, a much, much larger audience, television does, than a magazine. But probably the staying power of an essay in a magazine, or a column every week for a few years, has a greater resonance. It's an interesting question; I've never pondered it before.

The fact that Buckley couldn't rule out that *Firing Line* was his most influential vehicle spoke to the centrality of Steibel to his life. Peers in age, the two were otherwise a study in opposites: Where WFB was Catholic, conservative, lean, elegant, and patrician, Steibel was Jewish, liberal, pudgy, and volatile. What they shared was a love of laughter and a commitment to high standards. Where WFB's aim was ideological, Steibel's was to produce good TV—and each reveled in the other's contribution to the winning alchemy that made *Firing Line* an Emmy winner and the longest-running single-host talk show in TV history (1966–1999). For Steibel that meant booking interesting guests; lighting, wiring, and shooting them correctly; fostering lively discussion; and—it must be said—herding cats, of which the largest, and dearest to the producer, was the host. How poorer we are for the absence of a Steibel memoir! That the man who knew most intimately how Bill Buckley approached the making of thirty years of iconic television never talked about it, never wrote an account of it, leaves *Firing Line* at once the most public and well-documented segment of WFB's professional life and the most obscure and unchronicled. Theirs was a genial two-man conspiracy, a long-running buddy movie that was equal parts *Butch Cassidy and the Sundance Kid* and *The Odd Couple*. The closing lines of this brief yet deeply moving eulogy show how hard WFB took the loss.

"Warren Steibel, R.I.P."

National Review, January 28, 2002.

Warren Steibel, producer, friend, character, died on January 3 in New York Hospital after a miserable week. The cause of death was cancer.

Warren's offices were at *National Review,* an arrangement that began when he took over the production of *Firing Line,* a few months after its launching in April 1966. Neal Freeman, sometime Washington correspondent for *NR,* had at age 24 acted as de facto producer, but left town to work out his destiny in Washington, where he thrives. Steibel, age 40—disheveled, corpulent, dogged in his views about how the program should be produced—came to us after having done work with Andy Rooney at CBS, as also with others at NBC and ABC. *Firing Line* was still something of a problematic enterprise—its original commission, by RKO, had been for 13 weeks, and it was running on its second or third renewal when Steibel took it over.

That seems many years ago, because it was. Warren had produced a movie, *The Honeymoon Killers,* which is now recognized as something of an art classic. He took time, that summer of 1966, to do an hour's documentary featuring Nancy Reagan, whose husband was running for governor of California. In the ensuing 35 years, he dabbled in sundry enterprises, but until *Firing Line* ended, with the millennium, he gave it most of his time. After we closed shop, he continued his fascination for exchanges of opinion with a program called *DebatesDebates,* the singular feature of which is the absence of a referee. His manner, in approaching guests to appear, was forthright. I don't really know at first hand what techniques he used over the telephone, but it seemed to me that everyone whose last name was other than Kennedy or Rockefeller acceded to his invitations, or importunities. He was unique, and unforgettable; stern as regarded duties, but enormously thoughtful in small ways (he never made me appear at the studio more than 15 minutes before air time). He made thorough and fruitful use of his assistants, first Paul Sweeney and then George Kahookele. Every now and then he had a quite extraordinary fit of temper, one of which, coming in in medias res, I witnessed, wondering that the object of it would ever speak to him again, let alone continue to work with him.

But everybody stayed friends with Warren Steibel. His extravagant kindnesses, his comprehensive seizures of laughter, his love of the races and of the casinos, of music and opera, roped everybody in. He liked to tell journalists (he won an Emmy award for *Firing Line*) that he was a dedicated liberal, notwithstanding his prolonged exposures to alien thought (1,504 episodes of *Firing Line,* 45 *Firing Line* debates). I never challenged him (or cared, really). I was never entirely convinced that his liberalism was anything more than attitudinal.

What mattered was the sense of substance one had in associating with him. His was a very large presence, and when he died, there was stillness at *National Review* that day, the measure of a true sense of loss.

Charles Wallen

◆━━◆

(1920–1997)

In July 1972, a writer named Charles Wallen debuted in *NR* with an article titled "Hoffa—Baptized," arguing that the civil rights of former Teamsters leader Jimmy Hoffa had been "trampled all over" by Attorney General Robert F. Kennedy and that the restrictive terms President Nixon set when he commuted Hoffa's prison sentence in December 1971—forbidding him from engaging in any union activities until 1980—were "cruel and unusual." The article's byline noted only that its author "has been in the trucking business for thirty-five years." How did such a person, his background so unusual for an opinion journal, come to write for *National Review*? The previous year, Wallen had met WFB during the latter's visit to San Francisco for a speech before bank executives; their friendship would extend twenty-six years, until Wallen's death. It took the form of infrequent get-togethers, WFB's gift to the older man of a dog, and a correspondence so regular, extensive, and heartfelt, so marked by what WFB called "Biblical lyricism," that it plunges the reader—even when sampled in small doses, as in

WFB's eulogy—into melancholy. It is noteworthy that Buckley accepts the description of himself as Wallen's "best friend" without any nod toward reciprocity; however, the length and tone of the eulogy surely reflect WFB's love for the man, and equally noteworthy is that it is the loss of Wallen that sets Buckley to ruminating, for the first time, on his reasons for publishing eulogies of personal friends unknown to the general public: namely, to wring "catharsis" from "pain."

"Charles Wallen, RIP"

National Review, January 26, 1998.

Most of our friends aren't listed in directories that record eminence. When the loss is of a public figure, public attention is expected, and obituaries are published and read. But of course the pain is no less when the death is that of a personal and private friend. Then there is no catharsis, no public or semipublic mourning, no public tributes. The consolation, in this corner of *National Review,* is the accessibility of this page. I have treated it, over the years, most exploitatively—as something akin to personal property; yet always aware that its longevity depends entirely on its capacity to engage your interest. From time to time I use my half-acre of space to recall a friendship purely personal, as I do now, on learning of the death of Charles Wallen, Jr.

Three days after he died I had a letter from Bill Gillen, of Novato, California, whom I've never met. He wrote of his own grief and added, "I am writing to you because I know you were his best friend, and I know that because he told me so in his last letter."

It was so, I am honored to reflect. Charles died at

seventy-seven in San Mateo, just out from San Francisco; silver-haired, slightly stooped, quick to laugh and smile, engrossed in whatever book he was reading. When did we meet?

> I was thinking this morning about one of your trips to San Francisco in 1971 . . . 26 years ago. I had joined you in your suite at the St. Francis Hotel and you had been engaged to speak before a meeting of Bank of America employees and there were several hundred of them there. . . . Then we went on to Trader Vic's and had a happy lunch. Memories— memories—you have provided me with so many happy memories over the years.

Charles Wallen was a purebred American whose interests were books, letters, and friends. He spent the great body of his time reading and rereading his books, which he stored in the huge cellar in his house in Millbrae, overlooking the airport at San Francisco and the surrounding hills and mountains. He was born in Tennessee, wandered about the country, and settled down for most of his professional life in San Francisco as a minor executive in a trucking company. His friends never knew what exactly he did for the DiSalvo Company, and we assumed, I'd guess correctly, that DiSalvo was not much more for him than the office where he worked to provide for his wife and three sons and to gain the leisure time to read his books and write his letters to his friends.

He wrote tenaciously, but I have to suppose that he wrote most often to me, as the laws of time & space make it unlikely that there are others who received two or three letters from Charles Wallen every week for 27 years. And this on top of the memoirs he began a few years ago. "The narrative goes on now way beyond the 1,214,000 words I mentioned to you last month. . . ." That would be about three times the length of *Gone with the Wind*.

Who did he write to? Everyone who interested him or caught his attention.

> I have just bought a copy of Father Patrick Samway's (S.J.) biography of Walker Percy. He mentions you on pages 302 and 303. I watched that *Firing Line* with Walker and Eudora Welty. I started writing to Walker in 1980 and we corresponded till his death in 1990. Once he sent me his privately published little book *Bourbon,* which is hilarious. What a blow he dealt to the 1960s with *Love in the Ruins.*

The Walker Percys of this world (as if they were a breed) don't maintain correspondence with listless minds or boring writers. It was so with others, some of whom I had introduced Charles to.

> Got a note from Tom Wolfe last week. He said he was doing OK. Also am rereading David Niven's two autobiographical works and enjoying them. We corresponded from 1972 when I met him with you until his death. He called me on his last trip to SF. . . .

> [Again:] I carried on some correspondence with [Malcolm] Muggeridge in the '70s and '80s & I think I have all his books . . .

> [A week or two later:] . . . Got a note from Tom Wolfe last week. He said he was doing OK.

He sometimes circulated answers elicited by his letter-writing, even when one such left him bloody. He was well and truly zonked by the fearful Hugh Kenner's reply to his complaint about my use of a word:

> I looked in your *Right Word* book for *solipsism* first &
> found it on page 427. In April 1973 Hugh Kenner
> wrote me about this word. You had written me that if
> I could find a substitute you would stop using it. Part
> of Hugh's letter: "Dear Charles:
>   ". . . But Bill's point is precisely that there is no
> substitute for 'solipsism.' If what pains you about it
> is simply the fact that you seldom hear it, then the
> fault is not in the man who grinds it against your
> ears, but in the millions of part-time and largely
> inadvertent solipsists who are so convinced the
> universe emanates from them that they feel no need
> of a word to designate such a condition. Fish, on
> the same principle, know nothing of water, and for
> aqueous terminology you should not apply to a fish."

Hugh Kenner, having gone this far, did not stop, and Charles, though presumably chastened, did not mute the full thunder of the closing lines:

> "If on the other hand your ears are assaulted by
> its impacted sibilants (as the ears of Tennyson
> were aggrieved by the word 'scissors') then I can
> only fetch you the cold comfort that for a graceless
> condition the wisdom inherent in the language has
> afforded us a graceless word. And if, finally, your
> grievance is that Bill uses it too often, then I can
> only tax you with inconsistency, since you report that

after one to two years of not hearing it from his lips
you were wounded anew by a single occurrence—
perhaps, I will grant, on the principle of a man
who has been sensitized to penicillin. Such a man's
comfort should be that others need the remedy that
inflames him, and that principle I commend to you.
Hugh Kenner."

Charles loved it. Stylistic grace enlivened him, though
his taste was not for the rococo, but for witty plain-
spokenness. His own literary opinions were emphatic.

In the [San Francisco] *Chronicle* this morning we had
the story of the death of William Burroughs. Patricia
Holt [the book editor] writes of it on the front page
and mentions Allen Ginsberg, his former lover, as
well as Richard Brautigan & Kurt Vonnegut. Happily
I have only an embroidered recollection of them. I
would not trade Jack London's *The Sea Wolf* for the
whole lot. Will they be remembered? I doubt it . . . I
am so shocked by some of the revelations of Pamela
[Harriman] that I can scarcely lay the book down.

Charles's health problems were recurrent, but he was
fatalistic. He had been an alcoholic, he once told me, but
he had quit drinking before I met him and seemed entirely indifferent to the absence of wine. But he persevered
with his small cigars, and was amused by medical proscrip-
tions. . . .

Bill: I noticed some other things the health freaks
forbid: STEAK, EGGS, SALT-CURED COUNTRY
HAM, SUGAR, TEA, COFFEE, COCA-COLA,

BACON—SO watch out for these dangerous items.
My cousin Joe Wallen of Johnson City, Tennessee,
about every 3 months sends me a good supply
of SALT-CURED COUNTRY HAM and several
packages of GRITS. When I was growing up at Kyles
Ford, Tennessee, my father raised Poland China
hogs—they were enormous . . . in the 600-pound
bracket. Hog-killing was a day I dreaded but we had
the year round plenty of SALT-CURED COUNTRY
HAM.

Tom Wendel, a historian and friend, recently examined the subterranean library. Charles, he reported, had
an ampler store of Mark Twain than anyone else this side
of a public library. The Tennessee of the young Charles
was Deep South country, where his cultural memories ger-
minated.

Going through some of my old family papers I was
reminded that my mother's family had slaves, and
several of them (after they were freed in 1863)
elected to stay on at my grandfather's farm and were
still there when Mama was married in 1900. My
paternal grandfather's family also owned slaves. One
was sold in 1850 for $800.00. But I probably have
told you this before. [He hadn't. But now his mind
turned, as so often it did, to his endless thankfulness
for all that went well.] . . . Not a day passes that I do
not think of all the things you have done for me over
the last 27 years. I am grateful.

Perhaps the Southern culture had something to do
with his rooted devotion to his family, to the pleasures of

literature, and the benefactions of his friends. I gave him a
puppy years ago, a Cavalier King Charles whom he named
Tres.

> I sent them [his cousins] a picture of you, me, and
> Tres taken in January 1983 . . . only three months
> after you sent me Tres on 8 October 1982. This was
> the most precious gift of my life. Tres has been gone
> to Heaven 43 months and 9 days today.

His sadness over the dog's death ("the doggie's death,"
I'd have phrased it if talking to Charles) was severe. He had
his melancholy moments, and I mentioned them once, in
talking with him.

> You quote Chesterton on page 158 [of my book.
> *Nearer, My God*] that despair is a sin, and years ago
> you quoted that to me when I came by the Hilton
> Hotel at the airport at 7 A.M. to pick you up. I was
> down . . . and then you cheered me up . . . I never
> thought of despair again.

There was never a favor done to Charles that was unre-
membered, uncelebrated. A few weeks ago he dispatched a
handwritten note to Frances Bronson in my office. "I still
love you, Frances, and will never forget your taking me to
Paone's for lunch in 1971, 26 years ago, and you picked up
the check. You are a darling. Regards, Charles."

The above are fragments of mail received from him in
the past three months. It would be a vigorous semester's
work to go through the bank of letters I have from him.
He maintained in so many of them a metrical cadence that
rang through with Biblical lyricism. As in the final sentence

of one letter a fortnight ago when he spoke of a projected visit sometime in the near future. You must come, he said. "We will sit out on the porch and discuss with light frivolity the meaning of glimpses dimly seen as in twilight." RIP, Charles Wallen, 1920–1997. —WFB

NEMESES

Alger Hiss

(1904–1996)

In 1955, one of the first articles Alger Hiss published after his release from prison—still denying he had been a Soviet spy, rejecting the perjury conviction that had so exposed him in one of the century's great political and courtroom dramas—was a spirited defense, in *Pocket Book* magazine, of Yalta. As a young State Department official, when he was actively spying against America, Hiss had helped organize the February 1945 conference at which the Allies divided up postwar Europe. Buckley, in an unsigned editorial in the very first issue of *National Review,* was incredulous; why hadn't the editors of *Pocket Book,* in their lengthy editor's note, mentioned anything about the author's treachery? Wasn't it pertinent? Buckley also seized on the moment in *Pocket Book* when Hiss conceded, "Soviet ascendancy in Eastern Europe has been dismaying to *many.*" "A Freudian slip," WFB declared, "if ever we saw one!" As for all politically conscious Americans in the twentieth century, the Hiss case, for Buckley, was foundational: How you assessed the clashing testimony of Hiss, the fallen golden boy of New Deal Democrats, and his chief accuser,

Whittaker Chambers, the rumpled ex-communist who produced
the State Department microfilm that helped convict Hiss—not to
mention the role of Richard Nixon, the young congressman who
doggedly pursued Hiss—immediately placed you on the ideological
spectrum, defined you, marked you for life. As the dominant news
story of Buckley's twenties, Hiss–Chambers propelled him into the
controversial arts—and he stayed with it for the rest of his career.
This included rebutting each new book or appeal from Hiss after he
left prison; hiring Chambers at *National Review* and publishing their
correspondence [*Odyssey of a Friend: Whittaker Chambers' Letters to
William F. Buckley, Jr., 1954–1961* (1969)]; defending the Hiss verdict
after Watergate ("To establish that Nixon was guilty of an impropri-
ety," wrote Buckley, "is not the equivalent of establishing that Hiss
was innocent"); and heralding the publication of *Perjury: The Hiss-
Chambers Case* (1978), the groundbreaking study by the historian
Allen Weinstein, whose access to declassified FBI files enabled him
to array, overwhelmingly, the evidence of Hiss's guilt. The fact that
The Nation and other liberal enclaves never admitted the obvious led
Buckley to sigh in 1980: "It all approaches neurosis."

"Alger Hiss, RIP"

National Review, December 9, 1996.

Those of us involved, however indirectly, in the Hiss case
waited with some curiosity to see how his death would be
handled in the paper of record, the *New York Times.* The
story was written by Janny Scott, and curiosity was justified.
The headline on page 1:

ALGER HISS, DIVISIVE ICON OF COLD WAR,
DIES AT 92

And, on the jump page, border to border,

ALGER HISS, WHOSE SPY CASE BECAME A
SYMBOL OF THE COLD WAR, IS DEAD AT 92

The reader had to wait until the sixth paragraph to be informed that Hiss "was convicted of perjury." The ensuing 68 paragraphs were given over to detailing both sides of the question on Alger Hiss. The writer did record the brief appearances on the scene of the Soviet general (Volkogonov) whose nonchalant statement (prompted by a Hiss devotee) to the effect that the KGB files had no evidence that Hiss had served as a Soviet agent had done an overnight facelift on the tatterdemalion Hiss loyalists. The general went on to divulge a few weeks later that he hadn't examined all the files. And yes, the *Times* story recorded all the legal appeals Hiss had made and lost; it informed the readers that biographer Allen Weinstein had begun his scholarly book on the case thinking Hiss innocent, but then changed his views as his research progressively undermined, and then collapsed, the Hiss case.

But the reader is left to conclude, after reading the long article, that in fact what we have here is nothing more than that some say tomato, some say tomahto. Indeed, we were specifically invited to think of it as in the category of the assassination of Kennedy and the murder of O. J. Simpson's wife and her friend. Some people say Oswald did it, and did it alone. Some people think O. J. did it; some, including the jurors, think he didn't do it. One wonders how the headlines would have read in 1935. "Alfred Dreyfus, Divisive Icon of Pre-War France, Dies at 76." "Alfred Dreyfus, Whose Spy Case Became a Symbol of French Confusion, Is Dead at 76."

.   .   .

The final paragraphs in the long story read: "Looking back, those who believe that Mr. Hiss was not guilty insisted he would never have accepted their support all those years had he not been telling the truth. In his long insistence, they found final proof. They said he had lived his life like an innocent man.

"As William F. Buckley, Jr., the founder of *National Review*, who viewed Whittaker Chambers as a moral hero and never doubted Hiss's guilt, put it recently: 'It's probably understandable that he would feel that he had let too many people down.' "

Back then, senior editors of *National Review*—James Burnham, Frank Meyer, Willi Schlamm, Priscilla Buckley—felt a personal involvement in the Hiss case, first as champions of Whittaker Chambers, later as colleagues. He came to *National Review* as a senior editor in 1957, arriving regularly in New York on fortnightly Mondays, until illness got the better of him (he died in July 1961). When Hiss was released from prison in 1954, the counteroffensive came in full thunder—legal appeals, books by his own hand, others by his sympathizers. The appeals failed, one after another, and the books were, one after another, overwhelmed. The forthcoming biography of Chambers by Sam Tanenhaus (a main selection of the Book-of-the-Month Club for April) will quiet anyone who has a remaining doubt.

Should there be such?

No, not really. Miss Scott of the *New York Times* was right to wonder why Mr. Hiss persisted in affirming his innocence. His supporters had the most obvious answer: To affirm one's innocence is what an innocent person does. My observation to the *New York Times* was to the effect that there is the other explanation, namely that Alger Hiss didn't want to let down his old dogged, loyal followers.

But there is a third explanation for his surviving followers, which is that, in silence, they came first to doubt, then to disbelieve; but pride kept them in the Hiss camp. To have crossed that aisle would have been to acknowledge a weakness of mind or of character. Some years ago, exasperated by yet one more curtain call taken in his magazine by a Hiss trouper, I wrote to the editor (an acquaintance) and told him I would send him or his charity one thousand simoleons if he would submit to a truth test whose findings documented that he truly believed Hiss innocent. He changed the subject.

Pride could account for the loyalty of the followers. But what, other than reciprocal loyalty, might account for Hiss's persistence?

There remains the reasoning of Nikolai Bukharin. In 1957, Chambers wrote me that he had been pondering two quotations. The second "is from Bukharin's last words [in 1938] to the court which condemned him to death. I do not understand how men, knowing that, in our own lifetime, another man spoke these words at such a moment, can read them and fail to be rent apart by their meanings. Yet these words are scarcely known. I would print them bold and hang them at the front of college classrooms, not to be explained as a text, but to be seen often and quietly reflected on. Bukharin, it must be remembered, is literally innocent [of the crimes imputed to him by Stalin]. . . . It is his uncommitted crime that he pleads guilty to. He said: 'I shall now speak of myself, of the reasons for my repentance. . . . For when you ask yourself: If you must die, what are you dying for?—an absolutely black vacuity suddenly rises before you with startling vividness. There was nothing to die for if one wanted to die unrepentant. This, in the end, disarmed me completely and led me to bend my knees before the Party and the country. . . . At such moments, Citizen Judges, everything personal, all personal incrustation, all rancor, pride, and a number of other things, fall away, disappear. I am about to finish. I am perhaps speaking for the last time in my life.'

"Is there not a stillness in the room," Chambers closed, "where you read this? That is the passing of the wings of tragedy."

I have from time to time thought that one measure of Alger Hiss as a man should never be overlooked. It is that he won the devotion of Whittaker Chambers, who knew him as friend and fellow conspirator. By continuing to plead not guilty, Alger Hiss was performing for his faith the same sacrifice Bukharin made by pleading guilty. —WFB

John V. Lindsay

❧

(1921–2000)

The first mention of John V. Lindsay in the pages of *National Review*, in May 1960, described him as "the young engaging, and intelligent congressman from New York"—but it went downhill from there. The unsigned editorial, which exhibited some of WFB's comic touch, mocked Lindsay's "bright idea" of establishing a cabinet-level Department of Urban Affairs (an idea adopted, in the form of the Council for Urban Affairs, by the Nixon White House). "Such a department could handle... relations between Chicago and Detroit (they have been very bad lately), and the smog problem over Los Angeles—you know that kind of thing," the editorial said, heaping scorn on JVL for "cutting right through all the deadwood notions about municipal government [and] state authority... by the Neanderthal Right." Thus was Lindsay, a liberal Republican with a Yale education and chiseled good looks, branded a heretic in the burgeoning conservative movement. WFB's campaign for mayor of New York City in 1965, on the Conservative Party ticket, was organized explicitly to blunt the forward progress of Lindsay. This derived neither from animus nor from obsession—WFB's brother, Jim, was a close friend of Lindsay's twin brother, David, and WFB noted drily that in the years preceding the campaign "I managed to go whole months at a time without thinking of John Lindsay"—but rather from the affront WFB regarded Lindsay as posing, by virtue of his posing as a Republican, to the foundations of American politics. "Lindsay is a Republican largely as a matter of baptismal affirmation," WFB wrote in *The Unmaking of a Mayor* (1966). "Lindsay's voting record, and his general political pronouncements, put him left of the center of the Democratic Party. As such he is an embarrassment to the two-party system." The record reflects no rapprochement between the two men save the "wan smile" WFB detected on his opponent's face when, during their televised debate, Buckley quipped that Lindsay could repay the great sense of obligation he was always saying he felt to New York by withdrawing from public life. Lindsay, of course, won, although WFB captured an impressive 13.6 percent of the vote, and vindication raced to Buckley's door swiftly and often: four years later, when JVL lost the Republican nomination for reelection, returning to office on the Liberal ticket; when JVL ultimately reregistered as a Democrat, only to see his electoral viability evaporate; and by Gotham's dismal arc. In *The Ungovernable City* (2001), Vincent J. Cannato reported that during Lindsay's mayoralty, the city's murder rate soared by 137 percent; its incidence of rape by 112 percent; assault, 64 percent; robberies, 209 percent; and car thefts, 84 percent; and that the percentage of New Yorkers receiving public assistance rose by an astonishing 16.4 percent *per year.* The fact that other major cities experienced similar trends provided little solace; even less so Gotham's slide into fiscal default, which prompted Buckley, in 1977, to reissue *The Unmaking of a Mayor,* stamping its cover with the words *VINDICATION EDITION.* WFB's two-paragraph eulogy is one of his shortest; his struggle to find *some*thing good to say remains palpable; his success, commendable.

"John Lindsay, RIP"

National Review, January 22, 2001.

John Lindsay died many years after history was done with him. In the late Fifties and in the Sixties he was the primary young star of liberal Republicanism. He edged into victory as mayor of New York and harbinger of enlightened Republicanism in a race in which Conservative Party candidate William F. Buckley resonantly cleared his throat, challenging Mr. Lindsay's political agenda and insisting that in the order of political reality, he belonged not with Republican gatekeepers of overweening government, but with Democrats. Four years later he lost the Republican nomination and ran (and won) on the Liberal ticket. Two years after that he left the GOP and joined the Democrats, who, however, discouraged his presidential bid. In 1980, he came in third in another bid, to win the Democratic nomination for senator.

What went wrong? An agenda, on questions of race and education and security, that didn't take hold because New York City had mundane concerns which weren't met by high rhetoric about welfare and racial integration and obligations by Albany and Washington to oblige Mr. Lindsay's extravagances. His departure from the political scene was soon followed by a dismal series of enervating and awful illnesses which he fought bravely, and from which, finally, he was relieved in late December, at his home in Hilton Head, South Carolina. He was a dashing figure who'd have done better as a star than as a tribune. And he always, or nearly always, gave theatrical satisfaction, and that's not something to be lightly dismissed. —WFB

Ayn Rand

(1905–1982)

In Ayn Rand, the novelist, screenwriter, philosopher, and cult object, Buckley found a vexing foe. Initially, it seems, he imagined that the author of novels such as *The Fountainhead* (1943), a best-seller that brimmed with antistatist fervor, might find common cause with the young publisher of *National Review,* but Rand's opening line to WFB at their first meeting, in 1954—"You are too intelligent to believe in God"—ruled out any alliance. "Religion is the first enemy of the Objectivist," WFB later noted. As with Bircherism, Buckley regarded Rand's concept of "objectivism," which exalted self-interest above fidelity to God and country, as a toxin to conservatism, urgently in need of expunging. To the task, no one at the time was better suited than Whittaker Chambers, whose review of Rand's latest best-seller in the December 28, 1957, issue of *NR,* lamenting the "dictatorial tone" of her writing, carried the greatest put-down in the annals of literary criticism: "From almost any page of *Atlas Shrugged,* a voice can be heard, from painful necessity, commanding: 'To a gas chamber—go!'" In his 1963 essay "Notes toward an Empirical Definition of

Conservatism," WFB reveled in how Chambers had managed to "read Miss Rand right out of conservatism." "Her philosophy," WFB wrote, "is in fact another kind of materialism—not the dialectic materialism of Marx, but the materialism of technocracy, of the relentless self-server, who lives for himself and for absolutely no one else.... Her exclusion from the conservative community was ... the result of her desiccated philosophy's conclusive incompatibility with the conservative's emphasis on transcendence, intellectual and moral."

"Ayn Rand, R.I.P."

Syndicated column, March 11, 1982; published
in *National Review,* April 2, 1982.

Ayn Rand is dead. So, incidentally, is the philosophy she sought to launch dead; it was, in fact, stillborn. The great public crisis in Ayn Rand's career came, in my judgment, when Whittaker Chambers took her on—in December of 1957, when her book *Atlas Shrugged* was dominating the best-seller list, lecturers were beginning to teach something called Randism, and students started using such terms as "mysticism of the mind" (religion), and "mysticism of the muscle" (statism). Whittaker Chambers, whose authority with American conservatives was as high as that of any man then living, wrote in *National Review,* after a lengthy analysis of the essential aridity of Miss Rand's philosophy, "Out of a lifetime of reading, I can recall no other book in which a tone of overriding arrogance was so implacably sustained. Its shrillness is without reprieve. Its dogmatism is without appeal."

I had met Miss Rand three years before that review was published. Her very first words to me (I do not exaggerate)

were: "You ahrr too intelligent to believe in Gott." The critic
Wilfrid Sheed once remarked, when I told him the story,
"Well, that certainly is an icebreaker." It was; and we con-
versed, and did so for two or three years. I used to send her
postcards in liturgical Latin; but levity with Miss Rand was
not an effective weapon. And when I published Whittaker
Chambers's review, her resentment was so comprehensive
that she regularly inquired of all hosts or toastmasters
whether she was being invited to a function at which I was
also scheduled to appear, because if that was the case, either she would not come; or, if so, only after I had left; or
before I arrived. I fear that I put the lady through a great
deal of choreographical pain.

Miss Rand's most memorable personal claim (if you
don't count the one about her being the next greatest philosopher after Aristotle) was that since formulating her
philosophy of "objectivism," she had never experienced any
emotion for which she could not fully account. And then
one day, a dozen years ago, she was at a small dinner, the
host of which was Henry Hazlitt, the libertarian economist,
the other guest being Ludwig von Mises, the grand master
of the Austrian school of antistatist economics. Miss Rand
was going on about something or other, at which point
Mises told her to be quiet, that she was being very foolish.
The lady who could account for all her emotions at that
point burst out into tears, and complained: "You are treat-
ing me like a poor ignorant little Jewish girl!" Mr. Hazlitt,
attempting to bring serenity to his table, leaned over and
said, "There there, Ayn, that isn't at all what Ludwig was
suggesting." But this attempt at conciliation was ruined
when Mises jumped up and said: "That iss eggsactly what
you ahrr!" Since both participants were Jewish, this was not

a racist slur. This story was mortal to her reputation as the lady of total self-control.

There were other unpleasantnesses of professional interest, such as her alienation from her principal apostle, Nathaniel Brandon [*sic*; Branden]—who was so ungallant as to suggest, in retaliation against her charge that he was trying to swindle her, that the breakup was the result of his rejection of an, er, amatory advance by Miss Rand. Oh goodness, it got ugly.

There were a few who, like Chambers, caught on early. *Atlas Shrugged* was published back before the law of the Obligatory Sex Scene was passed by both houses of Congress and all fifty state legislatures, so that the volume was considered rather risqué, in its day. Russell Kirk, challenged to account for Miss Rand's success if indeed she was merely an exiguous philosophic figure, replied, "Oh, they read her books for the fornicating bits." Unkind. And only partly true. *The Fountainhead,* read in a certain way, is a profound assertion of the integrity of art. What did Miss Rand in was her anxiety to theologize her beliefs. She was an eloquent and persuasive antistatist, and if only she had left it at that—but no, she had to declare that God did not exist, that altruism was despicable, that only self-interest is good and noble. She risked, in fact, giving to capitalism that bad name that its enemies have done so well in giving it; and that is a pity. Miss Rand was a talented woman, devoted to her ideals. She came as a refugee from Communism to this country as a young woman, and carved out a substantial career. May she rest in peace, and may she experience the demystification of her mind possessed.

Nelson Rockefeller

— ~ —

(1908–1979)

"We have nothing, nothing in the world, against Nelson Rockefeller," *National Review* declared in August 1958 on the eve of the Republican Party's nomination of Rockefeller for governor of New York State. "We have maintained, very simply, that he is not a Republican. Or, if it is better put another way, that if he is a Republican, Republicanism is a farce." As governor of the Empire State from 1959 to 1973—when he joined Gerald Ford in the White House as an unelected vice president serving an unelected president—Rockefeller championed a brand of liberal Republicanism that resulted in a massive expansion of state enterprise, authority, and debt. This made him, along with John V. Lindsay, a favorite target of WFB's polysyllabic derision. At the 1964 GOP convention, Buckley assessed that the "well-financed obstinacy of Nelson Rockefeller" constituted the chief obstacle to the consolidation of the pro-Goldwater forces. "The public's reaction to Mr. Rockefeller is embarrassingly plain," WFB wrote in a syndicated column at the time headlined "WHY DOESN'T ROCKEFELLER QUIT?" "He is well on his way to Stassenization: i.e., he has become half-ridiculous. (He would have become totally ridiculous except that no man with a couple of hundred million dollars to deploy is ever totally ridiculous.)" Buckley's eulogy, published fifteen years later in the same column, noted with begrudging admiration: "Nelson Rockefeller never gave up." However, neither the geniality of Rockefeller's company nor the putative absolution that death confers served to dissuade WFB from pronouncing Rockefeller, in the eulogy below, "the central figure in the progressive decline of the economy of New York and New York City."

"Nelson Rockefeller, R.I.P."

Syndicated column, February 1, 1979.

Some years ago—it was during the period of indecision in 1967–68 over whether to contest Richard Nixon for the Republican nomination for the presidency—Henry Kissinger called to advise me that Governor Rockefeller would like to meet me. Meeting me is terribly easy to arrange, so not long after, HK and I rode up the elevator to the Fifth Avenue apartment, and Happy opened the door. What would I like to eat, drink, smoke, etc., and in a few minutes—powerful men, it is my experience, generally let a visitor cool for a moment or two to heighten the suspense: but it was easy to pause there, because within eyesight lay several million dollars of nicely distracting art treasures—he strode in. We exchanged pleasantries while I wondered what was the purpose of the meeting.

In due course I found myself listening to an hour-long recitation of his early career on the Latin American desk, at the Chapultepec Conference, and at San Francisco,

where he had labored continually to counter Soviet machi-
nations. All this was done quietly, in the tones, I gradually
perceived—of a postulant. Nelson Rockefeller wished to
convince me that he was profoundly anti-Communist.

I always believed this true of him, but notwithstanding
his consistency on the question—marred by an ambigu-
ity on Vietnam when, briefly, Adviser Emmet Hughes prevailed over Adviser Henry Kissinger, respectively the dove
and the hawk in the inner circle—Nelson Rockefeller permanently alienated the right wing in America. He did this
in 1963 when he was induced to denounce in extravagant
terms the whole of the conservative movement as though it
were a branch of the John Birch Society. His reward was the
distasteful episode in San Francisco when delegates who
went there grimly determined to nominate Barry Goldwater gave Rockefeller the Bronx cheer—as if to say: "If that is
what you think of us, this is what we think of you."

But Nelson Rockefeller never gave up. And so now, in
1968, he made a gesture to a representative of the right
wing. During the convention itself, against the forlorn possibility that he might actually be nominated over Nixon
and Reagan, a special representative of Rockefeller kept me
regular company, his mission to guard against the preemp-
tive denunciation of Rockefeller by certain quarters, which
denunciation would have had on Rockefeller's candidacy
the same effect that the virtual denunciation of him by the
labor leaders had on George McGovern in 1972.

Then, too, there was the image of Rockefeller the Big
Spender. He was unquestionably the central figure in the
progressive decline of the economy of New York and New
York City. But he came gradually to recognize that there
were limits to all of this. And so he quarreled with John

Lindsay, who finally joined the Democratic Party, where he had always belonged. And on one occasion, with several dozen persons present, Nelson Rockefeller rose to toast Governor Ronald Reagan at the other end of the room:

"I feel the urge to confess," said Governor Rockefeller, "that I tried a different approach to state welfare than Governor Reagan. And his has proved more successful than mine."

In 1970 we met to discuss the senatorial race in which my brother James competed, and won. The incumbent Senator Charles Goodell, having been appointed by Governor Rockefeller upon the death of Robert Kennedy, had switched radically to the left, proving an embarrassment to Rockefeller. On that occasion he told me he would give only formalistic support to Goodell, to whom as a fellow Republican he was organizationally committed. "I really am a conservative, you know." And then, winking, "I've got a lot to conserve."

Classically, Nelson Rockefeller is another example of the man who, having nothing left to animate him, dies; like Napoleon at Elba, or Robert Taft after Eisenhower's nomination. He was a very strong man, persuasive in conversation, dogged in his pursuit of his goals, unsentimental, yet generous.

Henry Kissinger believes he would have been a great president. I think it altogether possible that this is true. He had the strength of character to profit from his own mistakes. If he had been kinder to Nixon during the years of exile, Nixon might have appointed him to replace Agnew. If that had happened, Rockefeller would almost surely have been president last week—in which event, almost surely, he would still be alive.

Eleanor Roosevelt

(1884–1962)

How, in retrospect, did *National Review* go seven whole issues before taking on Eleanor Roosevelt? The former first lady represented just about everything Buckley, his family, and his fellow editors abhorred about midcentury America. In the eighth issue, which hit the newsstands in January 1956, WFB set to work. The pretext was Mrs. Roosevelt's joining in a petition that urged President Eisenhower, in the spirit of Christmas, to grant clemency to sixteen leaders of the Communist Party serving prison sentences under the Smith Act. Buckley reminded Mrs. Roosevelt that the antisedition law had been signed "during the reign of" her late husband, President Franklin Roosevelt, and that much of her latter career had constituted an "indirect" rebuke of FDR's legacy. Galled that the petitioners, including prominent socialists, had claimed to be motivated "by their intellectual attachment to the democratic way of life," WFB argued that the petition in fact "discloses a deep contempt for the democratic way of life. . . . Those who are prepared to defend democracy must be prepared to

execute democracy's decisions." As a woman, a former first lady, and
an intellectual darling of the Eastern Establishment, Eleanor Roosevelt
presented an especially tricky target for WFB and other conservatives
in the Eisenhower and Kennedy years, when she used her newspaper
column and television appearances to advance causes she had championed, in some cases for decades: civil rights and humanitarianism,
the value of the United Nations, the imperative of negotiating with
the Soviet Union. To Buckley, she embodied the worst of what in
subsequent decades would be called political correctness: the mind-
less application to every issue of a platitudinous egalitarianism whose
practical effect invariably is to expand the reach of totalitarianism.
Amid the tributes that poured in from around the world, the critical
treatment in WFB's eulogy below surely stood out; dissenting from
the beatification of Eleanor Roosevelt was "standing athwart history"
in its rawest form. But it paid handsome dividends historically: At their
very first meeting, in 1961, a random encounter at a restaurant, the
very first thing that Ronald Reagan said to WFB was to quote, with
relish, one of his recent wisecracks about Eleanor Roosevelt.

"Mrs. Roosevelt, RIP"

National Review, January 29, 1963.
[signed by "Wm. F. Buckley Jr."]

I have been sharply reminded that I have not written about
[the death of] Mrs. Roosevelt, and that only a coward would
use the excuse that when she died, he was in Africa. There,
there are lions and tigers and apartheid. Here, there was
Mrs. Roosevelt to write about. Africa was the safer place.

People get very sore when you knock the old lady. And
it isn't just the widow who thinks of Mrs. Roosevelt as the

goddess who saved her children from getting rickets during the Depression. It is also the Left—intellectuals. "When are you going to stop picking on Mrs. Roosevelt?" a very learned writer asked me at a reception a few years ago after one of my books was published. (I had a sentence in it that annoyed him, something like, "Following Mrs. Roosevelt in search of irrationality is like following a lighted fuse in search of an explosion: one never has to wait very long.") I answered: "When you *begin* picking on her." I meant by that that people are best reformed by those they will listen to. Westbrook Pegler could never reform Mrs. Roosevelt, or her legend. But Adlai Stevenson, or Max Lerner, might have.

A GREAT MIND?

The obituary notices on Mrs. Roosevelt were as one in granting her desire to do good—she treated all the world as her own personal slum project; and all the papers, of course, remarked on that fabulous energy—surely she was the very first example of the peacetime use of atomic energy. But some publications (I think especially of *Time*) went so far as to say she had a great mind. Now is the time for all good men to come to the aid of Euclid.

Does it matter? Alas, it happens to matter very much. For Mrs. Roosevelt stamped upon her age a mode. Or, it might be said by those who prefer to put it that way, that in Mrs. Roosevelt the age developed its perfect symbol. Hers is the age of undifferentiated goodness, of permissive egalitarianism.

Mrs. Roosevelt's approach to human problems, so charming in its Franciscan naivete, was simply: do away with them—by the most obvious means. The way to cope with Russia is to negotiate. . . . The way for everyone to be free in the world is to tell the UN to free everyone. . . . The way to solve the housing shortage is for the government to build more houses. . . .

All that is more than Mrs. Roosevelt writing a column. It is a way of life. Based, essentially, on unreason; on the leaving out of the concrete, complex factor, which is why they call it "undifferentiated" goodness. Negotiation with Russia, you see, implies there is something we are, or should be, prepared to yield. . . . And everyone in the world cannot be free so long as freedoms are used by whole nations to abuse the peoples of other nations or the freedoms of their own people. . . . Latin American poverty is something that grows out of the pores of Latin American institutions and appetites, and cannot be seriously ameliorated by mere transfusions of American cash. . . . And the way to get houses built is to reduce their cost, so that poor people can buy them, without paying crippling wages to monopoly labor unions, or crippling prices to manufacturing concerns that have to pay the taxes of a government which among other things decides it needs to get into the housing business. . . .

PRINCIPAL BEQUEST

Mrs. Roosevelt's principal bequest, her most enduring bequest, was the capacity so to oversimplify problems as to give encouragement to those who wish to pitch the nation and the world onto humanitarian crusades which, because they fail to take reality into account, end up plunging people into misery (as Wilson's idealistic imperialism plunged Europe into misery for years, and spawned Hitler), and messing up the world in general (under whose statecraft did Stalin prosper?). Above all it was Mrs. Roosevelt who, on account of her passion for the non sequitur, deeply wounded the processes of purposive political thought. "Over whatever subject, plan, or issue Mrs. Roosevelt touches," Professor James Burnham once wrote, "she spreads a squidlike ink of directionless feeling. All distinctions are blurred, all analysis fouled, and in the murk clear thought is forever impossible."

Some day in the future, a Liberal scholar will write a definitive thesis exploring the cast of Mrs. Roosevelt's mind by a textual analysis of her thought; and then history will be able to distinguish between a great woman with a great heart, and a woman of perilous intellectual habit. "With all my heart and soul," her epitaph should read, "I fought the syllogism." And with that energy and force, she wounded it, almost irretrievably—how often have you seen the syllogism checking in at the office for a full day's work lately?

Arthur Schlesinger, Jr.

$\sim$

(1917–2007)

Asked if he had recruited Arthur M. Schlesinger, Jr., to the White House to write the president's memoirs, JFK reportedly told aides he would handle the chores himself before adding: "Arthur will probably write his own, and it will be better for us if he's in the White House, seeing what goes on, instead of reading about it in the *New York Times* and *Time* magazine." Kennedy needn't have worried; Schlesinger's books about the president and his brother—*A Thousand Days: John F. Kennedy in the White House* (1966) and *Robert Kennedy and His Times* (1978)—offered hagiographic portraits of the Kennedys, who afforded the owlish liberal historian his only proximity to power. The son of the chair of Harvard University's history department, the younger Schlesinger first captured national attention with his publication, at the age of twenty-seven, of *The Age of Jackson,* which won the 1946 Pulitzer Prize. (*A Thousand Days* would garner Schlesinger his second Pulitzer, for biography, as well as the National Book Award.) "Last night," Schlesinger wrote in his diary in January 1995 (unpublished until six months after WFB's death), "Bill Buckley and I appeared on the Charlie Rose show. Our performances must have disappointed all those who looked forward to a slam-bang, no-holds-barred fight. Indeed, as I saw the show myself (it was taped at 6 P.M. and shown at 11), I thought that here were a couple of old gladiators who in their genial decline were substituting jollity for combat."

> Thirty years ago Bill Buckley and I went on occasion from city to city like a couple of professional wrestlers. We really disliked each other then, and no holds were barred. Once, out of my own sense of mischief, I entered a *National Review* contest of some sort and won a prize. Buckley, out of his bolder sense of mischief, awarded me a live donkey, which lived on our back-yard on Irving Street for a couple of days until I hired some-one to take it away. Our relationship in those times was one of incessant—and heartfelt—reciprocal insult.
>
> Then I came to New York. I liked Pat Buckley. Bill liked Alexandra. Alistair Horne, Bill's old friend and my new friend, took it on as his mission to bring us together. Bill's views moder-ated; today he would no longer defend Joe McCarthy, as he did forty years ago. My attitudes mellowed with age. I developed a regard for Bill's wit, his passion for the harpsichord, his human decency, even for his compulsion to épater the liberals (which is about all that remains from the wrathful conservatism of his youth). So now we are friends—and go easy on each other.

For Schlesinger, the rapprochement had been years in the mak-ing. A diary entry from May 1984, after a joint appearance on *Night-line*, had found Schlesinger reflecting: "I did the Ted Koppel show with Bill Buckley.... I am compelled to confess that my old dislike of Buckley has given way to a certain liking, if not affection. I surmise that a reciprocal change has taken place on his side.... We differed, of course, but amiably; we had enjoyable talk off camera; and when we went our separate ways in the night, Buckley said improbably, 'Good night, my dear.'" If WFB never quite reciprocated Schlesinger's conciliation, it may derive from how central Schlesinger was to Buckley's mission: Bow-tied, egg-headed embodiment of all WFB aimed to stand athwart, the Harvard historian was present at the creation. Writing in *Facts Forum News* in June 1955—identified as the editor of *National Weekly,* which was set to launch in September— WFB recounted a kind of baptismal tale:

> I first caught on to the Liberal political game many years, I am certain, after you did. It happened to me rather suddenly, in the spring of 1950, after reading an article in the *New York Times Magazine* called "The Need for an Intelligent Opposition." The article was written by Arthur Schlesinger, Jr. He was reading not only the Republican party and its leaders, but all conservatives as well, a little lecture, the gist of which was this: We Liberals, said Schlesinger, think it's important for you conservatives to be around. It gets stagnant otherwise; it keeps us on our toes to have to cope with you. We're all for you. . . . Mr. Schlesinger then proceeded to tell us how to be intelligent. What it amounted to was for us to desert our principles and embrace his.

The first sentence WFB published about Schlesinger in *National Review,* in April 1958, stated: "Arthur Schlesinger, Jr.'s, obsessive partisanship has disqualified him as a historian." For *NR*'s "Books in Brief" section, he reviewed Schlesinger's 1960 pamphlet *Kennedy or Nixon—Does It Make Any Difference?* in three savage sentences:

> A cream puff for Jack, by a historian whose simple-minded partisanship strips him here of style and manners. He sits at table gorging with his fingers and spilling food down his front, in his

ravenous desire to feed the gnawing hunger-at-large for a plausible set of reasons why anyone in his right mind should vote for Mr. Kennedy. Professor Schlesinger's recipe: Hate Nixon.

Two years later, after Schlesinger claimed he had denounced the fringe left, WFB demanded the evidence: "I shall always be glad to give publicity to any lapse by Professor Schlesinger into sanity, and do not worry that such a guarantee will heavily mortgage my future time." After quoting from the speech Schlesinger supplied, WFB mocked his adversary's appearance: "One wishes the eloquent Professor Schlesinger had sunk his pointed teeth a little deeper." As late as May 1977, Buckley devoted an entire column to dissecting a sycophantic memo Schlesinger had sent JFK in April 1961, unsealed by the Freedom of Information Act, in which the eminent historian had counseled Kennedy at length on how to lie. "In later years," WFB wrote, "a successor courtier would call that stonewalling." Schlesinger's diary recorded his fury, as in October 1976: "The egregious William F. Buckley, Jr., printed a flat lie about me in his column ... filled with Buckley's usual malice. ... The last thing in the world that Buckley wants is to have the facts violate his prejudices."

> It is odd: whenever I encounter Buckley, he is excessively genial, as if he wanted to be friends; but whenever I begin vaguely to soften under his personal courtship, something like this reminds me how odious he is.

The opening line of WFB's eulogy shows that the distance between the two men remained unbridgeable to the end, most acutely on the very point that Schlesinger had made in his diary twelve years before his death about him and Buckley emerging at last as "friends."

"Arthur Schlesinger, R.I.P."

Syndicated column, March 2, 2007; published in *National Review,*
April 2, 2007.

I always regretted that we didn't become friends, because
the thousands who succeeded in doing so found friendship
with Arthur Schlesinger very rewarding. For one thing, to
behold him—listen to him, observe him, read him—was to
coexist with a miracle of sorts.

It is an awful pity, as one reflects on it, that nature is
given to endowing the wrong men with extraordinary productivity. If you laid out the published works of John Kenneth Galbraith and of Arthur Meier Schlesinger, Jr., the
line of books would reach from Galbraith's house in Cambridge to Schlesinger's old house in Cambridge.

A week or two back, Schlesinger acknowledged to someone that he wasn't quite on a par with his old self, his old
self having been just fine until about age 86, three years
ago, after which the decline began. He walked more slowly
and, he said, his speech was not as fluent as usual.

Any reduction in his productivity must have been shattering to him, as to his many clients, beginning with Clio,
the muse of history, which he served so diligently, beginning with his first all-star history, *The Age of Jackson,* and
going up to his last book, published a couple of years ago,
deploring President Bush for one thing and another.

Schlesinger wrote serious studies, of the age not only of
Jackson, but also of Roosevelt and of Kennedy, for whom
his enthusiasm was uncontainable. Arthur proceeded to
write not one but three books on JFK, whom he venerated.

He lived with the risk entailed in following so uncritically the careers of his favorites. Professor Sidney Hook dismissed one of his Kennedy books as the work of a "court historian." Schlesinger minded the derogation not at all, so much did he cherish public controversy that cast him as maintaining the walls of the fortresses that protected his idols.

He was, I record regretfully, not very deft at close-up political infighting. I say this as the survivor of a half-dozen encounters designed, by Arthur, to kill, which failed. In one of them he hurled a sarcasm, saying of me, "He has a facility for rhetoric which I envy, as well as a wit which I seek clumsily and vainly to emulate." I thought that so amusing, I copied the words exactly on the jacket of my next book as though they were a great, generous compliment. If you see what I mean about Arthur's awkwardness in combat of this kind, he actually sued me and my publisher, drawing much attention to his careless use of sarcastic praise, and, of course, to my wit.

But we kept on bumping into each other with less than mortal exchanges, and I had to endure my wife's huge affection for him, which unhappily did not quite effect a personal rapprochement. He died in New York on February 27, after being struck by a heart attack at dinner in a restaurant, and I think back on the lunch we shared after the funeral of Murray Kempton, and of the sheer jolliness of the great and productive historian when he didn't feel that his gods were being profaned.

There is no honor payable to an American historian that he did not earn. One of his books got the National Book Award *and* a Pulitzer. Meanwhile he entertained himself by writing movie criticism, and hordes of others by writing essays on every subject that interested him, including what it is in society that creates history. He was a liberal partisan, but he did not turn a blind eye to transgressions by accommodationist liberals who permitted themselves to follow the Communist Party line. He was devastating in his expulsion of them from his movement, which he served more diligently than perhaps any other human being in modern history.

Acknowledgments

There we sat, Bill Buckley and me, in the *National Review* library, shooting the breeze. It was September 17, 1991: George H. W. Bush was president and the Soviet Union was collapsing. A recent Johns Hopkins graduate, I was seated across from my hero because I had stumbled, in a used bookstore, upon a book that had belonged to him and had mailed it to him. He invited me to meet him.

Toward the end, I mentioned a Kurt Vonnegut essay titled "Who in America Is Truly Happy?" *What year?* WFB asked. "1979," I said. It had described Buckley's writings as "uniformly first rate," examples not only of "unbridled happiness . . . but as shrewd comedies and celebrations of the English language."

He is a superb sailor and skier as well—and multilingual, and a musician, and an airplane

pilot, and a family man, and polite and amusing
to strangers. More: He is, like the Yale-educated
hero of his novel *Saving the Queen*, startlingly good-
looking. . . . So whenever I see Mr. Buckley, I think
this, and, word of honor, without an atom of irony:
"There is a man who has won the decathlon of
human existence."*

"Never more so than now," I said. WFB shot me a quiz-
zical look. "If there is any reason to envy a man like you,"
I said, "it's not because of the trappings that surround you
but because you've accomplished what you wanted to when
you were a young man. Domestically and internationally,
communism as an ideology is entirely discredited. You've
won! Game over!"

Except, WFB replied, *in the sense that there are no final vic-
tories. But essentially you're right.*

It pains me to disagree with Bill, but I regard *A Torch
Kept Lit* as a final victory and owe my first expression of
gratitude for it to WFB himself: for the example of his life,
his massive body of work, and his many overtures of friendship and support. I never met Pat Buckley, but suspect I
owe her deep thanks as well.

Jack Fowler, publisher of *National Review,* understood the
need for this book and opened *NR*'s archive and licensing,
and his own big heart, to make it possible. Christopher Buckley gave his blessing, and, late in the process, wise counsel.
NR editor Rich Lowry, a friend for two decades, was always
available when I needed him. Senior editor Jonah Goldberg,

---

* Kurt Vonnegut, *Politics Today* (January–February 1979); reprinted in Vonnegut,
Palm Sunday (Delacorte Press, 1981).

also a dear friend, offered support on many fronts. Editor at large Linda Bridges, who whipped my very first published article into shape—for *NR*, in 1992—provided encouragement. Executive editor Reihan Salam, managing editor Jason Steorts, literary editor Mike Potemra, Madison Peace, and Rachel Ogden were all very kind.

At Crown, I am indebted to Campbell Wharton and Mary Reynics, Derek Reed and Julia Elliott, Owen Haney and Jennie Pouech. Nowhere in publishing is there a finer team.

Keith Urbahn and Matt Latimer, and everyone at Javelin, the literary agency that represents me, are the best in the business. My thanks also to those who provided the blurbs for the dust jacket.

At Fox News, there are always more generous people than can be listed, and by way of thanking them all, I offer my gratitude, once again, to chairman and CEO Roger Ailes, whose vision provides working space for so many talented people.

By divine coincidence I received the Earnest C. Pulliam Fellowship to teach at Hillsdale College, which maintains the indispensable online archive of WFB's canon, just as work commenced on *ATKL*. My thanks to Hillsdale's president, Dr. Larry Arnn; John J. Miller, *National Review* writer and director of Hillsdale's Dow Journalism Program, and his wife, Amy; Matthew Bell; Kathy and Craig Connor; Jim Drews; Soren Geiger; Margie King; Marcy Rader; Laura and Paul Rahe; Calvin Stockdale; and not least to the uniformly bright and kind students I met on campus. Deep thanks also to the Hoover Institution, which catalogued and transcribed portions of the *Firing Line* archive, available at the Hoover website.

My thanks also to Neal Adams, Eduardo Arteaga, Mary and Denny Barket, Marty Baron, Dr. Jennifer Barron and Ryan Durkin, Vince Benedetto, Shelbi Bivons, Brad Blakeman, Karna Bodman, Katie Boothroyd, Rick Borman, Brent Bozell, Greta and Billy Brawner, Donald Bryant, Inez and Joao Cabritas, Kim Caviness and Lyn Vaus, Shaun K. Chang, Bronwyn and David Clark, Susan Coll, Monica Crowley, Mark Cunningham, Lorraine and Joe Durkin, Josh Earnest, Al Felzenberg, Rainey Foster, Mark French, Dr. Ashley and Hugh Gallagher, Philip Glass, Susan Glasser and Peter Baker, Juleanna Glover, Lauren Guaraldo, Jacob Heilbrunn, Hugh Hewitt, Connie and Chris Hillman, D. J. Hoek, Rick Hohlt, Elodie and Austin Hunt, Hollis Hunt, Heather and Derek Hunter, Matt Jones, Patrick Judge, Greg Kelly, John Kirby, Kathy Lash and Joe Trippi, Matt Lee, Kevin B. Leonard, Daniel Lippman, Maia and Dan Magder, Tony Makris, Christopher Malagisi, Tom Mallon, Seth Mandel, Andrea Mays and James Swanson, Skip McCloskey, Edward F. Meehan III, Hilary and Noah Mehrkam, Dan Miller, Amy Mitchell, Rob Mitchell, Dan Moldea, Vida and Rob Myers, Bobby Nash, Chuck Nash, George H. Nash (who first suggested the need for a volume like this), Graham Nash, Larry O'Connor, Tracy and Todd Pantezzi, Mark Paoletta, Kaja Perina, Dana Perino, Susan and Mike Pillsbury, Charles Pinck, John Podhoretz, Michelle Rice and John Hamilton, Peter Robinson, Dr. Shilpa Rose, Eric Rosen, Regina and Mike Rosen, Eric Roston, Ryan Samuel, James Schneider, Julie and Will Schrot, Cindy and Ryan Schwarz, Ellen Shearer, Nancy Shevell, Ricky Skaggs, Kiron Skinner, Juli and David Smith, James Sprankle, Jim Steen, Beth and D. J. Sworobuk, Gayle and Joel Trotter, Michael Von Sas, Ildi and Mory Watkins, Craig Weiner, Rachel Westlake, Brian Wilson, and Matt Yurus.

My apologies to anyone I've forgotten. Any errors that appear in my introductory material are solely mine.

Finally, no words can adequately thank my wife, Sara, for her love and support and grounding. I strive with intermittent success to be worthy of her and our sons, to whom this book is dedicated.

James Rosen
Washington, D.C.
June 13, 2016

WILLIAM F. BUCKLEY, JR. (1925–2008), was the architect of modern American conservatism. As the founder of *National Review* magazine, the host of TV's *Firing Line* (1966–99), a widely syndicated columnist for more than fifty years, and the author of several dozen books—ranging from critiques of higher education to sailing travelogues to spy novels, most of them bestsellers—WFB cut a singular figure in American public life and media. He also served in the Central Intelligence Agency, founded Young Americans for Freedom, captured 13.4 percent of the vote in the 1965 New York City mayoral race, and received the Presidential Medal of Freedom. Ronald Reagan called Buckley "perhaps the most influential journalist and intellectual in our era."

JAMES ROSEN is the chief Washington correspondent for Fox News, where he has been a reporter since 1999. He has covered the White House and State Department beats and reported from Capitol Hill, the Pentagon, the Supreme Court, nearly all fifty states, and forty foreign countries across five continents. Rosen's exclusive reporting made him a target of the Obama administration and a rallying point for civil liberties groups and champions of the First Amendment. Rosen's articles and essays have appeared in the *New York Times*, the *Wall Street Journal*, the *Washington Post*, *Harper's*, *The Atlantic*, *National Review*, and *Playboy*, among other periodicals. He is the author of *The Strong Man: John Mitchell and the Secrets of Watergate* and *Cheney One on One*. He lives in Washington with his wife and their two sons.